Craig Kennedy

STACKPOLE
BOOKS

Published by
STACKPOLE BOOKS
5067 Ritter Road
Mechanicsburg, PA 17055

Printed in the United States

10 9 8 7 6 5 4 3 2

First edition

Illustrations by Cathi Beers
Cover design by Tracy Patterson with Wendy Baugher

Library of Congress Cataloging-in-Publication Data

Kennedy, Craig.
    Pennsylvania fairs and country festivals / Craig Kennedy. — 1st ed.
      p.   cm.
    ISBN 0-8117-2494-8 (pb)
    1. Fairs—Pennsylvania. 2. Festivals—Pennsylvania. 3. Pennsylvania—
  Social life and customs. I. Title.
GT4610.P4K45   1996
394'.6'09748—dc20
                                         95-20300
                                             CIP

To my family, and to Raggs, who sleeps on my feet as I write

Contents

May

June

July

January

Pennsylvania Farm Show

Harrisburg, Dauphin County

On the first Wednesday of the new year, a snowstorm crippled Central Pennsylvania. The following day's ice storm immobilized the state from Philadelphia to the Ohio border. Businesses shut down, schools closed, and patrol cars herded vehicles off Interstate 81 as efficiently as a pack of Scottish border collies let loose in a sheep field.

As most of us slept through the freezing rain that night, all over the state trailers and vans backed up to open barn doors. Loading ramps dropped to the ground with a noisy clatter, and drowsy animals clomped out of their stalls. Ramps swooshed back into place, doors slammed shut, suitcases landed behind truck seats, and engines roared to life as the trucks headed for a sixteen-acre brick complex in Harrisburg. It was Farm Show Week, and the weather was typical.

Inside the warm front lobby of the Farm Show's main building, in a refrigerated glass enclosure, an eight-hundred-pound butter sculpture of a Penn State football player spun on a spotlighted dais. But it wasn't the sculpture that lured me inside, it was the smell. The country's largest agricultural fair under one roof, the Farm Show has a nose all its own. Well-oiled machinery, new paint, livestock, chocolate cakes, apple pies, leather harness, Christmas trees, nursery stock, grain, corn, fertilizer, and the food court all create an aroma found only in January under the Farm Show roof. The smell and the building's warmth wrapped themselves around me and pulled me in.

The Main Exhibit Building just beyond the lobby was filled with commercial exhibits from all aspects of farm life. Mailboxes, toy tractors, seedlings, bare root stock, large equipment, fertilizers, silos, seeds, and lobbyists all vied for attention. It was easy to tell the farmers from the townies, for the farmers moved slowly, studying the exhibits with keen interest. More often than not, they were snagged by the undertow of stroller-propelling, pretzel-eating city folks out for the afternoon. I found the passing lane to be safest.

As I walked into the West Hall, the temperature dropped about twenty degrees and the livestock smell went up about twenty notches. The state's elite hogs and sheep alternately murmured, muttered, bleated, oinked, squealed, and shrieked, depending on their humor at the moment. In the Small Arena, a Scottish judge made dreams come true for some young exhibitors and broke the hearts of others. Meanwhile, the contestants themselves, unaware of the difference between breeding stock and lamb chops, idly chewed their lead ropes and nuzzled their penmates.

In the North Building, the dairy farmers had moved in and had turned the sprawling building into a comfortable week-long home for themselves and their cattle. Empty stalls were set up with card tables, toaster ovens, televisions, and easy chairs. Occupied stalls were decorated with gingham curtains, straw hats, silk flowers, and scarecrows. While some exhibitors watched football games, others napped on cots. The smells of brewing coffee and Crockpot dinners added to the at-home feeling.

For others, however, there was the serious business of the show to deal with. The cattle-washing booth was hot real estate, and a blow dryer the size of a vacuum ran constantly. Cows were being clipped, coiffed,

---

Blue-Ribbon Honey Caramel Apple Pie

Crust and Cover:

1 $1/3$ cups flour	Pinch of salt
$1/2$ cup butter	3 tablespoons ice water

Combine flour, butter, and salt with pastry blender until the size of small peas. Add water until dough forms a ball. Roll out dough on floured board and place in a 9-inch pie pan. With remaining dough, cut out apple shapes to decorate top of pie.

Filling:

10 to 12 apples, peeled and sliced	$1/4$ cup brown sugar
$1/4$ cup flour	1 cup honey caramel sauce
1 teaspoon cinnamon	(below)

Toss together apples, flour, cinnamon, brown sugar, and honey caramel sauce. Pour into unbaked pie crust. Decorate top with pie-dough apples. Bake at 400 degrees for 1 hour or until apples are tender.

Honey Caramel Sauce:

1 $1/2$ cups honey	1 teaspoon vanilla
$1/2$ cup heavy cream	$1/8$ teaspoon salt
1 tablespoon butter or margarine	

Combine honey and cream in a heavy saucepan. Cook and stir over medium-high heat until mixture reaches 238 degrees. Stir butter, vanilla, and salt into mixture. Makes 1 $3/4$ cups.

—Julie Freeman

Blue-Ribbon Chocolate Caramel Cookie Bars

$3/4$ cup butter or margarine
2 cups graham cracker crumbs
$1/4$ cup Hershey's cocoa
$1/2$ cup powdered sugar
2 $2/3$ cups shredded coconut
$1/2$ cup slivered almonds
1 can condensed milk

1 12-ounce bag Hershey's
   chocolate chips
$1/2$ cup Reese's creamy
   peanut butter
14 Kraft caramels
2 teaspoons butter
2 teaspoons water

In microwave oven, melt $3/4$ cup butter or margarine. Add graham cracker crumbs, cocoa, and powdered sugar. Spread mixture in a 9 x 13-inch pan.

Drizzle some condensed milk over crust. Put 1 $1/3$ cups of coconut on crust and drizzle condensed milk over coconut. Place slivered almonds on top of coconut layer and drizzle condensed milk over almonds. Put the remaining 1 $1/3$ cups of coconut on almonds and drizzle remaining condensed milk on top. Pat down to compact and bake 20 minutes at 350 degrees.

On hot stove, melt chocolate chips and peanut butter. Spread this over warm cookie bar mixture and let cool.

Melt caramels, 2 teaspoons butter, and 2 teaspoons water together. When chocolate is firm, put caramel mixture on top of cookie bars. Garnish with a Hershey's Hug.

—*Jennifer Intrepido*

---

buffed, and polished like Vegas showgirls being readied for a date with the producer. Exhibitors also manned the manure shovel, and it was the spectator's responsibility to avoid a full load, or a cow on the way to the beauty parlor. I bumped into someone and offered an automatic "Excuse me," then turned to find that I'd just excused myself to a Holstein. But that's all part of the Farm Show experience.

I moved through the beef cattle quickly, stopping for a moment to gather recipes from the Beef Council's booth. Time was running out, and I wanted to see the draft horses in the large arena. I arrived in time for the obstacle course, one of twelve events. Wagon teams had to pass through a serpentine, over a dummy, back into a narrow passageway, rotate 360 degrees while keeping the back pivotal wheel in a chalked circle on the ground, run both wheels on one side along a straight painted line, pass over a piece of plastic on the ground, put a paper in a mailbox high on a pole, and pass through a gate. Contestants were judged on time and faults.

The audience held its breath as a pair of dappled gray Percherons backed into the passageway at a sharp angle. One side of the smart red wagon was two feet off the ground and it seemed almost certain to topple over, but at the last minute, the driver readjusted his position and the wagon dropped to the ground. Third-place winner Elwood Zinn of Newville said, "When you work your horses every day of the year like I do, plowing and harvesting, this obstacle course is no big deal. These show horse breeders are concentrating on raising horses that look good trotting around the ring, but they never really work them. This course separates the men from the boys!"

My last stop was the food court, a twenty-seven-thousand-square-foot village green complete with a gazebo and landscaping. In addition to the legendary Farm Show favorites—baked potatoes and milkshakes—were a variety of Pennsylvania food items, from apples to zucchini. Pennsylvania Aquaculture Association offered fish and chips, fish sandwiches, and smoked trout. Pennsylvania Livestock Association served pork barbecues, lamb stew, ham and cheese sandwiches, and roast beef. Breaded mushrooms, mushroom soup, and mushroom salad were popular choices at the

---

Pennsylvania Mushroom Growers' Mushroom Salad

3 pounds fresh button mushrooms, quartered or sliced
1 tablespoon salt
1 tablespoon lemon juice

In a 4-quart saucepan, add salt and lemon juice to 2 inches of water. Bring mixture to a boil, add washed mushrooms, and bring to a boil again. Drain.

In a large bowl, combine:

1 cup chopped celery	$1/4$ cup cider vinegar
$1/2$ cup grated carrots	1 tablespoon salt
$1/3$ cup chopped onions	$1/2$ teaspoon black pepper
3 to 4 ounces pitted black olives	1 tablespoon parsley
$1/3$ cup olive oil	1 teaspoon garlic powder

Add drained mushrooms and mix together. Refrigerate, covered. Keeps up to ten days.

Maple Growers' Glazed Carrots

8 medium carrots $1/4$ cup maple syrup
3 tablespoons butter $1/2$ teaspoon ginger

Slice carrots. Cook until tender. Melt butter. Add maple syrup and ginger to melted butter. Simmer carrots in maple syrup mixture until glazed.

The Pennsylvania State Beekeepers' Association's Honey Gingerbread

1 egg, beaten   1 teaspoon baking soda
1 cup dairy sour cream   2 teaspoons ginger
1 cup honey $1/2$ teaspoon cinnamon
$2 1/2$ cups flour $1/4$ cup vegetable oil
$1/2$ teaspoon salt

Preheat oven to 350 degrees. In a small bowl, beat together sour cream and honey. Blend into beaten egg. Sift together dry ingredients. Beat well. Blend in oil. Pour into well-greased 9 x 9 x 2-inch pan. Bake 30 to 40 minutes until done in center. Cool on rack 5 minutes. Remove from pan. Serve warm with ice cream or whipped cream.

Pennsylvania Apple Growers' Old-Fashioned Apple Dumplings

6 medium-size apples $1/2$ teaspoon salt
2 cups flour $2/3$ cup Crisco
$2 1/2$ teaspoons baking powder $1/2$ cup milk

Pare and core apples. Leave whole.

Sift flour, baking powder, and salt together. Cut in shortening. Sprinkle milk over mixture and mix well. Roll dough as for pastry and cut into six squares. Place an apple on each square. Fill cavity of apple with brown sugar and sprinkle with cinnamon. Pat dough around apple to cover it completely. Fasten edges securely on top of apple. Place dumplings 1 inch apart in a greased baking pan. Bake at 375 degrees for 35 to 40 minutes or until nicely browned.

—*Velma Brubaker*

Pennsylvania Livestock Association's Lamb Stew

300 pounds lamb (braker plate)	.6 pound black pepper
300 pounds water	.9 pound paté spice
60 pounds diced onions	1.2 pounds garlic powder
75 pounds diced carrots	1.2 pounds provencal herbs
80 pounds diced potatoes	3.6 pounds Kitchen Bouquet
80 pounds sliced mushrooms	14 pounds food starch
80 pounds green peas	30 bottles Marsala wine
9 (#10) cans diced tomatoes	3.6 pounds crushed garlic
6 (#10) cans tomato puree	6 pounds parsley
10 pounds salt	7.2 pounds sugar
Makes 600 pounds.	

—Lion's Den Catering

Pennsylvania Mushroom Growers Association booth. Pennsylvania Poultry Federation offered chicken nuggets and wings, chicken breasts, chicken corn soup, chicken hot dogs, and pickled eggs. Pennsylvania Bakers Association offered cinnamon buns. Pennsylvania Vegetable Growers Association served vegetable soup, tomato juice, and batter-dipped vegetables. State Horticultural Association of Pennsylvania offered apple cider, apple butter, and apple dumplings. Pennsylvania Maple Growers Association served maple syrup sundaes and frozen maple yogurt. Apparently many other people had thought that supper would be a good idea before leaving, for lines were long and stand-up table space short. Before long, however, I was in the shuttle bus line spiraling around the front lobby.

Outside, menacing and malicious, the winter night stalked the barren parking lot. The last shuttle bus dropped its passengers and pulled away. The echoing crunch of departing footsteps rattled around the parking lot and rolled out into the silent city. While the car warmed up, I turned on the radio. "More snow on the way, with continuing record lows! It's Farm Show weather!" the forecaster intoned. To the farm folks inside, however, the weather was simply another contestant to beat.

❖ The Farm Show is held the second week of January, from Saturday through Thursday. Doors open daily at 8 A.M., closing Saturday, Monday, Tuesday, and Wednesday at 9 P.M., Sunday at 5 P.M., and Thursday at 4 P.M. Admission is free, but there is a small fee for parking on the sixty-acre lot. Overflow parking is available in the adjacent Harrisburg Area

Community College parking lot, and shuttle bus service is convenient and inexpensive.

The Farm Show truly offers something for everyone. In addition to five thousand animals, 325 commercial exhibitors, hundreds of home products, and the popular food court, there are hourly demonstrations and lectures in the Family Corner in the Northeast Building. Cooking demonstrations in the West Lobby are held frequently every day of the show. Saturday's high school rodeo is held at 2 P.M. and again at 6 P.M. in the Large Arena. Sunday, after the Governor's Review at 11, the draft horse events begin. The sheep-to-shawl contest is held on Monday, horse pulling on Tuesday, pony pulling on Wednesday, and the sale of champions on Thursday.

The Farm Show is located at 2301 North Cameron Street in Harrisburg, one mile off the Cameron Street exit of I-81. For information, call 717-787-5373.

Marienville Winterfest

Marienville, Forest County

After weeks of imprisonment at winter's hands, I was of two minds when I left for the Marienville Winterfest, a trip that would take me northwest across the state. Although I was happy enough to throw my daypack of writing gear into the car and take off, I had a healthy respect for the 250 miles of unfamiliar roads ahead of me.

As it turned out, the roads proved kinder than the temperature that Sunday morning. The brittle sunlight was no more convincing than a used-car salesman's smile. Mile by mile as I headed farther north, populated areas gave way to broad expanses of gleaming white porcelain fringed in green-black evergreens that slumbered under a cobalt sky.

On the edge of the Allegheny National Forest, Marienville comes up almost as a surprise. Like most villages on a first-name basis with winter, it is compact. Surrounded by isolated hunting camps and three hundred miles of snowmobile trails, houses, churches, schools, and businesses huddle together, seemingly for warmth and safety. In January the streets are snow covered, and more snowmobiles than cars jockey for parking spaces at local diners. With Knox, Kane, and Kinzua Railroad cars hibernating on sidetracks at the edge of town, the effect is much like a Christmas train set come to life.

After an unfruitful tour of the village, I hailed a pedestrian and asked where the Winterfest was being held. "It's in the MACA Building," she told me, as confused by my ignorance as I was by her assumption that everyone would know. "Turn between the Unimart and the Bucktail Inn. Take a right, and then the first left. It's the long log building." I followed the directions, and a minute later, I was stretching road-weary muscles by the side of my car.

Except for a woman tidying the edges of the empty parking lot with a snow shovel, at 11 A.M. the Marienville Area Civic Association's home base showed no signs of life. For a moment I thought there had been some confusion on the dates of the event. Inside, however, the smell of vegetable soup wafting from the kitchen and the accompanying clatter of pots and pans were encouraging. From across the room, a voice boomed, "Hi! We won't get rolling for another half hour or so."

"For a minute, there, I thought you might have canceled."

"Oh, we never cancel."

When I finished explaining the purpose of my visit, Don Stevenson told me, "My wife's the chairperson of the Winterfest. You should talk to her." We went out the back door to watch a lone skater gliding across the skating rink.

"We built that rink ourselves," Don told me. "Two weeks ago, my brother and I pushed the snow back, then I came out each night and hosed it down until it was thick enough. I resurface it every night. We're looking into grants to build a permanent rink."

Downstairs, while several people dealt with the aftermath of Saturday's children's carnival, Micky Stevenson outfitted children with ice skates. Between customers, she shared the schedule of events with me. From the time the kitchen opens at 6 P.M. on Friday until it closes Sunday afternoon at 3, Marienville offers its guests a full weekend of family-oriented events.

Many of the activities throughout the weekend are designed with young people in mind. In addition to the carnival on Saturday morning, featuring games of chance in the basement, there is a scavenger hunt that sends participants all over the village. There's a snow sculpture contest on the grounds, and one of Saturday afternoon's features is a children's craft session.

Ice skating and a tube slide as well as Saturday's horse-drawn-sleigh rides make the most of the season. Saturday's ice-sculpting demonstrations appeal to all ages.

Games of chance are a big drawing card for the older set. As many as four hundred people attend "Little Las Vegas Night" upstairs in the MACA Center, from 7 till 11 Saturday night. At the closing of the casino night, there's a 50/50 drawing and a Chinese auction, and prizes are substantial. For those who don't enjoy risk taking, the Friday-night auction is a happy choice.

Winterfest Barbecued Ham Sandwiches

1/3 cup oil	3/4 cup brown sugar
1 medium onion	3 6-ounce cans tomato paste
2 cloves garlic	1 1/2 cups water
1 tablespoon mustard	1 green pepper
3 tablespoons Worcestershire sauce	1 onion
1 cup vinegar	5 pounds ham

Mince onion and garlic and sauté in the oil. Add the next six ingredients. Simmer for 20 minutes, stirring occasionally. Slice green pepper and onion into strips and add to sauce. Pour over 5 pounds of thinly sliced ham. Bake at 300 degrees for about 45 minutes. Serve on a bun.

It should come as no surprise that Marienville, billed as the snowmobile capital of Pennsylvania, features several snowmobile events. With so many miles of trails, the Saturday morning route varies from year to year. Another event, Saturday evening's torchlight parade around MACA's grounds, features 125 to 150 snowmobilers carrying torches.

The most popular event, however, is the Poker Run on Saturday morning. About seventy-five contestants follow a thirty-mile course beginning and ending at the Kelley Hotel in the center of the village. Along the way each rider stops at five checkpoints, picking up random playing cards. Back at the hotel, they turn their cards in, and the best hand wins.

Sunday's activities include lunches, a final raffle, some entertainment, and an ice skating competition.

Upstairs the lunch crowd was arriving. An odd mix of snowmobiling outfits and dress clothes divided the sporting set from the churchgoers, but that was the only divisive element. Friends greeted friends, and the temperature seemed to rise in the room. The kitchen was serving chili, vegetable soup, hot dogs, sloppy joes, ham barbecues, and a variety of homemade pastries and beverages. Popcorn danced in the big glass corn popper.

As I ate my ham barbecue and vegetable soup, I couldn't help thinking that this is what a community festival is all about. It takes not only the folks who organize these events but also those community members who support them to make them work.

I left town as the sky faded to a softer shade of late-afternoon blue. I still was far from home when the sky turned to apricot. Before long, the sun melted a hole in the horizon and slipped beneath its surface. But the world seemed warmer since I'd met the folks at Marienville.

❖ The Marienville Winterfest is held the last weekend of January each year, regardless of the weather. Although it is a two-day event, most activities are held on Saturday; many are held at the MACA building. To get there, at the center of town turn between the Unimart and the Bucktail Inn. Then take a right, then the first left. The MACA building is a log structure. Several motels in the area accommodate winter visitors. For more information, contact the Marienville Area Civic Association, Marienville, PA 16239.

February

Groundhog Day

Punxsutawney, Jefferson County

It was dark when I closed the door to my house behind me, deep in the night that slumbered between the first and second days of February. The winter stars pricked pinpoints of light through the onyx vault, and a pale sliver of moon glittered cold as a silver candlestick.

Almost two hours later on Tussy Mountain, the snow began, like the glitter that falls from a Christmas card and scatters on the lap of its handler. Soon cinder trucks joined me on Route 322, the spraying gravel clattering and bouncing across the highway. I welcomed the noisy missiles and the flashing yellow lights. Dawn and destination were both a long way off. I was headed for Punxsutawney, the self-anointed weather capital of the world.

To fight sleep on the all-night drive, I recounted what I knew about Groundhog Day. Although Groundhog Day was first proclaimed in 1886, the mock pagan ritual has its roots in ancient history. The Greeks believed that an animal's shadow was actually its soul, darkened by the past year's sins. During the animal's winter hibernation, his soul was cleansed, rendering it invisible once again. If the animal awakened before winter had time to finish the cleansing process, he saw his shadow and returned to his den. The belief passed into an old European legend: "For as the sun shines on Candlemas Day, so far will the snow swirl in May." Pennsylvania's German folk had kept the tradition alive. It was an ethnic tradition zany enough to capture the hearts of the country.

It was just after six and I was seven miles from town when I saw the first flash of fireworks from Gobblers Knob. The nighttime sky was darker than the inside of an old four-buckle arctic when I pulled into the Country Market parking lot on Route 119 and boarded a shuttle bus for the final leg of the journey. Many of the houses along the Woodland Avenue hill wore Christmas lights that twinkled and glittered across snowy yards. Farther up the hill, a seven-foot-tall snow groundhog watched the parade of yellow school buses crawl to the top of the knob. As my bus neared the top, the grand finale of the fireworks display went off.

Just inside the gate, a large welcome sign with a painting of Punxsutawney Phil drew the crowd's attention. Folks handed cameras over to complete strangers and posed by Phil's portrait.

The atmosphere at the top of the hill was decidedly fraternity party. Straw covered the snow and ice, and two gigantic bonfires outside of the inner sanctum of the ceremony attracted circles of revelers, six deep. The temperatures in the teens did not deter a number of young people from running around in their underwear, but I suspected that they had already loaded up on antifreeze. It seemed that I had arrived at the tail end of an all-night party.

The media were out in force. Five satellite dishes aimed at far-away broadcasting stations. I counted ten radio stations, seven of which were broadcasting from wooden booths facing the stage. Cables ran through the snow in the woods. One station was broadcasting live, and rock music blasted out from the hilltop.

It was impossible to get close enough to see the ceremony. Some folks climbed trees. Others stood far up on the hill on piles of firewood, binoculars in hand.

It was after seven when the popular sixties group, the Vogues, sang the national anthem. The Inner Circle of the Punxsutawney Ground Hog Club came to the stage, dressed in top hats and tails.

The spokesman began: "The Inner Circle got into an argument. We were divided between those who wanted Phil to see his shadow and those who didn't. I put the winter rooters on this side and the spring rooters on the other."

Each group held up its signs, Shadow and No Shadow.

"Let's hear it for the winter team! If you want spring let's hear it for this side!" The crowd went wild, equally divided between winter and spring.

"It doesn't matter what you want! He decides! Let's bring Punxsutawney Phil out and find out!"

At 7:29:43, Punxsutawney Phil, carried out by handler Bill Deeley, looked around and saw no shadow. His long sleep was over.

Dr. Paul Johnson of the Inner Circle read his proclamation to the world. There would be an early spring.

As the crowd dispersed, the radio station began playing "Me and My Shadow," "Enjoy Yourself, It's Later than You Think," and "Almost like Being in Love," songs from the popular movie *Groundhog Day*. Bill Murray's voice followed. "So what if there isn't a tomorrow? There wasn't one today."

Eight thousand people slipped and slid out to the road, most to await shuttle buses off the knob. I waited for an hour and a half. My feet were ice by then, and the cold seemed determined to burrow between the layers of clothing I wore. Nevertheless, the atmosphere was partylike and spirits were high. Groundhog hats, sweatshirts, and stuffed animals were everywhere.

I sat with Jeanette and Ivert Mayhugh from Dallas on the way down the hill. This was their second trip to Groundhog Day.

"We were here last year," Jeanette explained. "He proposed to me on Groundhog Day."

"In 1958," Ivert added.

"He thought he was going to the Caribbean, but I brought him here instead."

"When we landed in Pittsburgh, I knew we weren't going to the beach!"

"I rented the movie and played it again and again to get the spelling of Punxsutawney. Then I subscribed to the *Punxsutawney Spirit* to get the schedule of events. I had the paper under our bed for three months so that he wouldn't find out. We had such a wonderful time that we came back this year."

I heard similar stories throughout the morning. People had come to celebrate birthdays, engagements, anniversaries. Of course, most of us had come to celebrate anything and nothing at all, simply to dispel midwinter doldrums.

Spicy Groundhogs

2 cups sifted all-purpose flour	$1/2$ cup soft butter
$1/2$ teaspoon salt	1 cup sugar
$1/2$ teaspoon baking soda	$1/2$ cup molasses
1 teaspoon baking powder	1 egg yolk
1 teaspoon ground ginger	1 egg, slightly beaten
1 teaspoon ground cloves	currants or raisins
$1 1/2$ teaspoons cinnamon	

Sift flour, salt, soda, baking powder, and spices together. Set aside. Cream butter and sugar together until fluffy. Blend in molasses and egg yolk. Stir in flour mixture and mix well. Form into a ball. Wrap in plastic wrap or waxed paper. Chill 1 hour or longer.

Roll out a small amount at a time on a sugar-sprinkled board. Roll $1/8$ inch thick. Cut out cookies with lightly floured groundhog cookie cutter. Place cookies on greased baking sheet. Brush with slightly beaten egg. Decorate with currant or raisin eyes, buttons, and so forth. Bake 8 to 10 minutes in a preheated 350-degree oven. Cool slightly before removing from cookie sheet. Makes 12 to 15 large groundhogs or 3 to 4 dozen smaller ones.

There were breakfasts all over Punxsutawney that morning. Restaurants had a two-hour wait. I stopped by the chamber of commerce to kill a little time before braving another line out in the cold air.

The office was packed. Groundhog souvenirs were leaving in surprising quantities. The phone was ringing nonstop as one of the members of the Inner Circle announced to the country Phil's prognostication. The crush of bodies was warming, and as I thawed out, I bought official Groundhog Day cookie cutters and picked up a recipe.

Later, I talked with Jeanna Winebarger and Jennifer DiBlasio, both from Dubois, at breakfast. This was their third trip to Gobblers Knob.

"You have to come here to experience this," Jeanna said. "People just don't understand otherwise." After a pause she added, "Will you come back, do you think?"

"It's too crazy not to do it again," I replied.

❖ If you plan to attend Groundhog Day and want to stay in town, book a room by June. Activities are scheduled throughout the week, so you might consider making a week of it. If you are driving in only for Phil's appearance, take a shuttle bus to the Knob. The most accessible bus stop is at the Country Market on Route 119. There is ample parking there. The buses run from 5 A.M. from various locations all over town. Fireworks begin on Gobblers Knob at 6. For more information, contact the Chamber of Commerce, 124 West Mahoning Street, Punxsutawney, PA 15767, or call 814-938-7700.

Warren County Winterfest and Sled Dog Races

Chapman State Park, Warren County

The photos I took of Chapman State Park at the Winterfest and Sled Dog Races are lovely but deceptive. My Pentax camera faithfully recorded the snow-covered lake, its lifeguard chairs up to their knees in a sea of snowy whitecaps at winter's high tide. Just as it was that day, the sunlight arcing through the firs and hemlocks is as brilliant as lightning. Watercolor-blue shadows punctuate every variation in the endless snowy carpet.

But there, all similarities end. In my photos, ice skaters freeze forever in midspin, cross-country skiers hold impossible poses, and dogs leap and smile at the camera, forever in harness. No camera can capture in one shot the vast and barren winter beauty of the park, or the terrible cold. No camera can capture the noise or the crackling energy of the races. No camera can capture the relationship of musher and dog.

Pulling into Chapman State Park, I stopped at the ranger station to ask where the sled dog races were being held. As soon as I opened the car door, I knew that I needn't bother asking anyone. From far away, I heard the dogs' barking ringing clearly in the icy air. It was easy to crack a window and follow the racket.

Actually getting to the starting gate from the car was another matter altogether. I walked up and down the parking lot looking for a shoveled path. Eventually I climbed over the wall of plowed snow and, still following the yipping of the dogs, waded through the snow to the lake.

Dave Shaw, a veteran of twenty-five years behind the dogs, was announcing the races. Between events he told me, "Racing dogs requires total dedication and a lot of work. Those dogs have to be taken care of 365 days. Even on a sloppy day, a gray day, you have to be out there to train them. And then you have vet bills, food bills, and other expenses. And, if something goes wrong—anything—you never, never blame your dogs!"

At 11:30, Dave announced the Eight-Dog Sprint. The first team arrived at the gate promptly, chattering like a busload of high school students on the way to a football game. When they got into the starting chute, they really began to wail. The high-pitched whining, yapping, and keening could only be what Iditarod veteran Gary Paulsen calls "the Dog-song." One after another, teams arrived at the post, and each team sang another verse of the same eager chorus.

In the lull between departure and arrival, Dave Shaw wisecracked with his audience. "Anyone here named John?" he asked. "There's a fellow here looking for him!" And then, to a teenager in a Bulls jacket, he said, "You're the first kid I've seen in a long time with his own picture on his coat. As a matter of fact, you're better looking in that picture than you are in person." When a woman wearing ankle-high boots waded by in the foot-deep snow, he barked, "I really like your cocktail boots!"

After an interval that seemed surprisingly short for the dogs to run 9.8 miles, the first team appeared at the edge of the woods above the lake. "Clear the area of pet dogs," Dave Shaw commanded. "I don't know if you've ever had a team of dogs come at you, but they don't take kindly to dogs not in the same business as they are. If you've never been run over by an eight-dog team, it's an experience you won't soon forget coming out of the emergency room. Clear the track, please."

Venison en Daube

3 pounds venison steak, cubed
  as for stew
12 ounces lean salt pork, cut in
  small pieces
1 pig's foot, washed
1 $1/_2$ pounds tomatoes, peeled,
  seeded, and chopped, or 1
  large can tomatoes, chopped

1 pound carrots, cut in
  thick rounds
pepper to taste
12 ounces beef stock
1 pound mushrooms, sliced
1 pound small onions,
  peeled
4 ounces pimiento olives
4 ounces black olives, pitted

Marinade:
1 tablespoon white vinegar
3 cups dry red wine
1 onion, sliced
1 large bouquet garlic
1 strip thinly pared orange peel

2 cloves garlic, crushed
6 peppercorns
1 clove
$1/_2$ teaspoon coriander
2 tablespoons olive oil

Marinate venison in refrigerator 24 to 48 hours.

Preheat oven to 300 degrees.

Remove venison from marinade. Strain marinade, reserving liquid. Tie solid marinade ingredients into a piece of muslin.

Layer venison, salt pork, pig's foot, tomatoes, and carrots in an ovenproof casserole. Pour marinade over top. Add pepper and beef stock. Add bag of marinade vegetables.

Bring to boil, cover, and bake 2 $1/_2$ to 3 hours in oven.

Remove pig's foot, debone, and add meat to the casserole. Remove marinade bag. Add mushrooms, olives, and onions.

Cover and bake an additional 15 to 20 minutes or until onions are done.

Before the 12:30 Open Class, I walked up to the last bend of the trail and stood on a picnic table. The ice-covered lake spread out in front of me like a picnic tablecloth, and on it, revelers enjoyed a smorgasbord of winter sports. Ice fishermen manned their holes; cross-country skiers raced along the northern shore; ice skaters whirled and spun on a cleared area; snowmobilers buzzed the edge.

By the time the last team raced by me and headed into the home stretch, I had to admit defeat to the cold. Even my pen was frozen.

Luckily, the organizers had sheathed a summer picnic pavilion in plywood and fiberglass, heating it with an electric furnace and a fire in the stone fireplace. Tarps covered two entrances, and a few picnic tables were crowded into one end. Few things have ever given me more pleasure than the warmth that the coffee and the steaming bowl of chili gave me that afternoon.

When my fingers worked again, I borrowed a pencil from the woman beside me (sled dog race people know that pens freeze) and took a few notes. I stayed until guilt made me vacate a seat for another frozen spectator to thaw out.

Out in the parking lot, where the dogs were kenneled in their owners' trucks, Sharon Dennis was feeding her team. I stopped to ask what was in the mixture she was ladling out.

"It's a combination of chicken and horse meat," she told me. "We buy a thousand pounds of chicken necks and backs a month and I grind them and freeze them until I need them. We came onto the horse meat by accident. Our neighbor is Amish. His Percheron mare, Kit, got into a fatal kicking match with a stablemate. He asked if we could use her for dog food. He said he'd rather see her live through the dogs than rot away in the woods. So we pulled her home and butchered her."

Competitors were hitching their dogs for the next event. First the long main line was stretched out in front of the sled. And then, as each dog was hitched, it jumped up to lick the face of its master. In return, each received a pat, a few gentle words, a playful box of the ears. So great was the desire to run that each dog required a handler to hold it until the team was in place and the driver ready to take off.

Later that evening, I talked to Caroline Lobdell, the organizer of the sled dog races, which are a memorial to her husband, Jim Lobdell. I couldn't help commenting about the close relationship between team and musher.

"Your dogs are like your kids," she told me. "I know each one of my dogs' voices. I don't even have to look out the window to know which one is barking."

❖ The Warren County Winterfest and Sled Dog Races go into gear on the first Friday night in February with a Wild Game Feast in Warren, weather permitting. In addition to the Jim Lobdell Memorial Sled Dog Races, the park hosts a variety of winter sport contests. Snow sculpting, ice fishing, cross-country ski tours, ice skating races, inner tube races, sled races, toboggan races, ice golf, volleyball, and boccie ball are all featured during the two days. There is also a venison cook-off on Saturday afternoon. Plan on spending the weekend.

Chapman State Park is on Chapman Dam Road 8.6 miles east of Warren via U.S. Route 6. Turn at the light in Clarendon; follow signs. For more information, alternate dates, or Wild Game Feast reservations, call 814-723-3050 or contact the Warren County Chamber of Commerce, Suite 409 Integra Bank Building, Warren, PA 16365.

Ligonier Ice Fest

Ligonier, Westmoreland County

On the Saturday of the Ice Fest, I awakened to the sound of icicles dripping. One by one, sections of the snow cover on the roof pulled loose and went sledding to the ground, landing with a sloppy *flump*. When I stuck a tentative nose out from under the covers, I found that the cold that for weeks had lurked around the corners of the house had stolen away in the night.

Outside, it was even more obvious that winter was out of town for the weekend. I stepped off the curb onto what had been solid ice the evening before and promptly sank in up to my ankle. The cold stream running underneath dammed up, filling my shoe with icy water.

All along the turnpike, the snow was melting so rapidly that a haze frosted the morning air. The sunlight got lost in the snow cloud, lighting it with an opalescent glow. On the southern slopes of western Pennsylvania's rolling hills, the elbows and knees of the bare earth ripped through winter's fabric. Knowing that winter would return to patch up her torn snow cover only made the day more exhilarating. The February thaw: a perfect day for anything—except an ice festival!

Half the charm of the Ligonier Ice Fest is the setting. Surrounded by snow-covered hills, on a February day Ligonier is a precious gem sparkling in a white satin jewelry box. Carefully groomed houses line the wide pavements of the village. Shops cluster around the center of town. On the Diamond, a parcel of land at the intersection of Market and Main Streets, sits the Victorian band shell. It looks like the top of a wedding cake.

My first stop was an antiques shop, right by my car door. I bought a FireKing batter bowl, then crossed the street to check out the first ice sculpture. Sitting on blocks at curbside, the ice cowboy boot had a ten-gallon hat perched on top, and it was sweating ominously. I was afraid it wouldn't make it through the day, so I photographed it before the sun could do more damage. At another antiques shop I spent a friendly fifteen minutes dickering with the dealer over the price of an Empire sideboard. In the end, the only thing standing in the way of my purchase was the size of my VW convertible.

And so my pattern for the day was established. I spent the morning ricocheting between shops and sculptures, indulging my whims on both sides of Main, and then Market. Twenty-eight ice sculptures melted all over town. A bird in flight dripped in the shadows by the Ligonier Tavern. Farther on, in front of the Davis Real Estate Office, a blocky Celtic harp wept into the pavement. Betsy's of Ligonier, purveyors of fine ladies' apparel, showcased two large birds on its brick porch. On the corner of Market and Main, two elegant (if icy) ladies held aloft melting vases of fresh flowers. Another sculpture sweated under a beach umbrella.

By noontime, the Diamond was wearing an edging of snow no wider than a friar's tonsure. Shadows from the wintry trees latticed the lawn and brick patio, and the green park benches filled with sun seekers. It was hard to believe that two days earlier, an army of workers had been chipping away the coating on the brick pavement to avoid Ice Fest lawsuits.

I walked around eleven sculptures on the Diamond, stopping to admire goldfish, a griffin, a wishing well, an anchor, and the call letters for the local radio station. The most elaborate sculpture on display was a nautical piece in the band shell. Protected from the sun, it also stood the best chance of surviving into evening.

I walked up North Market Street to Pondstone Park to watch amateur carvers at work. Ralph Schmidt, from Hartville, Ohio, was at the Ice Fest for his second year. A student in culinary arts at the University of Akron, he was hoping for a third- or fourth-place win. As we spoke, a lacy heart and flower sculpture fell in on itself. "Heatstroke," someone behind us murmured.

The professional carvers were beginning to carve at the Loyalhanna Parking Lot on South Market Street at 12:30, but I opted for lunch at the Masonic Lodge in the center of town, which was offering an all-you-can-eat lunch of meatloaf sandwiches, vegetable soup, and gingerbread. It was hard to resist Cheryl Noel, who was inviting people in from the street. "I was supposed to say, 'Come in where it's warm,' " she told me.

The following Wednesday's issue of the *Ligonier Echo* showed the winning professional carving, a winged female figure holding up one hand—a cross between the Nike of Samothrace and the Statue of Liberty. Robert

---

Presidents' Weekend Cherry Crunch

$^1/_2$ cup butter   2 cans cherry pie filling
1 package yellow cake mix $^1/_2$ cup chopped pecans

Preheat oven to 350 degrees F. Cut butter into cake mix until the mixture resembles cornmeal. Reserve 1 cup of crumb mixture. Pat remaining mixture into ungreased 9 x 13-inch cake pan. Spread pie filling over cake mixture to within $^1/_2$ inch of pan edge. Mix the nuts with the 1 cup of reserved crumb mixture. Sprinkle over top. Bake 45 to 50 minutes. Serve with whipped cream or ice cream.

Higareda of Indiana, Pennsylvania, took the $1,000 prize sponsored by Eat N' Park Restaurants. Ralph Schmidt, in the amateur division, didn't place, but he did receive a $50 savings bond.

I was tempted to book a room and stay for dinner—several restaurants looked as inviting as the town itself, the Valley Players were presenting "Noises Off" that night, and Sunday morning's ski race at Laurel Mountain Summit would have been fun to watch—but with "miles to go and promises to keep," I reluctantly headed home.

The Ice Fest is held over Presidents' Weekend. Activities start on Friday afternoon with ice carving all over town and a snow sculpture contest for kids on the grounds of Fort Ligonier. A good plan would be to arrive on Saturday around noon. Spaced with hot chocolate breaks and visits to the town's shops, the walk around town would be leisurely and enjoyable. After dinner at one of many restaurants, attend the Valley Players' production in the Town Hall. A nighttime walk through the village would be a delightful closing to your day. Brunch and Sunday's ski races would polish off a perfect winter weekend, and you could be at home anywhere in the state by dark.

❖ Ice Fest events begin Friday evening and continue through Sunday afternoon of Presidents' Weekend. Ice sculptures are displayed on East and West Main Street, North and South Market Street, the Diamond area, Pondstone Park, and the Loyalhanna Municipal Parking Lot. Ligonier is located on Route 711, twelve miles from Exit 9 of the PA Turnpike.

Horse-Drawn Sleigh Rally

Forksville, Sullivan County

Day after day for a century or more, the Victorian houses that line Forksville's Water Street have stood drowsing to the music of the Loyal-sock Creek. On the rare occasion when they open their shuttered eyes, they look out on a scene with all the elements of a Grandma Moses paint-ing—rolling mountains that fold over and double back on themselves, a tumbling creek, a red covered bridge, a church spire. The water that rushes under the covered bridge moves faster than the traffic that bypasses town on 154, faster than life in the quiet hamlet, faster than time itself. On a February afternoon, Forksville seems as timeless and changeless as a Victorian snow globe.

On the day of the Horse-Drawn Sleigh Rally, winter was leaving Sul-livan County with reluctant footsteps. Snowbanks turned Route 154 into a slalom run, winding and twisting through World's End State Park; rocks sticking their heads out of the icy Loyalsock Creek wore snowy gnomes' hats. In nearby Muncy, however, the ancient maples that line the street were tapped and hanging with pails—the sap was running. Rally-goers shed coats and mittens in the teasing first taste of spring.

A string of parked cars lining the road signaled our arrival at the Sulli-van County Fairgrounds. Because of the deep snow piles squatting along the berm and the proximity of the Loyalsock, parking was a haphazard affair. Traffic was slowed to a crawl by pedestrians straggling down the road.

We had just entered the gates and were getting our bearings when the announcer started screaming from her perch on the back of a Ford pickup, "Clear the track! Clear the track! We have runaways!" I jumped up on a snowbank in time to avoid a smart little paint pony pulling a bas-ket sleigh, followed by a bay Arab in front of a green Albany cutter. Both were driverless; neither one could have run any faster if he were being chased by a knackerman with a pistol in one hand and a skinning knife in the other.

When they came to a bottleneck created by the announcer's truck and a bank of plowed snow, they plunged into the snowbank and went down. Although the horses were badly shaken, no one was hurt; the sleighs, however, were smashed: a white Lincoln wore a green racing stripe from the Albany cutter, and a Ford pickup lost a taillight.

Later in the afternoon, Ruthanne Gavitt, announcer and organizer of the event, told me what happened. "The paint was about to enter the ring when one of his sleigh runners got caught in the mud. The sleigh tipped, dumping its junior driver. The horse spooked and ran into the bay. His driver was out of her sleigh putting on her coat. He took off running, too. We're just lucky no one was hurt."

After all of that excitement, it took a minute or two to concentrate on the rally itself. Slowly, it came back into focus. The Sullivan County Fairgrounds is a movie-perfect setting for the sleigh rally. The narrow slice of land is bordered by Route 154 and the Loyalsock Creek on one side, and a huddle of mountains on the other. Painted red, gray, turquoise, and white, the fair's buildings resemble a family farming operation.

Classic sleighs, gleaming in shades of red, burgundy, green, and black lacquer, skimmed along behind sleek horses. Sleigh bells jingled merrily as competitors circled the makeshift show ring. Judged by John Grenall, a well-known Vermont-based official, eight of the nine events were performance classes. The other class—the real crowd pleaser—was the Currier and Ives competition. Judged solely on appearance and presentation, drivers and passengers wore nineteenth-century clothing appropriate to the vehicles. Bowlers, fur hats, muffs, wire-rimmed spectacles, furry lap robes, and even a meerschaum pipe were details that separated winners from losers.

I ate lunch at the only concession set up on the fairgrounds, the Kiwanis Club's dining room. Choices were limited to burgers, barbecues, hot dogs, chili, warm Danish pastry, chips, and beverages. It was an interesting meal. I spent most of my time moving from table to table, dodging the icy drops of water that found their way through the roof. The first topic of conversation at each stop was the runaways, but that deteriorated quickly to laughter about the leaking roof.

At one three-bite stop, I asked my tablemate, Annabelle Hepburn of nearby Montoursville, if she planned to take the bobsled ride included in the cost of admission. "No!" she told me. "I did that often enough when I was young. I don't need to do it now."

Bill Fogelman, seated beside her, also declined. "One time when I was a kid, I went to the neighbor's house to get some butter, and the sleigh went over. No sleigh rides for me!"

Since I'd had no previous bad experiences, I stood in line waiting for my turn to tour the fairgrounds in a bobsled. There were several running the course and I ended up on Dave Peterman's log sled, sitting on a hay bale behind a pair of black Percherons. During the ten-minute ride, I learned that the bobsled was his grandfather's and that he still uses it for logging despite the four tractors parked in his barn.

Julio's Mediterranean Beef

Use a round roast or a rib roast. With your hands, rub it with Tabasco, Worcestershire sauce, salt, pepper, oregano, and crushed garlic. Rub well to work seasonings into meat. Then, rub roast with olive oil. Cover and refrigerate at least 24 hours.

Peel and chop coarsely carrots, onions, and potatoes. Place them in roaster around beef. Douse liberally with Burgundy wine.

Bake covered at 250 degrees F to desired doneness.

—*Cherry Mills Lodge*

Although it was only three o'clock, the events were over and folks were leaving. I drove down to the Forksville Bridge and looked across the Loyalsock at the Victorian houses of Water Street. Like ancient dowagers who line the walls at a ball and awaken only at the sound of a song from their youth, I imagined these old ladies pulled into consciousness by the sound of hoofbeat and sleighbell. And then, as evening drifted over the valley on Rally night, only a creaking shutter or a groaning floorboard signaled that they were settling back into their timeless sleep.

❖ The Sleigh Rally is held on the Sunday of Presidents' Weekend each year. Contestants register at 9:30; gates open to the public at 11:00. Being there at 11:00 is advisable.

Food choices are limited, and you may want to consider tailgating. Depending on the snow, parking may be limited to the berm of Route 154. Plan ahead.

There is ample lodging in the surrounding area. For reservations, call Flora Villa Inne, 717-525-3245; Eagles Mere Inn, 717-525-3273; Forksville Inn, 717-924-3251; Cherry Mills Lodge, 717-928-8978; or Sonestown Country Inn, 717-482-3000.

For more information, write to Sullivan County Chamber of Commerce, Box C, Dushore, PA 18614, or call 717-928-9550.

Eagles Mere Toboggan Slide

Eagles Mere, Sullivan County

Many years ago I stood on the porch of the old Crestmont Hotel, looking down on Eagles Mere Lake. The smell of pine crept around the porch, batting my nose with velvet paws. The porch was filled with golden oak bedroom suites that morning. Some of the tall dresser mirrors reflected the silvery brown cedar shakes of the hotel, others studied the porch's peeling floorboards, and more than a few stared out over the lawn, taking one last look at what had been home for a century.

A regiment of oak wardrobes stood in line against the wall. One by one an auctioneer sent them on their way. A panel truck wearing North Carolina license plates swallowed them up.

Bit by bit, the other contents of the old hotel followed the armoires off the porch and into waiting trucks, trailers, and station wagons. Rumors of bankruptcy, demolition, and condos circulated through the crowd, in hushed whispers, as if no one wanted the old hotel to hear. As I watched that morning, an era ended, was torn up, and disseminated on the winds of progress, piece by piece. I couldn't help wondering about the fate of the tiny hamlet below: Would it follow the hotel down the road to progress?

A decade or so passed before I returned to Eagles Mere. To my relief, few changes had taken place in the village proper. Townhouses hadn't elbowed their way between the grand old homes on Eagles Mere Avenue. Fast-food restaurants hadn't knocked down the old mansions. There were still wide lawns instead of parking lots. Small-paned shop windows glowed in the afternoon light.

My friend Jage and I lingered in Someplace Special, Kay Thomas's shop in the center of town, before walking up to the slide on Lake Avenue. Kay shared her recipe for the Welsh cookies served in her shop during the Victorian Christmas weekend. And then, like two truants on the way to the principal's office, we procrastinated by stopping at the little Irish shop on the corner. Finally, we trudged up to Lake Avenue and got in the toboggan rental line.

"Are you sure you want to do this, my dear?" Jage queried. "I know how much you hate heights."

"For the sake of literature," I intoned.

"Well, it really doesn't look too steep . . . here, take my arm. I left my glasses in the car."

One by one parties of four or six got their toboggans and left for the slope. The rental line was getting shorter. Around us a soft, gentle snow swirled and danced, obscuring the lake below and muffling the sound of laughter.

All too soon we had our toboggan and were in line for our departure. We stood back, inviting sledders on a second or third run to cut in front of us. After several minutes of contrived courtesy, we couldn't stall any longer.

"You're in front," Jage told me. "Wind break."

"Neck break," I thought to myself, and decided that if we broke through the ice, I wouldn't save her.

A little paddling, and we were off. Jage had her legs under my arms and her arms around my waist. At first, it seemed like a Sunday afternoon sleigh ride in the park. Families pulling their toboggans up the hill smiled and waved. We smiled and waved back.

And then the bottom dropped out. The gentle slope gave way to a cliff. The soft snow turned to icy pellets. Trees whirred by and then became a blue-gray blur against the snowy countryside. The cold tore at my face, and I closed my eyes. The only sound was the shush of the toboggan against the ice. A soul-shattering scream ripped through the snowy silence, just behind me, and continued until, after a lifetime, the toboggan glided to a stop far out on the lake.

We unwound ourselves and brushed off the snow lodged in every crease of our clothing. I shook out my scarf and hat.

"Well, what did you think?" I asked.

"I didn't think. I was praying."

"You were praying very loud. I'm sure God heard you."

Gentleman that I am, I started pulling the toboggan across the lake and up the hill. It was amazing how heavy it had become. Chivalry soon exhausted itself.

"Here, you pull it awhile," I told Jage. "Part of the experience."

That didn't last long. Then we pulled it together. I counted steps, then lost count.

"Some little kid could make a fortune pulling these for people," Jage rasped.

"What little kid is that stupid?" I wheezed back.

And so we continued up the slope, mostly in silence. We were not two of the smiling, waving pedestrians.

At the top we decided, to my surprise, to try it one more time. Down the slope we kited, two veteran toboggan sliders. When we got to the top

Welsh Cookies

....

4 cups flour	1 level tablespoon nutmeg
2 cups sugar	1 level tablespoon salt
3 level tablespoons baking powder	

Mix together.

1 cup currants

Coat in dry mixture.

Add 1 cup butter to make crumbly mixture. (I use $^1/_2$ cup margarine and $^1/_2$ cup butter-flavor Crisco.)

Put 3 eggs in a cup measure. Add milk to make 1 cup.

Add to dry mixture. Refrigerate dough.

Roll and cut into slices $^1/_4$ inch thick.

Fry on 350-degree griddle 5 minutes a side.

the second time, we turned our toboggan in and headed for coffee and a warm fireplace.

On the way home Jage read the booklet Kay Thomas had found for us. "Did you know that the slide has been in operation since 1904?" she asked. "A Captain E. S. Chase designed it for his grandchildren."

She read on in silence. Then, out loud, "They're more mechanized now, but they're still using the same methods to build the slide. When the ice on the lake reaches twelve inches thick, workers cut twelve hundred blocks of ice, each fifteen and a half by forty-four inches. Then, using an elevator operated by a tractor, the ice is transported from the lake to a waiting pickup truck. Each block weighs at least two hundred fifty-six pounds.

"It takes a whole day to lay the blocks of ice down the hill from Lake Street out onto the lake. That night, the crew hoses the track down to seal it. The next day, they cut the groove. After they sweep it, the slide is tested by volunteers.

"It says here that the toboggans reach a top speed of forty to forty-five miles per hour."

"No wonder my teeth are still chattering!" I said as she closed the booklet.

❖ Eagles Mere is located in the heart of Sullivan County on Route 42. The toboggan slide starts in the center of town at the intersection of Eagles Mere Avenue and Lake Street. Opening date depends on weather conditions—too much snow or unseasonable warmth delays construction. If the slide hasn't been built by Presidents' Weekend, plan on waiting until the next winter. It's best to call ahead, 717-525-3244, or write Eagles Mere Village Inc., Box 2, Eagles Mere Avenue, Eagles Mere, PA 17731.

If you plan to try the slide, dress warmly. Avoid loose-fitting clothing, and take your Dramamine.

March

Gordonville Auction

Gordonville, Lancaster County

In early March, winter hangs around Lancaster County like the old-timer seated before the potbellied stove in the general store. By March, her tales are so worn that none of her repertoire excites or alarms us as it did in December, for now, winter has more past than future.

Held on the second Saturday in March, the Gordonville Fire Company's auction provides the Amish and Mennonites with one last fling before spring. In several weeks the alfalfa will be planted; corn and wheat will follow a month later. This is the last leisure the Lancaster County farming community will know until winter sets in again, and so, finishing barn chores before dawn, they hitch up the horses for a day of socializing.

From Route 340 East, I drove south into Gordonville on the Old Leacock Road—a huge mistake on sale day. Every barnyard along that narrow road was filled with horses—as many as fifty to a farm. Shining black and gray buggies stood in neat rows in front pastures. Cars and trucks rubbed noses with plowed snowbanks on both sides of the narrow road, reducing the road to one lane.

Traffic turned to a rolling boil near the Gordonville Fire Company, and with no parking, there was nothing to do but drive on toward U.S. Route 30. From there, I followed parking signs to the St. John's Church parking lot, a mile or so west of the Old Leacock Road on Route 30, one of four parking areas on the shuttle bus run. After a twenty-minute wait, a school bus picked us up, taking us on a pleasant drive through Amish countryside.

By the second stop, bus seats were filling rapidly. An old man tottered aboard at the end of the line. Wearing a plaid shirt, argyle sweater, bold plaid slacks, and a polka-dot bow tie, he had dressed up for his big day out, but he'd obviously left his glasses at home.

"Hey lady!" he bellowed. "Hey lady!"

Everyone turned—the only remaining seat was beside a middle-aged man. Paunchy and balding, he sat there in shock, a look of stony horror and disbelief etched on his face, willing himself to disappear in a flash of smoke.

"Mind if an old guy sits with you?" the aging dandy said in a voice that could wake the dead. His rakish wink as he creaked down into the seat was the final shovelful of dirt on his seatmate's coffin. For most of the passengers, the ride was a short, laughter-filled ride through the snowy fields, but for that poor fellow it must have seemed an eternity. When the bus stopped, he shot out of his seat, crawled over the old man, and disappeared into the crowd, first off the bus. As we watched him go, my friend Matt said, "Kinda makes you wonder what the old guy's wife looked like, doesn't it?"

As we walked toward the firehouse, we were surrounded by thousands of Amishmen. "I feel like we've just walked into *Witness*," Matt said.

We stood looking down into a makeshift arena. Half of the Amish, encouraged by early spring, wore summer straw hats, while the other half held on to winter in black felt toppers.

A pair of five-year-old mules were brought out from a striped tent, lot numbers taped to their rumps. Judging from their size and tawny color, there was a Belgian mare in their ancestry. Bidding was fast and increments were high. In a minute or two, the mules sold for $5,800. Another pair of mules followed, bringing $700 less.

Then horses began to appear in the ring. A handler brought out a flashy bay standardbred with a pedigree. As cart horses go, this one was a Porsche. Her handler knew it and trotted her around the ring. Even so, she failed to bring $2,000. The woman beside me said, confidentially, "He bought it for his son, so he did. Isaac's sixteen now and needing a horse of his own."

The next offering, a smaller, more docile creature, was led out. "Here's a good family horse!" the auctioneer boomed. I watched the family horse bring $1,200 before turning my attention to the mountains of snow pushed back along the railroad track to clear the arena area.

There, three little Amish boys played king of the mountain. Two more inspected large yellow snowplows. Another group splashed each other in the mud puddles—like children everywhere, despite the gravity of their clothing or the seeming harshness of their lifestyle.

Quilts were the main attraction in the firehouse across the street. The building was standing room only, and the crowd flowed out onto the blacktop beyond the bays. This crowd was "English." A fan pattern quilt went from $50 to $375 in less than a minute. The woman beside me spoke in hushed tones about a $1,200 quilt sold the year before—the highest price ever paid at Gordonville. Meanwhile, one quilt followed another, all in the $250 to $550 range. At the end of an hour, seventy-one quilts had been sold—old, new, pieced, appliquéd, and embroidered. By the end of the day, more than eight hundred quilts had crossed the auction block, and judging from the license plates in the parking lot, many went far from their place of origin.

Later, my friend Judi Shunk, a veteran of many Gordonville quilt sales, explained the pricing to me. Quilts made entirely by one person

---

Oyster Stew

Boil 1 quart of oysters in their liquid until the edges curl. Add 1 gallon milk and 1 quart of light cream. Heat to boiling but do not boil. Add one stick of butter, and season to taste with salt and plenty of pepper. Allow to cool or season. Reheat just before serving. Serve with generous amounts of oyster crackers.

---

generally fetch the highest prices. There should be ten stitches to the inch, all even. Color and pattern also affect price. Antique quilts seem to be in a league of their own. This little quilt lesson explained the magnifying glasses, sage nodding of heads, madly waving bidders' cards, and bored sighs of the cognoscenti in the Gordonville audience.

While the quilts were being sold, auctioneers outside sold all manner of goods. One man worked from the back of a produce truck selling flats of fresh strawberries, the first of the season.

Matt said, "You know, this is pretty clever of these sellers. All out-of-towners associate the Amish with fresh produce. They come here, get caught up in the spirit of things, and buy something to take home, assuming that they've bought something Amish. I'll bet these strawberries came from California."

I nodded, then stepped up to buy a flat of berries.

Across the parking lot from the berry truck were two yellow-and-white tents full of used household goods. Table lamps, a swivel desk chair, a crib, a hospital bed, sets of kitchen chairs, living room suites, end tables, and hanging lights awaited the auctioneers. Amish housewives inspected and appraised these items, pecking, scratching, and clucking like a flock of biddy hens looking for corn.

On the other side of the firehouse building, another tent held new items. Tube socks, socket sets, screwdrivers, and batteries stood in cardboard boxes on rows of folding tables.

Two twelve-by-twenty-foot storage sheds would be sold at the end of the sale. From one, crafts flowed out the door and into the parking lot. The other was a food concession. Inside, an Old Order Mennonite woman served bowls of oyster stew from a ten-gallon stockpot. Soon, Matt and I were seated at an oilcloth-covered table, shoveling oyster crackers into the creamy, buttery stew, laughing with the auctioneer, Sam Stoltzfus as the cook shared her recipe, but not her name.

"I use a milk can of milk," she said. "That's twenty quarts. Then I use a gallon of oysters and a pound of butter and some salt and pepper. I try to put three oysters in a bowl."

By the time we finished, it was midafternoon. The crowd was shoulder to shoulder. The Old Leacock Road was so blocked with pedestrians that a New York City cab driver would have looked for an alternate route. The crossing guard seemed headed for a nervous breakdown. And so we crossed the railroad bridge to the bus stop and left Gordonville and the crowds behind us.

❖ The Gordonville Auction is held on the second Saturday in March. If you attend, drive in on U.S. Route 30. Look for parking signs in Paradise and wait for the shuttle bus. For more information, contact the Gordonville Fire Company, Gordonville, PA 17529.

St. Patrick's Day Dance

Shunk, Sullivan County

After snaking along the Loyalsock Creek for miles, Route 154 suddenly takes off over the mountains at Forksville. Then, after a leisurely ramble over mountain ridges and plateaus, it barrels down a roller-coaster hill and rockets up the other side. There in the hollow, the tiny village of Shunk weathers the years. If you cup your hands together, you'll have a pretty good idea of the size and shape of Shunk.

In the center of the hollow, Baumunk's General Store and the U.S. post office hold court in a large, blocky building. The sawmill next to it sprawls over the center of the town, well aware of its crucial role in the citizenry's survival. Across from Baumunk's, one old garage faces down the road to Canton, proudly displaying a "Shunk, PA" sign across its forehead, and another relic of a garage, with auto showroom, sports an original Kaiser Frazer sign, still lighted on special occasions even though the last Kaiser Frazer rolled off the assembly line a half-century ago.

Ten or so houses climb the hillsides around the core of the village. The white spire of the Shunk United Methodist Church rises above the village on the Forksville side. Farther up that hill, the Endless Winds Volunteer Fire Company keeps watch over the village from its long, red, board-and-batten building. The population of the cemetery nearby far exceeds the population of the village below.

As I pulled into town, evening succumbed to night. Although lights twinkled on the surrounding hills, the village was deserted—Baumunk's was closed, the sawmill silent. Just as I was ready to leave town, a lone man emerged from the "Shunk, PA" garage. I raced across the street.

When I asked why there were no lights at the firehouse, he explained, "Well, the dance doesn't start until nine, and the equipment is all in this garage to make room up at the firehouse. Don't worry, they have the parking lot pushed out. There'll be a dance."

I looked at my watch. I had a good two and a half hours to burn before things got rolling at the Endless Winds dance. I'd already explored all four corners of Shunk, and there was no chance of a cup of coffee, let alone dinner. I considered my options. Forty-five minutes later, I was eating pizza at the only restaurant I could find open in Canton. From the look of that town, it seemed that the Endless Winds Fire Company's dance promised to be the hottest thing going on in three counties.

I ate as slowly as I could and drove back to Shunk in third gear. Even so, I was among the first arrivals.

The admission charge seemed a little steep until I realized that it included the fresh popcorn on the table, food from the kitchen, and an open bar. There was additional charge only for pitchers of beer. With live entertainment, the evening was a real bargain.

The truck bays of the Endless Winds Volunteer Fire Company were heated by a woodstove made from an old oil drum. Tables and chairs lined the back wall and the side along the doors. With its concrete floors, the building was a little cold around the edges on a wintry night, and the tables closest to the stove filled up first.

When I arrived, Kay Lynn and the Mavericks were setting up at the end of the building. The kitchen was abustle, and in one corner people were organizing a makeshift bar. As I settled in, strings of owl lights came on over the stove and the stage area. All the while, a steady trickle of villagers straggled in, got their hands stamped, and found seats. A volley of greetings and back-slapping hellos filled the engine bays.

Kay Lynn said, "Are you ready to square dance? Grab your favorite partner, and let's dance!" The music started, and few folks were too shy to get up on the dance floor. Coats came off in a hurry. Couples whirled, swayed, and do-si-doed. Despite the advertising of "square and round dancing," it was easy to see which style held favor. Two brave souls tried a few sequences of a country line dance and then left the floor self-consciously. Things don't change quickly in places like Shunk.

At my table, Eileen Henry told me, "I don't think I've missed too many of these dances. We have them for every major holiday except

Ham, Leek, and Potato Soup

2 ham hocks
1 pound potatoes, peeled
 and cubed
1 pound leeks (white and green
 parts), sliced thinly

1 teaspoon salt
freshly ground black pepper
 to taste
1 cup heavy cream

Simmer the ham hocks in plenty of water in a large soup pot. When meat is literally falling from the bone, remove and set aside. Measure stock—you'll need 7 $1/_2$ cups. Add cubed potatoes and sliced leeks to the ham broth, add seasonings, and simmer for 40 to 50 minutes. Meanwhile, when the meat is cool, remove from bone, chop, and add to soup pot.

Remove half of vegetables and meat, purée them in the blender, and return to pot. Add cream, reheat, and serve, garnished with fresh parsley—and a little country music!

Easter. I only live a mile and a half down the road . . . and besides, there's nothing else to do here."

Burdell Quail and his wife, Arlene, joined us. "So, you did make it," he said. "I talked to you earlier at the garage. My wife owns that garage—I used to work there—I don't anymore."

"Yeah—she fired him!" a passerby interjected.

As the evening progressed, I learned that Burdell had been a member of the fire company since its formation. He was also the first fire chief in Shunk, and his wife was serving her third term as company president. And once again, I was reminded of the importance of folks like the Quails in small-town life.

Conversation faded away in a country tune. With each change of tempo, the Mavericks controlled the roomful of guests. Couples swirled and danced the age-old square dance sets. The band kicked up "The Aunt Jemima Polka," and the dancers kicked up their heels. Then the lights went down, and dancers slow-danced to a country ballad.

When Burdell handed me the schedule of firehouse events, conversation quickly turned to firehouse dinners. All meals at Endless Winds are all-you-can-eat—including August's prime rib dinner. The menu that caught my attention, however, was the ham and leek dinner served in May. Obviously, this is a regional specialty.

Arlene explained the recipe. "First, we cook the ham and then we take the broth and cook the leeks in that. We dress them with salt, pepper, and butter, and serve them with vinegar on the table. We also serve mashed potatoes, baked beans, and orange Jell-O with cabbage and carrots. The meal is buffet style."

Burdell added, "We have raw leeks on the table, too, but if you eat them raw, you'll sleep alone that night!"

"And don't plan on going to church the next morning," Arlene added.

I looked at my watch, voiced my regrets and good-byes, and began packing my camera and notes into my backpack.

Burdell said, "You make sure you have something in your stomach— you have a long drive ahead of you!"

And then, with more good-byes and promises to return, I left Shunk, feeling as if I were walking out of an old and cherished family photograph.

❖ The Shunk dances are held on the Saturday closest to all major holidays except Easter. They run from 9 P.M. to 1 A.M. When the weather cooperates, expect a large crowd of folks from surrounding hunting camps. Firehouse dinners are held throughout the year. The ham and leek dinner is in May, the prime rib dinner in August, the chicken and biscuit dinner in October, and the all-day pancake and sausage dinner during the opening day of hunting season. There is also a gun raffle drawing early in December. For exact dates and possible weather cancellations, call ahead.

There are no overnight accommodations in Shunk, so it's best to book rooms in nearby Canton, Eagles Mere, Sonestown, or the Forksville area. The Endless Winds Fire Company is located just east of town on the top of the hill on Route 154.

April

Mennonite Relief Sale

Harrisburg, Dauphin County

Ask anyone why he attends the Mennonite Relief Sale and you're certain to get one of two answers: strawberry pie or quilts. Since 1958 those lures have drawn folks from all over the country to the Farm Show Building in Harrisburg on the first Friday and Saturday in April.

On that weekend springtime undid her bonnet and let down her hair, and April sunlight flirted with the winter-weary state. Daffodils exploded into bloom, walkers and joggers elbowed each other on Harrisburg's riverside, and the Farm Show Building threw open its doors to fifteen thousand spring-hungry guests.

As I pulled off Cameron Street into the parking lot, it was impossible not to recall my January trip to the Farm Show. I put the VW's convertible top up and threw my sweater into the backseat. I noticed a few mangy snow piles on my way to the entrance. The unmistakable smell of livestock hangs there, faint as a trace of wood smoke lingering through winter into spring. Ahead of me a large red-and-white sign read, "Welcome to the Pennsylvania Relief Sale." Other signs pointed the way to omelets, pancakes and sausage, crafts, the quilt display, and the antiques auction.

The quilts were displayed in a fenced enclosure—no one was taking chances with these valuable works of art. I had to chuckle to myself—just three months earlier, hogs and sheep had occupied that same floor space.

I didn't take time to preview the quilts but followed the red arrow to the country auction. A few months before, a Scottish judge, tweedy and self-important, had presided over this area, and the center of attention was a bleating and bantering flock of sheep. When I walked in on the day of the Relief Sale, antiques and paintings awaited sale. Verna Wagner was introducing lot number 122, a painting entitled "Lancaster County Farm," as I took a seat. Bidding rose rapidly to $575. That was followed by a watercolor bringing $65, and an antique saint painting that was a real bargain at $15.

Mrs. Wagner introduced one of her own paintings, an oil of the Star Barn, the 1868 landmark along Route 283 in Middletown. She shared the history of the barn with the crowd, but still it brought only $225.

Other donated items awaited the gavel: a barrel churn, a golden oak parlor table, a Lincoln rocker, an oak clothes tree, a wicker table, and a firehouse Windsor. The country auction had begun at 9 A.M., and by the time I got there many things had changed hands. The sale bill in the pre-view catalogue listed antique pattern glass, crystal, graniteware, brass, copper, textiles, toys, and tools. In addition to the antiques, a handcrafted scale-model Conestoga wagon by Earl W. Schmidt and a series 330 Speedway Express Wagon with a one-thousand-pound capacity received special advertising.

I headed for the strawberry pie stand in the east corner of the Main Exhibition Building but got bogged down by exhibits. Smart move, putting the pies in the corner of the building! I stopped at the Penny Power Project and was overwhelmed by the magnitude of the effort. Hun-dreds of bags of pennies collected at local Mennonite churches lay on skids, counted and ready for the bank. Although a painted thermometer registered $13,000, volunteers continued to pour bottles, jugs, and cans of pennies into an automatic counter. Like all of the proceeds from the Relief Sale, the Penny Power Project is used for missionary purposes— tree seedlings for Lebanon fruit farmers, canned meat for Third World countries, Bibles for Egyptian families.

I wandered through the other displays, always vaguely drawn to the pie stand. I rummaged through the book booth, stopped at the informa-tion booth, examined crafts, stopped at the International Self-Help Crafts booth, and considered a rug for my front hallway. I also looked at the needlework, art supplies, quilting supplies, baked goods, and tapes and records.

All the while, I scouted the food booths. With strawberry pie on my mind, I'd forgotten about the other homemade foods offered at the Relief Sale. It was a tough decision. I bypassed baked potatoes, pizza, fresh fruit, beef barbecue, cold platters, french fries, funnel cakes, homemade ice cream, ham sandwiches, hot dogs, Orange Julius, homemade donuts, pie, roast beef sandwiches, soft pretzels, and homemade soups. Finally, I set-tled on a turkey sub and a vanilla milkshake.

I sat at a table by the strawberry pie booth and watched the pies leave shelves, travel to the showcases, and then disappear in white pastry boxes. Through the shelves I saw workers assembling the pies.

Finally, I bought my pie. I talked with Shirley High, a Rheems resident who has been in charge of making the Relief Sale strawberry pies since 1987. She told me that eighty volunteers had been working since Wednes-day. The crusts were prebaked and donated by a bakery, but three people spent five hours on each of two nights making glaze and topping. Forty people spent two hours stemming berries. Then a full staff assembled the pies on Friday night and Saturday. The pies are sold whole or by the piece.

Strawberry Pie

1 9-inch or 8-inch baked pie shell   1 quart strawberries
Wash, drain, and hull strawberries.
Simmer together about 3 minutes:
    1 cup strawberries $^2/_3$ cup water
Blend and add to boiling mixture:
    1 cup sugar $^1/_3$ cup water
    3 tablespoons cornstarch
Boil 1 minute, stirring constantly. Cool.
    Reserve $^1/_2$ cup choice berries; put remaining berries in baked
pie shell. Cover with cooked mixture and garnish with reserved
berries. Refrigerate until firm—about 2 hours.

I carried my pie carefully as I made a few more purchases—two bags of homemade noodles, a loaf of fruit bread, and a peace lily. Finally, when I couldn't juggle any more packages, I went to the quilt auction.

Despite thousands of eager bidders already seated at the west end of the Main Exhibition Building, there were still catalogues. All told, 419 quilts and hangings were listed. I watched numbers 360 through 389 being sold.

Each quilt was brought out and opened on a rotating display stand. The auctioneer listed the number, pattern, size, and maker, and the bidding began. The crowd was large. Spotters worked in front, assisting the auctioneer with finding bidders. Excited bidders stood up to attract attention. After each quilt sold, its number and price were projected on a screen. Number 383, "Country Sweetheart" by Linda Zook, brought a round of applause when it sold for $1,000. Each quilt was folded, bagged, and taken to a pickup center, guarded more carefully than the bags of pennies at the Penny Power booth. Dealers from all over the country buy here. At first I thought it was a little incongruous—finished city folks devouring the country quilts. When I thought it over, it made sense: They can pay top price, and the money goes to charitable works.

❖ The Mennonite Relief Sale is held on the first weekend in April at the Farm Show Building in Harrisburg. Doors open late Friday afternoon for an auction of quilts, comforters, wall hangings, afghans, and rugs. There is also entertainment.

Saturday's schedule begins with breakfast at 6 A.M. and includes the quilt auction, a children's activity tent, and a country auction. There is no admission charge, and parking is free.

For more information, contact the Mennonite Central Committee, 21 South 12th Street, Akron, PA 17501.

Meyersdale Maple Festival

Meyersdale, Somerset County

Miles before you reach the small commmunity of Meyersdale for the Maple Festival, you begin to get a pretty good idea of what the town is all about. A restaurant window announces, "Maple Smiley Face Cookies Are Here!" Another sign advertises pure maple syrup over an autumn-hued maple leaf. Still closer to town, Hitties's Sugar Camp stands at the bottom of a hillside, supplying the gravity needed to get the sap down to the boiling tanks. Finally, coming into Meyersdale on Bleachley Street, you pass the Maple City Fire Department and "Welcome Pennsylvania Maple Festival!" banners. As you turn onto Meyers Avenue, you see the sap pails on the venerable maples. Welcome to Meyersdale, the Maple City!

Mary Neimiller was waiting for me at the festival office with Kathy McClure, the festival president. Both women have had a long association with the Maple Festival. Mary, a forty-three-year veteran, said, "I started out making pancakes for the Lions Club and worked my way up to this confusion."

Kathy added, "In Meyersdale, every little girl wants to be Maple Queen. I was first runner-up, but now I'm president."

Together they told me the story of the Maple Festival. The festival idea was born on a winter night in 1947 as a group of gentlemen sat around a potbellied stove in a local store. They were lamenting the loss of local stands of hardwood trees. This was after the war, when returning GIs married and began building and furnishing homes. Lumber was in demand and the maple groves of Somerset County were disappearing. These general-store visionaries realized that income from maple sugar products would protect the maple groves.

Then, on a 1947 radio broadcast, America's songbird, Kate Smith, announced that she was hungry for some good Vermont maple syrup. Somerset County responded instead, and in April 1947 Kate Smith told the whole nation that Somerset County maple syrup was the sweetest she'd ever tasted. Soon the first Maple Festival was in the planning.

Mary Neimiller gave me a tour of Maple Manor, the centerpiece of the compound. Begun in 1769, the simple log frontier structure grew to its present size after Jacob Meyers purchased it in 1805. With the proceeds from his business ventures—a tannery, a grist mill, a woolen mill, a distillery, a foundry, and a cattle farm—he and his family enlarged the log house and sheathed it in clapboards. Now it stands as a symbol of gracious, mid-nineteenth-century country life.

From the Federal farmhouse and 1850 Chickering concert grand piano in the double parlor to the bucket bench and walnut dry sink in the old log kitchen, the mansion is a wish book for antiques collectors. Yet it feels like a much-loved family home, and visitors feel like welcome guests. We visited the sugaring building and tasted spotza, hot maple syrup drizzled over snow. At the general store in the park, I bought maple syrup and

Grandma's Maple Cake

1 1/2 cups sugar
1/2 cup margarine, softened
3 eggs, separated
1 cup warm milk
2 1/2 cups flour
3/4 cup maple syrup
2 teaspoons baking powder
1 teaspoon vanilla

Beat together the sugar, margarine, and egg yolks. Add alternately 2 cups flour and milk. Beat for 2 minutes.

Add maple syrup, remaining flour (1/2 cup), baking powder, and vanilla. Mix well. Gently fold in stiffly beaten egg whites.

Pour into two prepared pans and bake at 350 degrees for 25 minutes (9-inch pans) or 30 to 35 minutes (9 x 13-inch pan).

—*Margaret Ackerman, Meyersdale*

Grandma's Icing

1/2 cup maple syrup
3 tablespoons margarine
1 pound confectioners' sugar
4 to 5 tablespoons milk
1 tablespoon vanilla

Boil the first two ingredients for 3 minutes, then cool.

Add the three remaining ingredients alternately to the maple mixture. Beat well until the right consistency is achieved.

—*Margaret Ackerman, Meyersdale*

Maple Oatmeal Bread

2 packages dry yeast	$^1/_3$ cup shortening
$^1/_2$ cup warm water (110 degrees)	1 tablespoon salt
1 $^1/_2$ cups boiling water	6 cups white flour
1 cup oatmeal	2 eggs, beaten
$^1/_2$ cup maple syrup	

Soften yeast in warm water and set aside.

Combine boiling water, oatmeal, maple syrup, shortening, and salt. Cool to lukewarm.

Stir in 2 cups of flour and the eggs. Beat well.

Add enough remaining flour to make a soft dough.

Form into a ball and put in a greased bowl.

Let rise until double in size, about 1 to 1 $^1/_2$ hours.

Punch down and divide in half and put into two greased loaf pans.

Let rise again for 1 hour or until double in size.

Bake at 375 degrees for 40 to 45 minutes.

Cool on racks.

—*Esther Mishler, Hollsopple*

maple cookies. The old-time doctor's office is completely equipped with antique surgical tools. At the cobbler's shop, two elementary schoolchildren demonstrated colonial shoe making. Their stage presence, knowledge, and polished showmanship were astounding.

Later, I met Pat Conn, a retired school librarian who does storytelling for younger Maple Festival goers. When I found that she had trained the young cobblers, I complimented her on a fine job. "I'm glad you enjoyed them," she told me dryly. "They apparently thought they were doing pretty well, too. They put out a bowl with a sign, 'Please tip the help.' "

After one more spin around Maple Festival Park and a quick inspection of the crafts on display, I walked to the pancake dinner at the old schoolhouse. A long line wound down the stairs, but the sausage and pancakes were worth the half-hour wait. There was no shortage of maple syrup on the tables, and waitresses served generous portions repeatedly at the long, family-style tables. My coffee cup was never below half empty. Part of the fun was feeling teleported to the 1950s; anyone of my generation would have had a sense of déjà vu in the school cafeteria.

I walked back to Main Street to see the antique autos on display. I felt I should have spent the weekend.

❖ The Maple Festival is held the last two weekends in April: Saturday and Sunday, then Friday, Saturday, and Sunday. An admission fee to the park includes the tour of the manor house, sugaring shack, doctor's office, general store, and cobbler's shop. Entertainment in the park area is continual. Parking is available around town, but there is a charge for convenient parking lot spots.

The schedule of events is extensive and includes three performances of "Legend of the Magic Water," a pageant that follows the history of Meyersdale from the Iroquois settlements in the area.

From the north, take the Pennsylvania Turnpike (I-76) and exit onto U.S. Route 219 South; from the south through Maryland take I-68 and exit onto U.S. Route 219 North. For more information, call 814-634-0213.

Look for Kathy and Mary—and tell them to save me some maple cookies.

Endless Mountains Maple Festival

Troy, Bradford County

On the weekend of the Maple Festival in Troy, spring won her final tug of war with winter and sent the old man tumbling to his knees. As I drove into town on Route 14, the bank sign flashed out 2:30 and 77° in rapid succession, as if even the computer that runs the mechanism was surprised and pleased to share the information with the northern-tier community.

The citizens of Bradford County responded enthusiastically with shorts, T-shirts, and sunglasses. By the end of the day, no doubt many of them would also be sporting the first sunburn of the season.

On that Sunday afternoon, the leaves were about halfway open, dots of silvery green splashed against a baby blue sky. The ancient trees were gearing up for summer's sunshine and another season of sheltering the clapboard homes that line the streets of the village. The running of the sap was over, and this celebration marked the end of the boiling season, the beginning of spring.

I followed Route 14 through town, looking for the festival until I saw a Ferris wheel glinting against the wooded hillside. I pulled into the main gate of Alparon Park and followed the crowd toward the track and arena.

I looked both ways for runaway horses and sulkies, but there was only a hay wagon loaded with spectators and pulled by two docile draft horses. Then, looking up at the nearly deserted grandstands, I felt a little foolish at my caution, for the track wasn't drawing any attention.

At the auto exhibit, there were about thirty vehicles, many from the forties, fifties, and sixties. A gaggle of folks walked along the line, paying cursory attention to the vehicles. I chocked up their lethargy to spring fever.

Then I noticed a flurry of activity under the grandstands. People were buzzing around the entrance, and the whole building was humming like a beehive. When I walked closer, I knew why. The unmistakable smell of pancakes and sausage wafted from the building. What better way to showcase the season's harvest?

Across from the Trojan Booster Club's makeshift cafeteria, the Endless Mountains Maple Producers had set up a display. As I was examining the samples of maple syrup, Carmen Barker, Pennsylvania's 1994 Maple Sweetheart, appeared.

The seventeen-year-old from Warren Center started out as Endless Mountains Maple Queen and had already attended both the Troy and Harford fairs the summer before, done school promotions, and appeared in parades. During her reign as State Maple Sweetheart, Carmen would appear at the Farm Show and at schools throughout the state. Like any good PR person, Carmen loaded me up with promotional pamphlets.

There was a compact midway between the stadium and the swimming pool. In addition to the Ferris wheel, there were bumper cars, a Twister, a slide, and a moonwalk. There were also several games and a sand art booth for the younger set. Without even looking over my shoulder for anyone I knew, I got in line and rode the Ferris wheel—it must have been the springtime air that brought on my foolishness, but I enjoyed every turn.

Three sap evaporators steamed throughout the afternoon. One, set up in a permanent building, promoted the sale of maple products. The other two were demonstrators promoting two brands of evaporators. I think that most of us cherish a Currier and Ives lithographic image of sugaring: draft horses pulling a large wooden barrel on sled runners through mountains brimming with snow. In our minds there are always old tin sap buckets hanging on the trees instead of the plastic tubing that feeds into a vat. Sugar shacks are stacked high with lumber as whole families work around the clock manning the fires. It's nice to know, sentiment aside, for the sake of those who still tap the sugar bush, that technology has made the task of sugaring just a little easier.

Maple Pork Chops

6 thick center-sliced pork chops   2 apples
$^3/_4$ cup maple syrup

Arrange pork chops in baking dish. Core apples and slice each in three thick slices. Place one slice of apple on each chop. Top with maple syrup. Bake covered for 1 $^1/_2$ hours in a 325-degree oven. Uncover and bake 20 minutes longer. Baste frequently throughout baking.

Vendors had booths behind the stadium and in the livestock barns. The usual T-shirts and flea market items were displayed next to wooden cutouts, stained glass sun catchers, crocheted dish towels, Adirondack furniture, and needlework. One enterprising soul was selling crosscut slabs of maple logs, but neither the locals nor the out-of-towners were interested in such high-priced firewood.

I stopped for a moment to listen to the local band. They were playing rousing Sousa marches to an appreciative lawn-chair audience. Then, my physical self won out over my aesthetic self, for my stomach was oompahing louder than the tuba. And so I headed for the Cub Scouts' hot dog stand.

Winnie Bowman, den mother for the Webelos, shared the recipe for maple dogs. "The festival has a rule that all the foods sold here must be maple related. We cook our hot dogs in maple sap. Our mapleade is lemonade made with maple sap as a sweetener."

My maple dog tasted just like any other hot dog. Considering that it takes forty gallons of sap to make one gallon of syrup, I guess it would take a lot of boiling to impart any flavor to the dogs in the pot.

My final stop was the Grange Exhibits Building. One of two structures on the ground that could be labeled vintage Pennsylvania fair, the Grange building is a hodgepodge of rooflines, gables, and angles—an architectural treasure.

A sign inside reads, "This historic building has been restored through the cooperation and hard work of the Grangers of Bradford County. Thank you to all and a special salute to Nancy Brackman for her leadership."

Spotlighted by the highest bank of windows, a colorful canvas theater drop hung, brightly lighted by in the afternoon sunlight. A lake scene was surrounded by quaint advertising, perhaps the sponsors for a long-forgotten theatrical production. "A city store in a country town. Selling at Country Prices: Harry S. Mitchell, Troy," one ad read. Another said, "Soper and Mosher, Sylvania, General Merchandise and Produce." Still another said, "F. L. Ballard: Jeweler and Registered Optometrist, Eyesight Specialist, Troy. Prices always the lowest." I had to agree with Nancy Brackman and her crew—this building and this backdrop were definitely worth the effort of restoration.

I left Troy feeling good about the day. Spring was finally assured, even in the northernmost edges of the state. And I'd found a community that was interested in preserving the heritage of Pennsylvania's fairgrounds.

❖ The Endless Mountains Maple Festival is held from 9 A.M. to 5 P.M. on Saturday and Sunday of the last weekend in April. Parking and admission are free. Alparon Park is located just north of Troy on Route 14. For more information, call 717-297-2791.

May

Shad Festival

Bethlehem, Lehigh County

Beside the Monocacy Creek, a small morsel of the eighteenth century lies untouched by ravenous time. A stone waterworks built in 1762, a stone tannery built a year earlier, and a log springhouse with a cedar shake roof look out over the waters. Across the Ohio Road, the imposing brick Luckenbach Mill rises five stories above this eighteenth-century industrial area. Since 1978, this tiny historic enclave has hosted the Shad Festival in celebration and remembrance of this oceangoing fish's contribution to life in early Bethlehem.

According to Linda Robertson, spokesperson for Historic Bethlehem, Inc., shad were important to the settlers' survival. A 1772 diary reads, "We caught 5300 fat shad this season." Many of the fish were sold for hard cash. The settlers served a shad feast to celebrate their spring migration and the end of the meager food supplies of the winter.

When my mother and I arrived, we were caught in the tangle of aromas from the festival. Wood smoke, cooking shad and bacon, and the odor of the hot planks wafted up into Bethlehem. For a moment the smells of the eighteenth century erased the smells of the present. It was easy to imagine the first shad festivals held here, and the joys that springtime held for the early settlers.

We walked down the pathway to the fish-roasting area. Two fifty-foot-long charcoal pits were surrounded by rows of oak planks. Each plank held two shad fillets with a strip of home-cured bacon nailed over each end. Occasionally, workers flipped the planks, so that the fillets roasted evenly. The bacon supplied continuous basting, helped by workers with long-handled brushes. When I leaned over the pit for a closer look, I almost singed my eyelashes. I didn't envy their job!

At the end of the pit, potatoes were baking on a large charcoal table. Costumed workers served up large platters of shad, potatoes, watercress salad, homemade bread, and mint tea.

We bought meal tickets and went through the line. I tried to exchange my mint tea for something else—lemonade, water, Kool-Aid—anything. No, the workers insisted: This meal was authentic, what the Moravians would have had in the eighteenth century. I hate mint tea.

Carrying our platters, we found seats in the dining tent. This was our first experience with shad, and the first forkful was full of tiny bones. Mother said, "This is like eating fish Brillo pad." I looked around. Other folks were picking out the meat with their fingers. We tried that and found the fish delicious.

After our lunch, we walked over to the chef's cook-off in a tent next to the tannery. Chef Mike Castle from the Hotel Bethlehem, Chef David Heiter from Youell's Oyster House, and Chef Drew Stichter from Glasbern were demonstrating shad and shad roe recipes to an enthusiastic audience. A row of judges, forks in hand, sat ready to evaluate the dishes.

Shad Stuffed with Shad Roe and Bacon

1 shad (3 $\frac{1}{2}$ pounds), boned and prepared for stuffing

1 pair shad roe

1 tablespoon vinegar

1 teaspoon salt

small onion, finely chopped

5 tablespoons butter

$\frac{1}{2}$ cup mushrooms, finely chopped

2 thin strips bacon, cooked and crumbled

$\frac{1}{4}$ teaspoon chives, chopped

$\frac{1}{4}$ teaspoon tarragon

$\frac{1}{2}$ teaspoon summer savory (optional)

1 teaspoon parsley, finely chopped

$\frac{1}{2}$ cup plus 2 teaspoons dry white wine

salt and freshly ground pepper

parsley and lemon slices for garnish

Preheat oven to 350 degrees.

Salt shad inside and out.

Poach roe in enough water to cover with vinegar and 1 teaspoon salt for 8 to 10 minutes. Drain, dry, remove skin, and chop finely. Set aside.

Sauté onion in 2 tablespoons butter until transparent. Add mushrooms and sauté 2 minutes longer until mushrooms are soft. Add bacon. Remove from heat.

Stir in 2 teaspoons white wine, herbs, chopped roe, and salt and pepper to taste. Stuff shad with roe mixture and carefully sew together with thread. Place stuffed shad on buttered pan lined with foil. Dot fish with remaining butter. Pour $\frac{1}{2}$ cup white wine into pan and bake until fish flakes (40 minutes), basting frequently.

Garnish with fresh curly parsley and lemon slices.

—*Karen Dolan, Easton*

Baked Shad with Zesty Orange Sauce

3 cups orange juice	2 ounces pimiento, chopped
8 ounces sugar	3 tablespoons orange zest
1 cup water	3 tablespoons scallions
3 tablespoons cornstarch	4 pounds shad
1 tablespoon ginger	

Sauce:

Combine juice and sugar; bring to a boil and reduce heat. Combine water and cornstarch and slowly add to hot juice. Stir until thickened. Remove from heat and stir in next four ingredients.

Shad:

Bake shad, covered, at 375 degrees for about 3 hours, then baste with orange sauce. Bake 2 hours longer or until shad has a nice firm texture.

For an additional fee, visitors could attend a Pennsylvania wine tasting. There was also an international beer tasting and hour-long lecture by beer expert John Harsell in the Luckenbach Mill. Later on, an international wine tasting was held.

Since one of the missions of Historic Bethlehem is education, many of the activities were informational. Three lectures, held throughout the day, were geared toward shad fishermen. David Arnold, regional supervisor for the Pennsylvania Fish and Boat Commission, discussed "The Lehigh River Shad Restoration." The shad have recently returned to the Lehigh River after an absence of 125 years. In the 1820s, dams constructed at the confluence of the Lehigh and Delaware Rivers in nearby Easton blocked their upstream route. Now new fish ladders have opened their route once again. Joseph Miller, fisheries biologist for the U.S. Fish and Wildlife Service, spoke on "The Life Cycle of the American Shad." Dennis Schroll, president of the Delaware River Shad Fishermen's Association, presented "Sport Fishing for Shad."

In the art tent, children explored the themes of ecology, fish anatomy, and the waterways. A casting contest was sponsored by the Dale Clemons Custom Tackle Shop. One of the kids' activities that also attracted many adults was the State Fish and Boat Commission's temporary shocking and stunning of the fish population in the Monocacy Creek so that youngsters could count and categorize the native fish population of the stream.

With the catch-and-release photo contest sponsored by Olympus Camera Company and the fly-tying contest sponsored by the Dale Clemons Custom Tackle Shop, there was a full day of activity. You didn't have to be a shad fisherman to enjoy the event. No restaurant in the world could compete with a planked shad dinner accompanied by the folk music of Andrew Roblin and Rick Starkey and served up amid the well-worn buildings of eighteenth-century Bethlehem, all seasoned with May sunshine.

During the day, dinner guests would consume 425 to 450 shad, 52 pounds of home-cured bacon, 13 cases of watercress, 5 quarts of salad oil and vinegar, 3,200 pats of butter, 100 loaves of freshly baked bread, 1,020 potatoes, and 70 gallons of mint tea. "Make that 69 gallons, 3 quarts, 1 $1/_2$ pints of mint tea," I thought to myself as I got in the car and pulled a bottle of water from the cooler in the backseat.

❖ The Shad Festival is held on a Saturday in May, but the exact date changes from year to year. From Route 378, exit from the Hill to Hill Bridge on the Main Street ramp. There is parking below the Main Street ramp, or look for a space in town. Don't forget to stop at the Moravian bookstore on Main Street. For information and exact dates, call Historic Bethlehem, Inc.

National Pike Festival

Brownsville, Washington County

The weekend after Bethlehem's Shad Festival, I went to Brownsville for the National Pike Festival. Brownsville sits on the banks of the Monongahela River, perfect access to fishing, I figured. I even wondered on the four-hour drive how these fish would be prepared—it would be hard to compete with the showmanship at the Shad Festival.

My guardian angel must have been working overtime that day. Even in my divine ignorance, I somehow managed not to say a word about fish for the first half hour of my visit. I was only a question away from total humiliation.

I drove into Brownsville on the kind of day that brings out sunbathers and yard sales. Several teenagers in period costume happily shared directions and sent me to the south side of Route 40. Soon I was being directed into a parking lot off Front Street with much brandishing of flags and flashlights.

An imposing brick mansion towers over the Front Street parking lot from behind a stone wall. To the left of the house, Brownsville cascades to the river's edge, far below. This was Nemacolin Castle, and its grounds were the site of the National Pike Festival. Judging from the rousing music that found its way over the stone walls, folks were enjoying a good time.

Once inside the grounds, I walked around looking for fish. There were wonderful foods for sale. Along the stone wall on the Second Avenue side of the lawn, the Calvin United Presbyterian Church was selling cabbage and noodles, cheese fries, and hot dogs. The Mount Zion Church booth advertised "Heavenly Treats"—chocolate-covered bananas and strawberries. There was a barbecue closer to the mansion, and smells of the cooking meat and the smoke from the pits wafted around the lawn and got lost in the ancient shade trees.

I checked out the bread from the baking contest, talked with the herb seller, and shopped for a birthday gift at the crafts vendors. I sat in the shade for a while and studied the pen-and-ink shadows on the lawn as I listened to the bluegrass music. There were no pike anywhere, in any form.

Finally, I walked over to the Brownsville Historical Society's table close to the mansion's back door. I looked at the festival T-shirt and examined some booklets, all the while chatting with the volunteers. I was just ready to ask about pike fishing when a pamphlet depicting a wagon train caught my eye. In bold letters it said, "Southwestern Pennsylvania's National Pike Festival. Ninety miles of fun food and entertainment. Travel the road that made the Nation. National Pike. Route 40."

"Thank you, Guardian Angel!" I said to myself. And then I explained my book project and asked to talk to someone about the *turn*pike festival.

The National Pike, or National Road, as it was called at first, was the first transportation link between the East and the western frontier. Eventually, the road ran six hundred miles from Cumberland, Maryland, to Vandalia, Illinois. President Jefferson signed a bill allowing money from the sale of land in Ohio to be used to build this road. Construction began in 1811.

Every old house should have a house fairy like Darlene Olsen, someone who cares for it, loves it to death, keeps it in good repair, and happily shares it with everyone who shows the least interest in it. As she walked me through the old mansion, I felt as though I were a guest of the Bow-

Nemacolin Castle Wassail

1 gallon sweet cider   1 cup sugar (or to taste)
10 2-inch cinnamon sticks $^1/_2$ cup lemon juice
1 tablespoon allspice

Heat all ingredients until mixture comes to a boil. Simmer for 15 minutes.

As with most traditional drinks, there are many recipes for the wassail bowl. Always a hot drink, it may be based on wine or cider. Mulled sweet cider makes a nonalcoholic wassail and can be spiced many different ways. This is the one most generally used for the castle's holiday tours.

man family, who built and occupied it from the 1790s until the last Mrs. Bowman died in 1959. Mrs. Olsen told me, "I feel like the Bowmans are my own ancestors," and it showed.

As we stood on the balcony overlooking the Monongahela, Mrs. Olsen told me that Nemacolin Castle, originally known as Nemacolin Towers, was named after Chief Nemacolin, who blazed the trail over which the National Road was built. The original building was a stone trading post built by Jacob Bowman, whose business successes included a nail factory, a paper mill, a machine parts business, and boat-building, shipping, and banking ventures. George Washington eventually appointed Bowman the first postmaster of Brownsville.

As his fortunes grew, the house grew in size. Its three sections, representing frontier, late colonial, and Victorian periods, are each furnished with Bowman family pieces. From the simple frontier-era trading post—a dark, low-ceilinged fortress against the perils of the wilderness—to the sunny interiors of the Victorian rooms, the house is a lesson in architecture and changing tastes and styles.

We walked into the nursery, silent for many decades. Mrs. Olsen showed me where the Bowman children kept their pet squirrels, and then, pushing back a curtain, she said, "I think the Bowman family would have enjoyed having people on the lawn."

When Mrs. Olsen left to meet the wagon train coming down Route 40 from Washington—she'd promised to take lemonade and cookies, and carrots for the horses—I sat on the lawn, watching the Mon Valley Cloggers perform. The sweet sound of laughter and hushed conversation mingled with the music, and I had to agree with Mrs. Olsen. Yes, the Bowmans would have enjoyed this afternoon lawn party.

On the way home, I drove down the National Pike to Washington. A far cry from the 1811 road, it's now lined with countless small towns, fast-food joints, bars, and gas stations. I think I was looking for a wagon train.

❖ If you plan to attend the Pike Festival in Brownsville, mark the third weekend of May on your calendar. Activities are held from noon to 6 P.M. on Saturday, and from 11 A.M. to 6 P.M. on Sunday. Take U.S. Route 40 into town, and turn south on Fourth Avenue. Go one block and turn right on Brashear Street. Go two blocks to the castle. For more information, call 412-785-6882.

June

World War II Commemorative Weekend

Reading, Berks County

It couldn't have been better planned. As I entered the hot, dusty tent encampment off an airstrip "somewhere in England," the vintage radio show broadcasting "Live from the Stork Club in New York" burst into "Sentimental Journey," the theme song for many folks attending the World War II Commemorative Weekend at the Reading Airport. The staccato snap and angry snarl of vintage planes overhead and the roar of their taking off and landing added another kind of music to the summer afternoon.

All around the encampment, authentic equipment added lifeblood to the reenactment. At one edge of the camp a sign read, "Danger! Keep Out! Unexploded enemy bombs in this area! Do Not Enter! Extremely Dangerous!" highlighted with a skull and crossbones. In the center of the camp, a street signpost with arrows pointing toward Hollywood, Brooklyn, Dayton, and Berlin gave the mileage to soldiers' homes. The tents were real, the cots were real, the uniforms were real, the vehicles were real—even the newspapers were real. One lying on a cot, as if thrown carelessly by an Air Force crew member, flashed the headline "Invasion: Allied Troops Land in North France."

The smells of the hot tarmac, the exhaust from the engines, and the smell of canvas added a final touch. Suddenly, I was immersed in a war that had ended the decade before I was born. I stood for a moment, taking it all in, as I would many times that afternoon.

As I stopped at the hangar, I overheard an older gentleman tell his grandson, "This is where we used to work on B-24s—in and out all day long, one after another. We prepared them for missions here."

There was a fine selection of memorabilia—uniforms, flight jackets, aviation items, squadron patches, guns, daggers, and swords. There was even a dealer selling reproduction K-rations. One side of the hangar was devoted to high-quality aviation and military art. Colonel Donald L. Currier was on hand to sign copies of his book, *Fifty Mission Crush*.

One of the highlights of the day was meeting Colonel Robert Morgan, pilot of the famous B-17 the *Memphis Belle*. Shamelessly, I stood in line for his autograph.

Later in the day, Colonel Morgan told the story of the *Memphis Belle*.

Broadcast over the grounds of the airport, his story stopped the busy crowd. Folks stood around, simply listening.

On that Sunday afternoon, over half a century had passed since Morgan had last piloted the famous heavy bomber. His association with her began in Bangor, Maine, where he first took her out on her shakedown run. After a few beers one night, he and the tail gunner christened the B-17 the *Memphis Belle* in honor of Morgan's fiancée. An artist from *Esquire* heard about the plane and sent Morgan a painting of a leggy pinup girl. An artist in Morgan's squadron copied the painting on the nose of the plane.

In 1942, Morgan flew the *Memphis Belle* across the Atlantic to England to help defeat the Nazis. The English were bombing German targets at night. In November 1942, the Americans began daytime bombing missions and inflicted devastating losses. There were no fighter escorts into Germany, for Spitfires couldn't fly that far.

As incentive the B-17 crews were told, "If you finish twenty-five missions, you can go home." To the crew of the *Memphis Belle*, this seemed an impossible goal, but one mission compounded on another, and the goal slowly became reality.

On the sixteenth mission, the *Memphis Belle* was chosen as the featured B-17 for a documentary film. For five missions, the bomber carried a cameraman aboard. The story of Morgan, his fiancée, and the plane became national news. The documentary film was completed, as were Morgan's twenty-five missions. The crew's twenty-sixth mission was a three-month promotional tour of the United States.

"We weren't heroes," Morgan told the audience. "We were just chosen for the film. The real heroes didn't come home."

Later that afternoon, I walked around the airfield looking at the planes. There were at least thirty vintage aircraft on hand, many belonging to the Mid-Atlantic Air Museum. There was a North American B-25, a Douglas DC-3 Navy R4D, a Fairchild M-62, a PT-19, and a Northrop P-61B. There were many visiting aircraft, among them a B-17G-105-VE, a Harvard MK IIA, and a Messerschmitt Bf-108. Many owners talked about their planes and their restorations. Most planes had required at least ten thousand hours of work.

I toured the Martin 404 airliner, a forty-passenger commercial aircraft owned by the museum. I spent a few minutes walking around a bomber like Colonel Morgan's, trying to imagine how it must have felt to have only this plane between me and certain death far below in Germany.

While I stood there, the 553rd Air Force Band of the Pennsylvania

War or Rationing Cake

Mix 2 cups brown sugar, 2 cups hot water, and 2 teaspoons shortening in a medium-size saucepan. Add $^1/_2$ to $^3/_4$ cup raisins and 1 teaspoon each salt, cinnamon, and cloves, and boil this for 5 minutes after it first bubbles. Remove it from the stove and let cool completely.

Add 3 cups flour and 1 teaspoon baking soda dissolved in a couple of teaspoons of hot water. Mix well.

Pour into a greased tube pan and bake for 1 hour at 350 to 375 degrees.

—*Grandmother Shoap*

National Guard struck up an old swing tune, "In the Mood." Standing far from the crowd, a lone woman watched the sky. Young during World War II, she had probably done this many times before. As the strains of the song made their way between the aircraft, her face lit up. And there, all alone on the tarmac, she danced.

For those too young to remember, the Reading World War II reenactment is a living history lesson. For those who lived through the war, however, it's a day for remembering, and a time for sharing. At the World War II reenactment, it's not unusual to hear a grandfather say to his grandchild, "Yes, this is how it was."

❖ The World War II Commemorative Weekend is held the first full weekend in June, Saturday and Sunday from 10 A.M. to 5 P.M. The Mid-Atlantic Air Museum is located on Route 183 at the northern end of the Reading Regional Airport. There is an admission charge, and advance tickets at reduced prices are available by mail. For more information, write to World War II Commemorative Weekend, Mid-Atlantic Air Museum, R.D. 9, Box 9381, Reading, PA 19605, or call 610-372-7333.

Pennsylvania State Laurel Festival

Wellsboro, Tioga County

Driving into Wellsboro on the first Sunday of the week-long Pennsylvania State Laurel Festival, I was surprised to find the town deserted. The gaslights that line Main Street glowed softly on that gray June morning. Shops wore "closed" signs. A few stray cars ambled down the street, apparently in no hurry to get anywhere. The town park, a likely spot for a festival, slumbered undisturbed, lulled to sleep by the gentle splashing of the fountain.

I turned onto Central Avenue and pulled over to the side of the street. Rummaging through my daypack, I pulled out cameras, notepads, film, pens, and a tape recorder. There at the bottom, I found the flyer I was looking for. Sure enough, the advertising promised Laurel Festival activities on this second day of the celebration.

At that point, my friend Rich Olsen spotted people coming out of a brick building—the chamber of commerce. "Let's go in and find out what's going on," he said.

Before long, assured that we hadn't driven four hours in vain, we were drinking coffee and chatting with Mary Worthington, executive director of the Wellsboro Chamber of Commerce, and Sandra Price, Laurel Festival chairperson, while waiting for the pet parade to begin.

I wanted to know about the wonderful chamber of commerce structure. With its brick gingerbread cornice trim, rounded lintels, bull's-eye attic window, and wide front porch, the old manse by the park looked more like a home than a commercial building.

The building was once the residence of the town sheriff. The adjoining jailhouse provided him easy access to his wards, and his wife prepared prisoners' meals. I wondered how the cells in the back compared with the inviting porch and bright, airy rooms of this gracious house.

Pushing the curtain aside, Mary pointed out the large elm tree on the front lawn. "We believe our elm is one of the largest in existence," she told me. "It's been here since the 1700s. It's older than Wellsboro. It was grown when the first settlers came in 1814.

"Some people call it the hanging tree. The first hanging in Wellsboro was from that tree. There was a murder in Mansfield. A man killed his girlfriend. He caught her in a buggy with another man—"

"But talk about blessed!" said a woman who had just bustled in. "When the rest of the world lost their elms, Wellsboro was blessed to keep theirs!"

A round of introductions followed. I learned that Louise Walker is a direct descendant of the Wells family, namesake of the town. "I have Mary Wells's sugar bowl," she told me before taking leave, and I never did get the end of the hanging tree story.

First held in 1938, the Laurel Festival was the brainchild of Harry Woodin, a local businessman. With his encouragement, the Lions Club organized the first event, capitalizing on the town's proximity to the fifty-mile-long Pine Gorge while also promoting the state flower. The first celebration had a parade, a block dance, a circus, and a ball. From the first festival, there has always been a Laurel Queen.

Like most of the state, Wellsboro canceled its festival during World War II. In 1946, though, the celebration resumed, growing each year. In 1959, organizers added a pet parade; in 1963, the Laurel Princess Program was started. In the years following 1972, an arts and crafts fair, a concert series, footraces, and bike races have been added. The latest addition is a mountain bike race. The festival has grown from three days to eight days. There is no central location for activities. Instead, they are held all over town at various times every day of the week.

On the first festival Saturday, the Laurel Classic bike race takes off from the green. This 18.8-mile touring race is for the serious cyclist and offers competitors spectacular scenery. There is also a family-oriented bike ride. Simultaneously, Packer Park hosts the Great Penny Extravaganza, in which children use pennies to create sidewalk art. The Laurel Princess Program is also held in the park in the afternoon. There is evening entertainment at the high school.

Sunday afternoon is the pet parade; everyone gets a prize. Then there's afternoon gospel music on the chamber of commerce lawn.

The Wellsboro Firemen's Carnival, running Monday through Saturday, offers visitors another entertainment option. There is also a weekday night concert series designed to appeal to a wide variety of tastes.

The second weekend of the Laurel Festival is the big one. The arts and crafts fair runs until dusk on Friday and Saturday and features strolling entertainment during the fair. A Queen's Preview is held at the high school Friday night at 8, with the coronation following on Saturday night. Saturday also features international foods on the streets, a 10K footrace, and a 2-mile fun run.

The festival closes on Sunday with the Union Church service held in the park.

Laurel Festival Special French Toast

loaf of Italian bread,
    sliced about $^1/_2$ inch thick on the diagonal
Dip bread in mixture of milk, egg, vanilla, cinnamon, and nutmeg.
(A splash of Grand Marnier is a wonderful option.) Brown dipped
bread on grill or in frying pan. Serve with warmed maple syrup and
butter. Top with fresh fruit and edible flowers, such as Johnny-
jump-ups, spring violets, borage, calendula, or nasturtiums.
    Debbie Keister, innkeeper at the Four Winds, serves this with
bacon, sausage, or ham to the judges for the Laurel Festival Queen's
Pageant.

—Four Winds Bed and Breakfast

I put down my pen when we heard the music of the middle school
band. The pet parade was on its way. We walked out into a very different
Wellsboro from the one we had seen an hour earlier. The pavements were
full of people.

There were children in costume, pets in costume, parents in costume—a thousand of them, it seemed, strolling down Main Street toward
the park. There were express wagon floats, lawn tractors pulling wagons,
decorated bikes, and all sorts of animals—dogs, cats, goats, a calf, ponies,
gerbils in cages, bunnies, birds, chickens, sheep, and even a monkey.
Helium balloons were everywhere.

The gray sky gave up completely, and rain began to fall as the last
tyke struggled into the park on his tricycle. We ran for cover under the
magnificent elm tree. Looking up, I couldn't suppress a shudder—I still
don't know whether it was awe at the spreading branches, or the man I
imagined I saw hanging there.

❖ The Laurel Festival in Wellsboro merits a visit. It is usually held
the second full week in June and most events begin in Packer Park.
While you are in the area, be sure to visit the Pennsylvania Grand
Canyon. Many motels are conveniently located in or near town. For an
exact schedule of events, contact the Wellsboro Area Chamber of Commerce, P.O. Box 733, Wellsboro, PA 16901, 717-724-1926.

Clearfield County
Gospel Music Festival

Clearfield, Clearfield County

Chicory and daisies lined the roadsides on the third Sunday in June. On the Nittany Mountain, laurel was in full bloom. Crown vetch flooded down the banks and collected in pink and lavender puddles in the rain gutters along Route 322.

It was one of the first breathless days of high summer. The sun melted the early morning haze, turning it to steam, and then got lost somewhere in the low clouds, burning brighter and hotter as it fought its way through. Mountains disappeared in the glaring heat.

Walking the short distance from the car to the grove of trees by the band shell at the Clearfield Fairgrounds was a sweaty ordeal. I picked my way through a maze of RVs and campers and found a seat on a picnic table in a pavilion at the back of the crowd that had gathered for the Sunday vesper service. Lawn chairs were placed strategically to take best advantage of the shade. The bleachers down front, in full sunlight, remained unoccupied, although they were the best seats in the house. It's not just at school, I thought to myself, that everyone heads for the back seats.

The service had already started by the time I arrived. The only other person in the pavilion introduced herself while the Knepp family, hosting the event, led the congregation in a rousing hymn tune. Mary Jane Lannen, from Lands, Pennsylvania, twenty-one miles from Clearfield, described herself as a "church pianist escaped from church for a Sunday morning." She told me excitedly that one of the Statler Brothers had been at the festival the day before, and the fairgrounds had been overflowing.

The minister began his sermon. Since it was Father's Day, he followed the progression of fathers through the Bible stories I'd grown up on, devoting a great deal of time to the nasty little prodigal son and his sainted father.

During the sermon, a poodle tied under the awning of a Winnebago started to whimper, then to whine. The minister preached louder. A woman craned around on her seat and willed the little white piece of fluff to quiet down. I figured howls were only a few minutes away, and apparently, so did the dog's mistress. Soon, woman's best friend was seated happily under a folding lawn chair, and the service went on.

Pistachio Pudding Salad

1 box pistachio instant pudding
1 can crushed pineapple
1 8-ounce container
   whipped topping
$1/_2$ cup chopped pecans or
   chopped pistachio nuts

1 bag miniature
   marshmallows
$1/_2$ cup maraschino cherries,
   chopped and drained

Combine dry pudding with pineapple. Mix well. Add remaining ingredients and mix. Refrigerate until ready to serve.

As ice cream containers were passed around for the offering, the performers sang another hymn. We ended the service with another singalong, "Clearfield for Jesus." I didn't know the words, but it was fun to hum along.

Mary Jane pointed out Carol, Bucky, and Bunny Knepp, organizers for the event. Started in 1985, the Clearfield County Gospel Music Festival now attracts more than twenty-five performing groups and fifteen soloists. The music begins on Friday night at 7. "On Saturday, it resumes at one and runs until whenever," Carol said vaguely. "It was pretty late last night. I think we quit at one A.M."

Tacked to the edge of the stage was a menu for Friday and Saturday. Hamburgers, hot dogs, sloppy joes, grilled cheese, and egg salad sandwiches had been offered at very reasonable prices. There were also macaroni salad, coleslaw, vegetable soup, potato soup, blueberry muffins, chips, popcorn, pie, and a variety of beverages.

Sunday lunch was a turkey dinner. I wandered over to the dining room and bought a ticket.

At 11:30, I found myself in a cafeteria-style line, my Styrofoam tray filling rapidly as Knepp family members served roast turkey, mashed potatoes (real, Mary Jane told me), stuffing, gravy, green beans, noodles, Jell-O salads, and a smorgasbord of homemade desserts, all prepared by the Knepp family.

At lunch Mary Jane and I joked about the problems of running church music programs, and shared sources for sacred music. Elizabeth Poole, from Clearfield, sat across the table from us. As conversation turned to the Gospel Music Festival, she said, "I've been here all three days. Believe me, I wouldn't miss this. Some people aren't Pentecostal, you know!"

❖ The Clearfield County Gospel Music Festival is usually held over Father's Day weekend at the Clearfield County Fairgrounds. RV camp-sites are available with hookups for a small fee.

From Route 322 on the west side of Clearfield, turn onto Weaver Street, then take a right on Mill Street to the fairgrounds. The best music is on Saturday, but the turkey dinner is on Sunday. Either day, take a lawn chair.

Cross Fork Snake Hunt

Cross Fork, Potter County

I sat on the top bench of the bleachers, as far away from the arena as I could get. Rummaging through my backpack, I unloaded my Pentax, and opening the zoom the whole way, focused it on the group of men in the pit.

"If you'd like to get a little closer, I'll trade seats with you," said the attractive young woman seated two rows down from me.

"No, this is fine," I replied. "I need to be up higher for the photo."

"I know what you mean," she said. Her smile told me that indeed she understood my need to be as far away from the entertainment as I could get. If I'd gotten any farther away, as a matter of fact, they would have had to send me a video.

Few things in this world terrify me as much as snakes. I've never won-dered for a moment why God chose the snake as Satan's alter ego in the Garden of Eden. I can't think of another creature so typecast for the role. And yes—I know they're not slimy—but neither is a land mine, for that matter. Step on either one once and see what happens.

Nope, I never wanted to build a meaningful relationship with a snake. And yet here I was at the Annual Potter County Snake Hunt and State Sacking Contest. Frankly, I'd just as soon have been on a tour bus in Chernobyl.

Below me, in the fenced arena, members of the Keystone Reptile Club lectured the audience on the habits, habitat, and physical character-istics of native Pennsylvania snakes. They also talked about snakebites.

"Remember, a snake's venom is designed to kill his food," the speaker said. "Few rattlers or copperheads could swallow a human being, and so the venom isn't strong enough to kill you.

"A copperhead's venom is real different from a rattler's. A copper-head's venom starts to digest his victim as soon as he's bitten.

"Say a copperhead nails a rabbit. The rabbit runs off and takes his time dying. The snake trails him, and by the time he gets there, the rabbit is already dead and the digestive process is under way. The snake unhinges his jaws and starts to swallow his dinner."

From somewhere in the bleachers I heard an old man say, "I got bit by a copperhead once. Lost the end of my finger. Musta been why . . ." I located him—the old-timer displaying a ragged finger for all of us to see.

While the snake fanciers spoke, a small collection of snakes slithered around their feet, Medusa's shower drain after her toilette. Occasionally one of the men would lean down and pick up a snake on a long metal rod, hooked at one end. Then, grasping the snake by the tail, he'd hold the creature up for all of us to see. I wondered whether I could jump to the roof of the Kettle Creek Firehouse from my perch on the bleachers.

When the lecture was over, the snake handlers urged the audience forward. They talked to individuals, holding the poisonous snakes out to the crowd, keeping the serpents' heads in plastic tubes. I walked behind the bleachers to get to the other side of the arena. I wouldn't have gotten that close to a snake even if I were encased in plastic.

At a row of folding tables just behind the snake pit, the Keystone Reptile Club held court, selling souvenirs and distributing information. Roger Wheeler, president of the organization, and his wife, Sherri, recording secretary, explained the event to me.

The snake hunt is just that. Folks are invited to bring in snakes until noon on Sunday. For the very adventurous, Pennsylvania law allows hunters to catch one rattlesnake a day, but a permit is needed for this sport. All snakes are measured and recorded. Prizes are awarded for the longest rattlesnakes and copperheads, the rattlesnake with the most rattles, and the longest snake in the hunt. All snakes are returned to their natural habitat after the contest.

Then there's the sacking contest for kids and women. Five nonpoisonous snakes are released in the pit. Contestants must pick them up and put them into a bag. The shortest time wins. Bill Wheeler stressed *nonpoisonous*, and I shuddered to think about the horrors of the men's sacking contest on Sunday.

I said, quite naively, that I had thought snake meat might be served.

"Oh, no," Melody Dynes assured me, "but we do sell it in cans."

She handed me a can of Shaker's Original Canned Rattle Snake Meat sold by the Reptile Club.

"Turn it around," she urged.

I did, and the can began to shake. Of course I dropped it on the table and jumped back. Everyone had a good laugh—snake fun.

While I was talking to the Wheelers, a young man appeared with two

C. J.'s Bar-b-Que Sauce

2 $^1/_2$ cups catsup   3 $^1/_2$ cups tomato puree

3 cups water   1 $^3/_4$ cups onion

4 tablespoons mustard   2 cups Pepsi (optional)

1 cup Worcestershire sauce   6 teaspoons salt

$^3/_4$ cup vinegar $^2/_3$ cup brown sugar, packed

3 $^1/_4$ cups tomato sauce   1 tablespoon paprika

3 $^1/_4$ cups tomato juice   4 tablespoons sugar

$^1/_4$ cup lemon juice $^3/_8$ teaspoon black pepper

1 $^1/_2$ cups tomato paste   1 tablespoon baking soda

Spices to Taste:

2 ounces hot sauce, 1 $^3/_4$ teaspoons chili powder, $^1/_8$ teaspoon cayenne pepper (add one, two, or all three, depending on hotness desired)

Combine all ingredients and simmer 1 hour or longer, depending on thickness desired, using a 6-quart saucepan.

Yields approximately 1 gallon.

—*Keystone Reptile Club*

snakes, his entries for the hunt. A huge blacksnake and a copperhead were measured and recorded.

After I escaped from the snake pit, I made a valiant effort to check out the craft show held in the field behind the firehouse. Heavy rains the day before had turned the field into a swamp. Water was ankle deep in places. Firemen were pumping water and trying to dig drainage ditches, but I fear that the craftspeople lost money that afternoon.

Farther afield, in what seemed like a separate celebration altogether, local fire companies were competing. In one game, a ladder with four ropes attached was lying on the ground. Four men raced to the ropes and pulled the ladder upright, and a fifth man scrambled to the top. In another game, five men ran to a tower topped by a fifty-gallon drum on a platform. The men had to fill the drum on top from a tank at the base. When water ran from a spout on the side of the drum, the stopwatch clicked off.

The firemen's games attracted a big crowd. Beer flowed freely. A sign at the entrance said, "Please buy your beer from the fire company. Support our volunteers by not bringing your beer onto fire company grounds." Things promised to get pretty lively by nightfall, and I was glad that there was a swampy field between this side of the festival and the snake pit.

The chicken barbecue, run by fire company volunteers, was one of the highlights of the food stand area. There were also several fast-food concessions.

❖ The Cross Fork Snake Hunt is held the last weekend in June at the Kettle Creek Hose Company, just off Route 114 in Potter County. For exact dates and more information, call 717-432-0472 or 717-923-2268, or write to Kettle Creek Hose Company #1, Crossfork, PA 17729.

The Groundhog Festival

Punxsutawney, Jefferson County

Mention Punxsutawney to any Pennsylvanian and you'll conjure up visions of an all-night vigil on a frozen mountainside and Phil the groundhog, always wearing his winter coat and blinking sleepy eyes at the pale sunrise.

There was no snow on the ground the day we drove into Punxsutawney for the Groundhog Festival, but it wasn't exactly the epitome of a day late in June, either. The sky hung low, heavy with rain, and the winds that shipped down Mahoning Street had a bit of leftover winter in them.

"This must be it," my friend Kay said as we passed the town park.

"What was your first clue?" I asked. "The seven-foot-tall groundhog statue, the twenty-foot-long 'Groundhog Festival Sponsors' sign, or the awning that says 'Groundhog Zoo' in foot-high letters?"

Yet only about thirty people were gathered around the back half of the park. There were a few tarps set up around the park's perimeter, and a row of booths looked like they might house games of chance. Although they hinted at a festival, they were empty. And the other features of a festival in progress—the blaring music, bell ringing, and crowd hums—were strangely absent.

Nevertheless, we joined the spectators gathered around a stone pavilion. Four grade-school girls dressed in gauzy harem outfits were dancing on the grass. The quartet was performing valiantly, in spite of the weather, the surface, and the proximity of onlookers. A row of judges was seated at a folding table under one of the tarps.

Prize-Winning Groundhog Festival Chili

2 $1/_2$ pounds ground beef
1 large onion, diced
2 large green peppers, diced
1 hot pepper, seeded and
    chopped
$1/_2$ cup oil
2 15-ounce cans whole
    tomatoes
2 15-ounce cans crushed
    tomatoes

2 15-ounce cans tomato
    sauce
1 16-ounce bag frozen corn
6 shakes hot sauce
salt
pepper
chili powder to taste

Brown ground beef. Drain excess fat. Put onion, green peppers, and oil in a large pot. Cook until soft. Add crushed tomatoes, whole tomatoes, and sauce to pepper and onions. Add spices to meat. Mix together in a large pot. Add corn; season to taste.

Lauri Lash, who typed this recipe for Mr. Steele, says, "I recommend adding two 15-ounce cans of kidney beans to this recipe."

—Roger Steele

Other performers followed, all of them four feet tall or shorter. Soloists performed pop songs along with backup tapes, and a few brave souls sang a cappella. The crowd responded to each act with enthusiastic applause.

We walked over to the Groundhog Zoo and visited with Phil and his furry family. They scrambled in and out of their den and squabbled over their bowl of dog food. At this point that was the most action we'd seen at the Groundhog Festival.

We asked the judges—the prizes had been awarded—where and when to find the festival. As luck would have it, Roger Steele, festival chairman, walked up, and as luck would have it, we'd come at the wrong time on the wrong day.

We'd missed the 8K run that morning, the rib cookoff, the dance and karate demonstrations, and the bike race. If we could hang around town until evening, we could catch the Punxsy Phil Harmonyck Symphonette Concert at the high school auditorium. From 8 till midnight there was also a country dance at the F. O. Eagles Club.

Mr. Steele directed us to the chamber of commerce for a schedule of the week's events. Having won the chili cookoff, he also offered his recipe. Soon, we were going over the schedule, lamenting the activities we would miss: a food fest, craft show, student art exhibit, daily appearances by local vocalist J. P. Michaels, vineyard tours, puppet shows, walking tours, a children's obstacle course, a magic show, a frog-jumping contest, miniature golf, real golf, concerts, a quilt show, a celebrity sponge toss, a clown, a strawberry festival, a model train display, and a duck derby at the creek.

For the second weekend, Friday's musical at the high school was to be followed by a full day of activities on Saturday. In addition to the continuing events, many at Barclay Square on Mahoning Street, a parade was planned for Saturday afternoon. The evening would include a Groundhog Cruise Night around town and an oldies dance on the square. Sunday night's plans included a fireworks display.

We walked around the town for a bit, and finding one concessionaire open, we bought hot sausage sandwiches. Kay bought two bowls of haluski—or cabbages and noodles—a festival staple in western Pennsylvania.

We left Punxsutawney late that afternoon. On the way home, Kay read one of the many pamphlets I'd picked up.

"Did you know that the Groundhog Festival predates the Groundhog Day celebration?" she asked. "It started in 1887, as a groundhog hunt. For a long time, it was more popular than the Groundhog Day festivities."

"Times change," I said, remembering the mob of eight thousand that came to meet Phil in February.

❖ The Groundhog Festival is held the last week of June. Most events are held at Barclay Square on Mahoning Street. Write or call ahead for a schedule of events to help you plan your visit. For further information, contact the Chamber of Commerce, Mahoning Street, Punxsutawney, PA 15767, phone 814-938-7700, or the Groundhog Festival Office, 124 West Mahoning Street, Punxsutawney, PA 15767.

Hay Days

Monroeton, Bradford County

Imagine a morning late in June, a morning when earth basks in the rich, ripe fullness of high summer. Picture the kind of morning when daylilies turn sunburned faces toward the road and daisies twinkle like stars fallen from a chicory-blue sky. Add to your picture a background of rolling hills, and top the hills with horse-drawn wagons. Blend in the smells of those horses, of well-oiled leather harnesses, and the sweetness of new-mown hay. As a final touch, add the background music—the sound of bees fussing over the clover, a meadowlark's song, the jingle of harness, the sound of clanking machinery, and the occasional whicker of a horse.

You don't need the family photo album to take you back to this summer hay meadow of long ago. You don't need a time machine or a magic carpet. At the Endless Mountains Draft Horse Club's Hay Days, years melt away in the June sunlight and wash the windows between *now* and *then*.

By the time I arrived at Ron Kring's farm, just outside of Monroeton, the hay fields were already mown. The old adage "Make hay while the sun shines" must imply "as soon as," for these folks had been up early to have so much accomplished before noon.

It didn't take long for me to see why the long hours were needed. Haying with horses was slower. Every minute of daylight would have to be used. Haying also required more manpower in the early days of this country. Willing helpers could spare only so much time from their own farms, a day or so at most, and even then essential chores like milking, feeding the stock, and caring for sick animals had to be attended to before the farmer could leave for the day. At haying time, help and sunlight were essential commodities.

As I walked up through the meadow, two strawberry roan draft horses pulled a wagonload of loose hay next to a contraption that looked like a torture device straight out of a gothic horror story. About six feet tall, the substantial wooden crate had a hinged lid on top. A system of chains, cranks, and pulleys hinted at a bottom panel that could be raised, compacting the unfortunate victim who found himself trapped inside.

Two men aboard the hay wagon started forking hay into the wooden contraption, and when they had filled it, they asked for a volunteer from the group of bystanders. Eventually, they "volunteered" a ten-year-old boy and helped him into the wooden box. He jumped up and down, compacting the hay until only the top of his head showed. They helped him out, and while he sat on the edge of the box, they filled it again. Again, the boy jumped up and down. The process was repeated. When the box was as full as it could be, the boy jumped to the ground. The wooden lid was closed and latched. A man began to crank the mechanism that raised the bottom panel. Six feet of hay was compacted to two feet. The men slipped binder twine around the hay bale, and when it emerged, the bale was as neat as a brick.

Nearby, another baler was operating. This one, once propelled by a steam engine tractor and a long belt, was a step beyond the older baler. Workers merely forked hay into a hopper and out came bales of hay. In the days of this machine's youth, it must have seemed like a gift from heaven.

At the information table set up under a tent fly, Alice Marks, secretary for the Endless Mountains Draft Horse Club, was on duty. Weather is always a good topic of conversation, for festival folks no less than for farmers, and soon we were chatting about the rainstorm the day before.

"My husband and I drove down on Saturday for the first day of Hay Days," she told me. "But the weather was so bad, we packed up and drove back home last night. This morning was so gorgeous we packed up and drove the two hours back down."

When I found out that she was from Groton, New York, I told her that we'd almost been neighbors back in the 1980s. After the "Do you know so-and-sos," and the "Is this still theres," and the "Have you ever been tos" were all explored, Alice shared the information sheets on the table. In addition to a brief history of draft horses, there were also fliers and pamphlets on characteristics of draft horse breeds, judging criteria for Belgians, measuring for a harness, directions for rolling a horse's mane, and a listing of classes for the upcoming Troy Fair Draft Horse Show. Along with a schedule of events and minutes from the last meeting, the club's newsletter listed new members from across the northern tier of Pennsylvania and the southern tier of New York State. There were also equestrian items advertised for sale, along with a Belgian stallion named Prince Did.

Club members prepared food on a Coleman stove under the adjacent tent fly. Although the choices were limited, the food was good. I opted for a cheeseburger and macaroni salad. While I ate lunch, Alice told me about the chicken barbecue held by the local fire company on Hay Days Saturdays. When the subject of recipes for the book came up, she shared her violet jelly recipe with me—she knew it by heart. She told me that it

Alice Marks's Violet Jelly

4 cups violet blossoms   4 cups sugar
3 cups boiling water   1 package SureJell
Cover blossoms with boiling water and let stand overnight. In the
morning, strain blossoms, reserving liquid. Add SureJell and sugar
to liquid, bring to a boil and continue to boil for one minute. Jar
and process.

came from Newark Valley, New York. "When I was little," she said, "any-time I got a new box of crayons, I went for the purple first. The color of this jelly is half of its appeal."

We also talked about the Endless Mountains Draft Horse Club. Formed in 1988, the purpose of the club is the promotion of the draft horse in northern Pennsylvania and southern New York. Members benefit from a variety of clinics on training, harnessing, grooming, logging, and equine health. The public benefits from living history lessons, such as Hay Days, Plow Days, and Corn Harvests.

When I'd finished lunch, I walked back to the top of the hill. Silhouetted against the afternoon sky, a hay wagon made its way to the stationary baler. The massive Belgians plodded along, placidly, as if across the years.

Watching the men and women who preserve our heritage and share it with us so willingly, I thought of Edna St. Vincent Millay's words: "For the sake of some things that be now no more, I will strew rushes on my chamber floor . . ." Yes, some things merit both preservation and celebration.

❖ If you attend Hay Days, the last weekend in June, dress casually. This is a living history lesson, and you may want to join in the hay making. Although food is available, consider bringing a picnic with you. Fried chicken, lemonade, and homemade biscuits spread out on a gingham tablecloth seem appropriate for haying. As a special treat, put a jar of Alice's violet jelly in your picnic hamper.

To get there, at Monroeton, turn onto Route 414 and go six miles. At the Center Cemetery and Franklindale Church, turn right onto Route 3035, go a half mile, and turn right onto Alexander Road. Ron Kring's farm is one mile on the right. For more information and dates, call 607-687-1622.

SCHOOL
← BLDG

REST
← ROOMS

GRANGE
BLDG →

RED
← CROSS

GRAND
STAND

FREE
STAGE →

CARNIVAL
← RIDES

82

July

Clarion County Fair

Alcola, Clarion County

For as long as anyone can remember, there have always been festivals at Alcola Park. At the end of the summer, as harvest time drew near, and then also at midsummer, the folks around Redbank Township gathered in the grove of trees.

A large, open-sided auditorium grew up under the trees. It was joined by a spacious dance hall, frame buildings for exhibitors, and a baseball field and wooden stadium that stretched down the first and third base-lines. Picnic tables were scattered about.

Folks came to the Harvest Home Picnic in wagons, buggies, on horses and bikes. The Pennsylvania Railroad ran special excursion trains for the event.

World War I changed all of that. Harvest Home Picnic stumbled along for a few years following the 1918 armistice, and then fell to its knees. With no one to tend it, the park fell into disrepair. Weeds choked the lawns under the trees. The only new construction was a "For Sale" sign.

The young veterans from the Walter W. Craig Post 354, American Legion, understood the value of home and tradition. They purchased the property, renaming it the American Legion Park, and brought the park back to life. At first, the intention was to revive the Harvest Home Picnic, but all efforts were unsuccessful, even a scheme to pit the Pittsburgh Pirates against the local team.

In the 1930s the Otto Milk Company came to New Bethlehem and began daily shipments of milk by rail to Pittsburgh. Merchants and farmers rose to prominence overnight. The new economic leaders decided to reward the community with a fair, which grew into an annual Farmers and Merchants Picnic at the Legion Park, styled after the old Harvest Home Picnic. As it expanded from a one-day event into a week-long affair, it changed its name to the Clarion County Fair.

I arrived fifty-six years after the young veterans finished their grandstand. It's a tall wooden structure. The main bank of bleachers is flanked by two shorter wings that wrap around the arena at forty-five-degree angles. It's rustic, thoroughly charming, and beautifully framed by century-old maples and oaks that overhang its shingled roof.

I walked up into the stands and took a seat. Looking out over the arena, I could imagine a baseball game from an earlier time. Babe Ruth undoubtedly started out looking up at grandstands like this one. Fairgrounds architecture is historically significant—it is an important indicator of how we live, laugh, and are entertained—and certainly the grandstand at the Clarion County Fair deserves to be on the National Register of Historic Places.

I pulled myself away from the grandstand to explore the rest of Clarion's fair. I found a petting zoo in one of the pavilions. The front of the pavilion had been turned into a barn, and a scarecrow sat on a hay bale by the door. Cheryl McCauley, leader of the CC Wranglers, the local 4-H group, was in charge. Each of the animals had a poem over its stall. The turkey's read:

> Gobble, gobble, gobble,
> Hi! Hi! Hi!
> My name is Henrietta,
> Thanks for stopping by!

Cheryl shared her week in the petting zoo with me. "The turkey is a pet of the Jones family," she said. "She usually sits on their pavement and

---

Blue-Ribbon Jewish Chocolate Brownie

Cream together:
    ¹/₂ pound softened oleo   1 ¹/₄ cups sugar
    3 eggs
Add:
    1 cup flour   3 heaping tablespoons
    ¹/₂ teaspoon salt   cocoa
Mix well, then add:
    1 cup chopped nuts.
Bake on greased cookie sheet at 350 degrees for 15 minutes.
Mix:
    2 cups coconut
    1 can Eagle brand sweetened, condensed milk
Spread mixture over hot cake and return to oven for 15 minutes.
Ice with chocolate frosting.
    Frosting:
    1 egg   ¹/₃ cup oleo
    1 cup powder sugar   2 or 3 tablespoons cocoa
    vanilla

—Fanny Adams

Clarion County Sweet Potato Casserole

3 cups cooked sweet potatoes, drained	$1/_2$ teaspoon salt
$1/_2$ cup sugar	$1/_2$ stick margarine, melted
2 eggs, beaten	$1/_2$ cup milk
	$1 \, 1/_2$ teaspoons vanilla

Mash potatoes; mix in sugar, eggs, salt, margarine, milk, and vanilla. Spread into 13 x 9-inch baking dish.

Topping:

$1/_2$ cup brown sugar	$1/_2$ cup flour
1 cup chopped pecans or walnuts	$1/_2$ stick margarine, melted

Mix brown sugar, flour, pecans, and margarine. Place on top of potato mixture.

Bake at 350 degrees for 35 minutes.

This recipe was submitted by Ann Truitt-Kopnitsky, a Clarion County Fair official.

—*1993 CC Wranglers 4-H Club Cookbook*

guards their house. This week, she's learned she can fly. When she flaps her wings, she scares people half to death.

"And then we put the sheep in with the baby goats. We thought they would go well together since they're both herding animals. The baby goats wanted nothing of it. They climbed out of their pen and took off."

Jim Snyder, another CC Wrangler leader, added his story to the collection: "We had a pony until the concert. He was fine all day long—very quiet. Then they started to do sound in the late afternoon. He went wild. He almost crawled over the fence. Then he started biting people. We had to get him out of here."

I scratched Halo, the quarter horse mare, under the chin and played with the puppies. When I found out they were free and I qualified as a good owner, I said my good-byes. I'd learned to resist crafts, french fries, and funnel cakes, but puppies were a different matter.

For free entertainment, Clarion offered a puppet show, a stage featuring local musicians, and a wild animal show. After the initial gate fee, it was possible to enjoy the fair without spending another nickel. Furthermore, with the livestock, the produce, and home products, and the crafts vendors, there was almost too much to do.

On the midway, there were carnival games, plenty of carnival food concessions, and bright lights. Indeed, the Clarion County Fair had something for everyone.

The big trucks were roaring in the arena as I left the fairgrounds that afternoon. With one last look at the veterans' grandstand, I turned toward home.

❖ The Clarion County Fair is held the first full week of July, from Monday through Saturday. Big-name groups play in the stadium several times during the week at an additional charge, but with the exception of food, everything is free. The fairgrounds is located in Alcola, two miles east of New Bethlehem on Route 28. For more information, write to the Clarion County Fair, Broadwood Towers, 400 Broad Street, New Bethlehem, PA 16242, or call 814-275-3929.

Bark Peelers' Convention

Galeton, Potter County

In the early years of this century, when lumberjacks still worked the mountains around my hometown, my grandfather Kennedy was a bark peeler for a lumbering operation. Though Grandpa's been gone for many years now, my father still repeats his father's tales of his early sawmill days, the days before he met my grandmother. The tales are so ingrained in my father's memory that a century later they come alive for me, even in a secondhand telling.

The bark peelers used a spud for their job. Two or three feet long, the metal pole flared at one end, angled like a spoon. The bark peeler would drive the spud into the bark, then lift and push at the same time, peeling the bark away from the log. In springtime, when the sap was rising, bark peelers would then send the slippery missiles shooting down the mountainsides.

I grew up on sawmill stories about lumberjacks bigger than life. Every story Grandpa told me had a little magic and mystery, a little supernatural, a little folklore, and a generous dose of country wisdom. When I saw the advertisement for the Bark Peelers' Convention at the Pennsylvania Lumber Museum, I marked my calendar.

It was not skidding logs that greeted me at the Pennsylvania Lumber Museum, but sounds: Dick and Mary Bogart's calliope, a steam engine display popping and puttering and wailing a bloodcurdling whistle at erratic intervals, and the strummed hillbilly tunes that found their way through the knotholes and chinking of the festive sounds.

I had arrived in time for the greased pole contest, Saturday's 1:45 feature. Folks were already seated on the banks around the arena, and I had trouble finding a seat within camera range. When manners failed, I resorted to rudeness, and within a minute or so, the woman who was "saving a seat for someone" left in disgust and I had my ringside seat.

The greased pole contest was fun to watch. Two by two, contestants came to the arena, climbed ladders, and sat, facing each other, straddled on a greased eight-foot-long log that hung five feet above a mound of sawdust. At the signal, contestants tried to knock each other off the log with pillows. It usually took no more than a few solid *whaps* to send one of the gladiators to the sawdust heap. One poor fellow lost his balance in the first volley but was so determined that he hung there upside down before dropping, with a thump, on his head. The longest round lasted for

Baked Squirrel Pot Pie

Cook meat until it falls from the bones. Line a baking dish with pie dough. Layer these ingredients, all precooked: potatoes, corn, hardboiled eggs, crushed crackers, and meat. Cover with pie crust and season the top with salt and pepper. Bake at 375 degrees until done. You may substitute chicken or duck.

Hazel's Squirrel Pot Pie

12 squirrels cut in pieces and soaked in salt water overnight. Simmer in fresh water and season to taste. Debone the squirrels and put meat back in broth. Add one onion and three potatoes, chopped. Let simmer for 20 minutes.

Your dough consists of:

2 eggs	$^1/_2$ teaspoon salt
$^1/_2$ cup milk	flour

Mix the salt and liquid ingredients together.

Start working your flour into the mixture until it forms a ball a little wet as you roll it out. You can still add flour. Roll it out and cut into squares. Put the squares into your cooking broth and cook it until you think it is done the way you like it.

eight exchanges before the wanna-be lumbermen fell off simultaneously, but I suspect laughter had more to do with their downfall than the pillows did. Remembering my grandfather's stories about sap-slippery logs shooting down the skid row in early spring, I was certain that in the early days, this game was part of spring revelry, and no grease had been needed to slick the pole.

I didn't stay at the arena for the entire contest. Strains of a familiar song rolled down from the hilltop, hooked me, and reeled me up the hill. There in the shade by the weathered sawmill buildings, the Allegheny Mountain Old Tyme Music Association played "Big Fun on the Bayou," an old hillbilly song I'd heard since my childhood. My grandfather had played it on his fiddle with me perched on his knee. My mother used to sing it to me in the afternoons when she was coaxing me to sleep. There in the maple shade, all the old stories came together for me—setting, music, wood smoke, new-cut lumber—it was all there. All we needed was a still.

I sat with the Allegheny Mountain Old Tyme Music Association for quite a while. Musicians came, sat in, left, and were replaced by other musicians—and the music went on. There were guitars, mandolins, fiddles, a banjo, and a bass. A few children showed up, grabbed a fiddle, played a tune, and moved on. When it began to rain, we all moved under a tarp, the group reorganized, and soon the music continued. They played "The Tennessee Waltz," "Redwing," and a treasury of other songs I remembered from long-ago family reunions.

Between songs, I chatted with Don MacBeth, president of the association, whose goal is to preserve the musical heritage of the Alleghenies.

"We support the true, traditional method of teaching music," he told me. "In olden times, many of the musicians were self-taught. Take Bob Shank, over there—he got a fiddle off a relative's attic and taught himself to play. It was missing a string!

"Many of us don't read music," he went on. "Our music is handed down, like old tales, or a family craft." And I understood. My grandfather, a champion fiddler, couldn't read music, either. He had gone blind.

I left the Allegheny Mountain musicians reluctantly to see the tobacco-spitting contest in the arena. Six brave contestants worked up mouthfuls of tobacco juice and took their places on the first line of a grid painted on the ground. Each one spit at the smoking potbellied stove in front of them. For a direct hit, the announcer yelled, "It's a sizzler!" and the next contestant took a shot at it.

Then they moved back one mark. When one contestant dribbled, the announcer yelled, "Buckshot!" and the line moved on. The third step back wiped out two contestants, and the next mark eliminated most of the field. The audience roared and cheered each contestant boisterously. The American Cancer Society would have had a stroke, I thought.

In the museum's Orientation Building was a collection of music boxes. The Tioga County Railroad Association had set up a model train display, something that never fails to attract my attention. I also spent time examining the collection of lumbering artifacts, tools, and photographs. When an afternoon storm came up, I took in the slide show.

The storm passed as quickly as it had arrived. I walked up to the rustic logging camp with its mess hall, kitchen, stable, blacksmith's shop, saw filer's shack, and old locomotive. By then I was far away from the festival and walking through our family's collective memory.

There were too many features of the Bark Peelers' Convention for the amount of time I had allotted for my visit. This festival is both entertaining and educational. Demonstrations include shingle making, blacksmithing, basket making, camp cooking, sawmill equipment, hewing, broom making, veneer production, log skidding, ax throwing, bark peeling, chopping, crosscut sawing, and operating a treadle lathe. On Saturday there was a fiddlers' competition. Sunday's schedule included a frog-jumping contest and a log cake cutting and serving competition. Log-skidding and burling demonstrations were also scheduled for both days, and the craft show was in place all weekend.

❖ The festival is usually held the first weekend in July, and the grounds open at 9 A.M. daily. The Pennsylvania Lumber Museum is on Route 6 between Galeton and Coudersport. For more information, contact the Pennsylvania Lumber Museum, P.O. Box 239, Galeton, PA 16922, phone 814-435-2652.

Red Suspender Weekend

Galeton, Potter County

What is your image of a fireman? Always, in my mind, the firefighter carries an ax in one hand and a child in a flowing nightgown in the other. His noble figure is garbed in tall boots and helmet. His long black coat is thrown open, his coveralls hitched to bright red suspenders.

I've also associated firefighters with the Fourth of July. Perhaps it's their obvious presence in July Fourth parades that forged the association—engines shining and bedecked with flags, proudly leading the procession down Main Street. Whatever the case, red suspenders and July Fourth belong to firemen as surely as dalmatians, and as soon as I saw the advertising for Galeton's Red Suspender Weekend, I knew that it was a firefighters' celebration.

On the day that I drove to Galeton, the Keystone State seemed eager to celebrate its part in the nation's independence. In the Sproul Forest, the mountain laurel still shone in bright clumps of pearl white along Route 144. Cabin windows, shuttered against the winter winds, were flying open as summer residents shook winter from their bedding. Houses wore red, white, and blue bunting. Here and there along the way, I was detoured and delayed by an occasional parade, while whole villages smelled of barbecues. Signs advertising sparklers along the road hinted that fireworks might also be available if one inquired in the right tone of voice.

When I attend a fair, I walk through the grounds quickly to see what's there, focusing on interesting events and displays the second time through. My first stop in Center Town Park in Galeton, however, broke my customary pattern. A display of tent flies and screened picnic table covers, with end-of-the-season prices, sent me back to the car with an unwieldy box. My next stop yielded a pair of red suspenders, and my third stop, at the Pine Creek United Methodist Church booth, landed a coffee cup in one hand and a piece of coffee cake in the other. And still, I hadn't made the rounds of all of the attractions.

I noticed a crowd of people sitting on the creek bank and lots of water flying everywhere. Two small red boats, each holding three helmeted firemen, were anchored twenty feet apart. Each team aimed a fire hose at the other boat and blasted it unmercifully. Some of the younger spectators scurried about, catching the spray from the hoses, while one or two braver kids waded into the stream. As the noontime sun gleamed down, I envied both kids and firemen. In a matter of minutes, one boat sank, and the firemen didn't hurry to leave the cool creek.

I talked with John Rossetti, fire chief at Galeton, about Red Suspender Weekend, which is a fund-raiser for the Goodyear Hose Fire Company. The local school ran a contest to name the festival in 1984. Each grade picked a name, and the eighth-grade class that year won.

We walked through the other firefighter game sites. A cable was stretched between two poles with a ball in the middle—"The Carolina Cable," Chief Rossetti told me. "This is the original firemen's water battle. In place of the ball, there used to be an empty beer keg. Two teams squirt water at the ball, and whichever gets it to the other end wins."

Crumb Cakes
....

2 $^1/_2$ cups flour

1 $^1/_2$ cups firmly packed brown
     sugar

$^1/_2$ cup softened butter or oleo

dash of salt

$^1/_2$ teaspoon nutmeg

1 cup buttermilk

$^1/_2$ teaspoon baking powder

1 teaspoon baking soda

Mix first five ingredients into crumbs.

Reserve 1 cup of crumbs for top. Put remaining ingredients into the first and mix. Pour into two greased 8-inch cake or pie tins. Sprinkle crumbs on top. Bake at 350 degrees for 25 to 30 minutes.

Let cool in pans.

This recipe was found in an old Grange cookbook.

—*Elaine Cloak, Grines*

The next game centered on a small house. "It's called the efficiency run," he explained. "Teams pump water from a holding tank and squirt it on the roof of the building. It runs down the spouting into a bucket, and when the bucket is full, the stopwatch clicks. The fastest time wins."

I bought half a barbecued chicken and a large fresh-brewed iced tea and began reading the schedule of events at a shady table in the pavilion. A roar overhead turned into a tornado, scattering my notes to the four winds as the *Guthrie I*, the local ambulance helicopter, landed behind the boathouse. I retrieved my notes with the help of several people and shoved them into my bag, the schedule still in hand.

The Goodyear Hose Company planned a full weekend of events, starting with live music in the pavilion on Friday night. A parade Saturday morning, the firefighters' water games, and live music followed. The Saturday night fireworks display was scheduled for 10, and according to John Rossetti, it would take two hours to get out of town after the last rocket.

There was plenty of good food on Saturday: alcohol-free strawberry daiquiris, fries, soda, beer, pizza, fresh fruit, soft pretzels, cotton candy, and candy apples. I can recommend the barbecued chicken and the coffee cake. Both were delicious. Baseball cards, tents, jewelry, wicker, wind chimes, T-shirts, and stuffed animals were offered for sale. There was also the usual flea market hodgepodge. If you cared to take a gamble, there was a drawing with a $2,000 grand prize.

❖ Red Suspender Weekend is always held over July Fourth weekend in Center Town Park. There are plenty of motels and campgrounds in the area for travelers who want to enjoy all the events. Since this is held over the same weekend as the Bark Peelers' Convention, plan on spending a weekend and attending both events.

Festival of the Candles

Lititz, Lancaster County

We sat in the lobby of the General Sutter Inn that evening, two old friends enjoying a favorite hostelry. Iced tea had led to dinner and then to more iced tea as afternoon slid into evening. The occasional clatter of the busy restaurant underlined our conversation. The aviary around the lobby added a descant to the musical score. As we sat and chatted, we watched the slow trickle of residents and tourists grow to a raging river headed down Broad Street for Lititz Springs Park.

"I suppose we should be going," Marian said, putting her glass down on the coffee table. "It's almost time for the crowning of the Queen of Candles."

"We have a few more minutes," I said, "To tell you the truth, I'm not eager to go out into that heat again. Tell me how you ended up in Lititz."

"You really are stalling! For the hundredth time, I came here when I was fourteen with my Sunday School class. I decided then and there, or then and here as the case may be, that I'd live here someday. It took fourteen more years, but I made it."

"How long ago was that?" I asked.

"Too long! And one more age-related crack out of you, and I'll crown *you*—forget the queen!"

We paid our bill, said good-bye to Richard and Joan Vetter, the innkeepers, and walked outside into a wall of steam. I shifted my leather camera bag to the other shoulder and resumed whimpering about the heat.

"You'll get used to it," Marian advised. "In a half hour you won't even notice."

"Tell that to a lobster."

Once we were through the gates of the Lititz Springs Park there was a noticeable temperature drop. The shade trees had insulated the park from the worst of the afternoon sun, and the stream had done the rest.

We hurried over to the band shell, ignoring french fries, funnel cakes, burgers, and hot dogs. Twelve young women from Warwick High School's Class of 1994, selected by secret ballot, were dressed in formal evening attire and carrying candles in nosegays of fresh flowers. Escorted by their fathers, each candidate was introduced and directed to the center of the stage for a moment of recognition—cheers, shouts, and whistles of encouragement and endorsement.

Then the master of ceremonies called the flower girl and crown bearer to the stage. With the court in place, he announced the Queen of Candles, and the crown of fresh flowers was placed on her head.

After lighting her candle, the new Queen of Candles lit the candles of her court, who then lit torches carried by the local Boy Scouts. In a matter of minutes, Lititz Springs Park was bathed in candlelight, my favorite part of Fourth of July weekend in Lititz.

Although Lititz Springs Park has hosted an Independence Day celebration since 1818, the Festival of the Candles didn't begin until 1843. Then, four hundred candles were lighted. As I watched, more than seven thousand candles sparkled on boards, pyramids, and floating swans between the stone-lined streamsides.

I grabbed Marian by the arm, and with a quick "Come on!" headed for the bridge that crosses the stream, camera in hand. Everyone else did, too. Folks were as crowded on the little footbridge as a pack of ship rats clinging to flotsam after their host has gone to meet Poseidon—and just as ruthless. I feared for the bridge.

"Let's go up to the head of the spring. If we climb the hill, you can get a shot of the stream the whole way down through the park," Marian advised. It proved a good idea. There were fewer people there, and the view was better.

After the rush, the push, and the climb, Marian said, "I thought you were hot."

"It has cooled down some," I said lamely. Her smile silenced me.

The crowd began to drift toward the open fields beyond the park for the patriotic fireworks display, and still, we stood watching until the last candle guttered out on its mounting.

"This is so simple and old-fashioned," I said. "I'm afraid that the fireworks will be too high tech and that they'll ruin the simplicity of this festival."

"Nonsense!" Marian snorted. "Fireworks predate Lititz Springs Park. The Chinese used them in battle to frighten their enemies."

"I take it you want to see the fireworks?"

Moravian Sugar Cake

1 cup mashed potatoes	1 $^1/_2$ cups butter, melted
1 cake yeast	2 eggs, beaten
$^2/_3$ cup warm water	6 to 7 cups cake flour
1 cup scalded milk	2 cups light brown sugar
$^1/_2$ cup white sugar	cinnamon
1 $^1/_2$ teaspoons salt	

Dissolve yeast in lukewarm water. Combine hot milk, sugar, and $^1/_2$ cup melted butter, stirring until sugar dissolves. Cool to lukewarm. Add mashed potatoes, yeast, and eggs. Beat until smooth. Add 6 cups of flour; knead 10 minutes, adding more flour as the dough becomes sticky. Place in a greased bowl, butter top; cover; let rise in a warm place about an hour and 15 minutes or until doubled in bulk. Roll into three 9 x 13-inch cake pans. Brush top with melted butter. Cover, and let rise to 1 inch in height. Sprinkle with brown sugar. Punch thumb into top of cake at 1-inch intervals, covering top of cake with holes. Pour melted butter in each hole. Sprinkle with cinnamon. Bake at 350 degrees for 20 to 25 minutes.

"You bet! They're set to computer this year."

And so we rambled over to the field. Most folks had come prepared, sprawling on blankets or seated on folding lawn chairs. We sat down on the cool grass, propped on purse, daypack, and camera bag. For forty-five minutes we *oohed!* and *aahed!* along with the crowd. Bombs exploded, Roman candles shattered, rockets roared and cracked overhead, lighting up the countryside around Lititz. Patriotic music rang through the town.

And then it was over. Marian and I followed the crowd out of Lititz Springs Park and down Broad Street to her house. It had been a long day and a half. We'd started Friday night with the parade and band concert. On Saturday we'd visited the photography show, watched the baby parade, checked out the antiques show, and fitted other local attractions, namely the Wilbur Chocolate Factory and the Sturgis Pretzel House, into the cracks.

"Tell me more about Lititz, how it was founded. Did Count Zinzendorf found this town?"

"Well, no, not exactly. Count Zinzendorf preached in Lancaster and so impressed John Klein, who owned a farm nearby, that Klein deeded his farm to a group of Moravians. This group, the Warwick Congregation, eventually founded the town of Lititz in 1756."

We talked late into the night and agreed that visitors to the Festival of the Candles should really plan on spending the weekend in the area to take advantage of Lititz's many historic attractions. No one should miss seeing the Moravian Church with its corpse house, where the winter's dead lay until a spring thaw allowed the congregation to bury them. The archives museum at the church, open Saturdays during the summer months, contains Lititz memorabilia as well as the congregation's instrument collection. The oldest viola of American manufacture, built in 1764 by John Andes, resides there. The museum also houses a fine late-eighteenth-century serpent—a leather-covered wooden bass horn.

The Sturgis Pretzel House is the oldest commercial pretzel bakery in the country. Tours are available and guests are encouraged to twist their own pretzels. Admission tickets are hard pretzels, and it takes discipline to keep yours in hand until the tour begins.

Chocolate lovers should also visit Wilbur Chocolate, next to Lititz Springs Park. It's difficult to forget that stop, for the smell of chocolate fills the town. There is a candy museum and an outlet in the front of the factory. Admission is free, but buy a bag of Wilbur Buds.

If you extend your July Fourth visit, the many attractions of Lancaster County are close by.

❖ To get to Lititz, take Route 501 North from Route 30 in Lancaster. Lititz Springs Park is located on 501 a block north of the square. If you plan ahead, lodging shouldn't be a problem. There are as many motels as cows in Lancaster County; nevertheless, the festival falls at the heart of vacation season, and rooms will be at a premium.

For more information on the Festival of the Candles, call 717-627-7112 or 717-627-4636.

Millville Firemen's Carnival

Millville, Columbia County

Manley Fought was 82 $^1/_2$ when I met him at the Millville Firemen's Carnival. He added the $^1/_2$ as proudly as a 4 $^1/_2$-year-old. He was taking money at the caramel corn and fresh roasted peanut stand when I caught up with him.

"I've helped with the carnival for better than fifty years," he told me. "I missed three years when I was in the service," he added, and you could hear the regret in his voice for those wasted summers.

Everyone I'd talked to in the hour I'd been at Millville that Thursday night had directed me to Manley Fought. Two questions, and every interview, ended with, "You should go see Manley Fought," and finally I took Millville's advice. It didn't take long for me to appreciate their wisdom. Why waste everyone's time when Manley has firsthand knowledge of the carnival?

Manley credits his sister, Edith Russell, with coming up with the caramel corn recipe years ago; the caramel corn is still the biggest money-maker at the carnival. "We usually buy three thousand pounds of shelled corn each year and that isn't enough," he said. "On Saturday nights, with the fireworks going, we pop fifty-five bushels of corn an hour—and no one touches it with his hands."

The 50th Anniversary Millville Community Fire Company's commemorative booklet tells a story that backs Manley's claims. In 1963 there was a friendly competition between the popcorn stand and the big game stand. Both claimed the title of King of the Carnival. The race was on. Though the game vendors did their best barking, wheedling, and cajoling, things were really popping across the midway. At the end of carnival week, the popcorn stand had made $1,200 more than the games, and no one since has ever doubted caramel corn's position as King of the Carnival—but Manley never had.

As I watched that night, a team of six women, stationed around a twelve-foot wooden trough, tossed the freshly popped corn in its caramel coating. Others bagged the confection, while another team popped corn and roasted peanuts. The smells coming from the open-sided pavilion were inescapable, and anyone within smelling range was a customer.

Manley gave me a bag of caramel corn, and when I'd tasted it, I bought some more. Little wonder that people drive miles for this yearly treat. I tried to get the recipe, but he wouldn't budge. "On, no," he said.

"Only a couple people have that. I'm one of them," he added proudly.

Manley and I also talked about the firemen's carousel, now permanently situated at the Millville Town Park. It was purchased from the old Columbia Park in 1939 and transported to the carnival grounds. According to Manley, it paid for itself the first year at a nickel a ride.

There is a story in Millville, repeated in the anniversary booklet, about Cleon Greenly, the first operator of the merry-go-round. He was so fond of the amusement ride that he named each of the wooden steeds. In the early years of its operation, the ride depended on an old Model T Ford motor, which had to be cranked. One Fourth of July, two of Greenly's helpers decided to play a trick on him. They planted two bombs on the motor. When Greenly got it started, the bombs would explode in a teeth-chattering whistle and scare Greenly out of his wits.

Their plan went awry. The bombs didn't detonate right away and Greenly began to open the gate to customers. The two jokers, afraid the bombs would go off with customers aboard, tried to stall him.

Finally, the bombs went off with a piercing shriek. Greenly grabbed Old Maude, one of the horses, and nearly squeezed her paint off.

The jokesters didn't have long to enjoy their laughter, though. The sparks from the bombs ignited some spilled gasoline. The firemen went to work and in a matter of minutes the fire was put out, but the carnival was also out of soup, lemonade, and coffee—all used to douse the fire.

For years, whenever Greenly was kidded about his death grip on Old Maude, he would respond, "I was just trying to calm the old girl down. She was shaking like a leaf."

I left Manley for a walk around the carnival grounds. Although the carousel was definitely a treasure, the other old rides also deserved a nostalgic visit. No doubt they've carried many Baby Boomers back to their childhoods over the years. The Ferris wheel was attracting quite a line, and it looked like the product of a child prodigy's 1950s erector set. The lovingly restored little train running around the Little League baseball field had also seen former riders grow to adulthood and then send their progeny around the tracks. My favorite ride, the kiddy cars, carried its joyful carloads in what may have been postwar pedal cars. For a low-budget evening, there were the town park's swings, sliding board, kid-powered merry-go-round, and sandbox.

I wandered down to the Toilet Toss, the Thursday night feature. Quite a few contestants picked up the commode and threw it across a sand pit. Throws were measured, and officials were more serious than the contestants about the event.

Caramel Popcorn

12 cups freshly popped popcorn,   2 tablespoons butter
    salted   1 tablespoon vinegar
1 cup sugar $1/_2$ teaspoon baking soda
1 cup molasses

Place popcorn in a lightly greased mixing bowl. Set aside.

Combine sugar, molasses, butter, and vinegar in a small Dutch oven. Bring to a boil, stirring until sugar dissolves. Cover and continue to cook over medium heat 2 to 3 minutes to wash down sugar crystals from sides of pan. Uncover and cook, without stirring, until mixture reaches hard ball stage (250 degrees).

Remove from heat; stir in soda. Pour syrup over popcorn. Stir until all popcorn is coated.

Note: This is *not* Manley Fought's recipe.

Local Millville vendors offered hot dogs, hamburgers, fries, steak subs, ice cream, cotton candy, snow cones, slushies, soup, clam chowder, and fresh fruit. I decided on a steak sub and fries and enjoyed the local banter almost as much as I enjoyed my dinner.

There were also games of chance run by volunteers. At the roulette wheel you could win a watermelon—I didn't. You could roll balls into muffin tins, toss a ball into glasses, or play a numbers game.

There was country music on the stage that evening, as there is every evening of the carnival. Other highlights during the week included the Independence Day parade, a play on the high school stage, and a Little League baseball game. The fireworks display would close the carnival on the last Saturday night, and then Millville's flying horses would rest for another year, their calliope would take a deep breath and then sigh into silence, and the corn popper would cool down.

I was impressed by this small town's carnival. Relying on no outside vendors or concessionaires, they do it all themselves, with extraordinary results. Perhaps their biggest success is the sense of community pride one feels in Millville.

❖ The Millville Firemen's Carnival is held from Friday to the following Saturday over the Fourth of July. There is no carnival on Sunday, but a vesper service is held at 5 that evening. Admission and parking are free. The carnival is held at the park in the center of town. From Bloomsburg, take Route 42 North for eleven miles into the square of Millville. Make a right onto Route 642. The park is about three blocks on the left. For more information, contact the Millville Fire Company or call 717-458-5092.

Big Butler Fair

Prospect, Butler County

Lesson One: If you are not familiar with the area, call ahead and ask for directions.

After spending four hours on the road, I arrived in Butler and began looking for signs to the fairgrounds. When they failed to appear, I spent another half hour riding around the city searching the horizon for Ferris wheels, bungee-jumping cranes, or any of the other landmarks that signify a fair. I had planned on having lunch at the fair, but as the sweltering day wore on, I stopped at Pizza Hut, had lunch, and asked for directions.

"It's on the other side of town," the waitress said with a vague wave at the back wall. She reeled off lefts and rights and forgettable landmarks. I said my thank-yous and tried anyhow—and ended up in a junkyard.

Lesson Two: Ask the person from whom you are getting directions whether he is a local.

I found a service station and got out with my tape recorder. The man on duty had an accent thick enough to require an interpreter. Still, he was friendly and smiled a lot, punctuating his unintelligible directions with sweeping gestures. I began to get the gist of it, thanked him, and took off. Too bad I hadn't used a camcorder. Without the visuals, his taped narrative sounded like my commode when the plumbing backs up—but at least I know what that means. In no time at all, I was on my way back to the junkyard, and so I turned in a direction I hadn't tried yet.

Lesson Three: Take advantage of being lost.

I found a lovely antiques shop and bought two Empire glass knobs for a night table I was working on. The dealer also gave me directions to the fair. "It's a shortcut," he told me. "You'll be there in five minutes."

Lesson Four: Don't take shortcuts in unfamiliar territory.

In five minutes I was driving into the woods. Civilization thinned out and then gave up completely. I'd been wilderness camping in better populated areas. I turned around, followed my nose back to the antiques shop, and went the other direction. And then I saw the sign: "Big Butler Fair. Turn Here."

As I walked past the draft horse arena just inside the gate, I saw a tiny pigtailed girl perched on the back of a two-thousand-pound Percheron gelding as the huge mass of muscle jogged placidly around the ring. She was so small and the horse's back so broad that her legs stuck straight out. I beckoned her over to the ringside, and when she had skillfully parked the behemoth next to me, I introduced myself.

"I'm Codee Jean Neff," she announced, and when she saw that I was writing, she spelled her name helpfully. "C-O-D-E-E—that's Codee," she explained. "N-E-F-F—that's my last name. I don't know how to spell Jean yet. I'm only five."

Codee told me that the horse, Moses, was really her father's. "But we share," she assured me. She also told me that she'd been riding since she was two and showing in the cart and wagon class since she was four. "One time I didn't win," she told me. "They runned out of ribbons."

It was easy to find the Neffs' stalls inside the draft horse barn. I was copying the stable's address when Traves Neff, Codee's sixteen-year-old brother, walked up.

"Does she really show in the cart and wagon class?" I asked.

"Oh yes she does!" he said, grinning from ear to ear. "I have to wrap my arms around her. She can drive the horses, but they pull so hard, and she's so little, they just pull her off the seat."

A 4-H horse show was in progress in the show arena on the other side of the east gate. A handful of anxious parents sat on the weathered bleachers or hung over the peeling rail. Fretful riders adjusted costumes and wiped sweat. Horses and ponies stamped feet and put their ears back. Dust competed with humidity to make it a truly breathless afternoon, heightening tensions in the ring and at ringside even further.

I listened as a young English rider behind me asked in disbelief, "Mother, do western riders actually lean back to ride?" I eavesdropped on a conversation between a prospective riding coach and the parent who would hire him if he said the right things. And I liked Traves and Codee even more.

I left the livestock buildings and walked through the midway. In addition to being a Class A agricultural fair, the Big Butler Fair had all of the customary state fair attractions to baffle, amaze, and amuse. There was karaoke, a reptile show, magic shows, a fun house, the clown Sonney Dayze, free stage shows, remote car races, miniature golf, bingo, games of chance, rides for all ages, bungee jumping, and pony rides for kids less fortunate than Codee and the 4-H'ers. There were hundreds of food choices on the midway.

Blue-Ribbon Hershey's Cocoa Brownies

2 cups sugar
4 eggs
1 cup oil
$^2/_3$ cup Hershey's cocoa
1 teaspoon vanilla

2 cups flour
1 teaspoon salt
1 teaspoon baking powder
$^1/_2$ cup chopped nuts

Grease and flour a 9 x 13-inch pan. In large bowl, combine sugar, eggs, and oil. Add cocoa and vanilla. Beat until smooth. Sift remaining dry ingredients and add to first mixture. Mix well and add nuts. Pour into prepared pan and bake at 350 degrees for 35 to 45 minutes. Cool completely before frosting.

—*Kayla Rogers*

I listened to music by the Keystone Music Association. I looked at the canned goods, the baked goods, and the produce. I stopped to see the needlework, too. By the time I left, I felt I'd gotten my money's worth at the Big Butler Fair.

The sun was going down and the lights were going up when I left the east gate. There was a "just for fun" competition in the draft horse arena. Each rider was carrying an egg on a teaspoon while obeying the announcer's commands, "Walk your horse . . . trot your horse . . ."

As I was getting into my car, I heard the announcer say, "I think that little girl has an egg up her sleeve!" There was no doubt in my mind he was talking about Codee.

❖ The Big Butler Fair is held during July Fourth week. It is located 7 miles west of Butler on Route 422. For more information, write to the Butler Fair and Agricultural Association, 1127 New Castle Road, Prospect, PA 16052, or call 412-865-2400. Ask for a map.

Richfield Dutch Days

Richfield, Juniata County

To most of the world, Lancaster County is synonymous with the Amish. Thousands of tourists arrive in Lancaster each summer to drive through Intercourse, Paradise, Blue Ball, and Bird-in-Hand. The adventurous intrude even more industriously on the Amish and Old Order Mennonites and load up on Amish cuisine, hex signs, distelfinks, straw hats, sunbonnets, and quilts.

Few realize that the Pennsylvania Dutch culture has flowed into the mainstream of the eastern half of the state. Indeed, it's not unusual to awaken to the staccato clip-clop of an Amish cart horse going down the road late at night, far from Lancaster County. The Amish influence is so ingrained that Pennsylvania has long forgotten its indebtedness to the Plain People. So many of us have grown up on pickled eggs, pot pie, chicken corn soup, scrapple, and shoofly pie. We "redd up the house" before company comes and eat sauerkraut for New Year's Day luck without even thinking about the Pennsylvania Dutch.

Even though Richfield is far north of Lancaster County, I suspected that, like many other Pennsylvania communities, the family tree of the town grew from good old Pennsylvania German rootstock, well fertilized with apple dumplings swimming in cream, cottage cheese and apple butter on thick slices of homemade bread, and pig stomach bursting with potatoes, cabbage, and country sausage. And I was certain that one of the main purposes of Dutch Days was the excuse to prepare and eat generous helpings of good food.

I arrived in Richfield late on Wednesday afternoon for the first evening of the four-day event. I was surprised to find a number of modern, well-maintained buildings. There was a home products building, a large commercial building, two food pavilions with kitchens, permanent concession stands, flush toilets, and another odd display building or two. The Dutch Days staff had craftspeople on the tennis courts and opened the horseshoe pits to fair goers.

I stopped in the commercial building to find the limited-edition trivets I'd read about in advance advertising. The punched tin trivets, produced by Irvins Craft Shop, were decorative, utilitarian, and attractively priced souvenirs. While I was there, I also stopped to see George Losch's limited edition print, "Airing the Quilts." Both pieces were designed for the Dutch Days celebration, and proceeds from their sale would benefit the festival association. I applauded Richfield for its good taste.

Beef Pot Pie

1 gallon beef (cooked) and broth   7 quarts pot pie squares
2 $1/_2$ gallons water   (dry)
2 quarts cut potatoes   1 tablespoon salt
Cook meat ahead of time and freeze with broth. On the day of the
event, add other ingredients and cook until tender.

I went to the Fancy House Arts and Crafts Building in search of the quilt that would be auctioned off at the end of the festival, the final benefit item. You couldn't miss it, spotlighted on one wall of the building. Designed by George Losch, the black-and-white quilt featured an embroidered picture of an early local fort. The border of the quilt was embroidered with hundreds of names, an autograph quilt. One of the volunteers explained that the names were sold for twenty-five cents each.

On my way to the food pavilions I marveled at the number of lawn chairs reserving spaces for the Country Legend concert that night. They gathered around the stage like a flock of geese in an October cornfield.

The two food pavilions offered seating under roof at long, oilcloth-covered picnic tables. They featured different menus but both were homestyle food—a chicken corn soup, barbecue, and pie menu, and a beef pot pie dinner platter. No contest. The pot pie was excellent, and the dinner included pepper slaw, a roll, a choice of dessert pie, and a beverage. While I was sitting down to my pot pie, I noted the menu for the rest of the carnival. Thursday night's specialty was a baked ham dinner, Friday's was pork and sauerkraut, and Saturday featured chicken barbecue after the parade.

In addition to these foods, local groups also offered apple dumplings, salads, fruit cup, baked potatoes, cheese steaks, pepper steaks, soft pretzels, pizza, lemonade, fries, cotton candy, and funnel cakes. The Freeburg Boy Scout Troop was running six freezers of homemade ice cream constantly, all night long. Scoutmaster Dave Hess told me that they would turn out twenty three-gallon containers on Wednesday and Thursday nights, thirty on Friday, and eighty-two to eighty-eight more on Saturday.

As I had expected, food was the big attraction in Richfield—but not the only attraction. There were a Ferris wheel, a Spinner, an Astro Top, a merry-go-round, a mixer, swings, cars, and a moonwalk. There were as many games of chance on the small midway. The crafts show on the ten-

nis court was small, but the merchandise was nice and the display area
was easily accessible. I was especially impressed by the Mill Creek Nursery's display: Black-eyed Susans, cornflowers, and lilies bloomed around a
brick patio, pool, and fountain. White birches and evergreens completed
the miniature park.

Before I left Richfield, I visited the food pavilion once more. Betty
Frontman, the head cook, told me that her crew of nine had arrived at
noon for the 4:30 meal, but their real work had begun two weeks earlier,
when they cooked the beef and made the rich stock for the pot pie. She
opened her worn notebook and copied the recipe for me.

The sun was an orange fireball hanging over the valley when I left,
but it was soon replaced by a glowing slice of moon. All along the way,
the smell of freshly cut hay rode over the valley on waves of humidity.

❖ Richfield Dutch Days are scheduled around the parade held on the
third Saturday of July. The festival is held from the preceding Wednesday
through that Saturday evening. Richfield is located midway between
Selinsgrove and Mifflintown off Route 35. Dutch Days are held at Basom
Memorial Park, one block north of Route 35 in the center of town. For
more information, write to the President of the Richfield Community
Center, Richfield, PA 17086.

Mifflin Fair

Newville, Cumberland County

The miles of cornstalks along the Steelstown Road made the already narrow road seem even narrower, nothing more than a silvery snake slither-
ing through the fields. At times that evening it was impossible to see
anything but the road in front of the car, the apricot sky overhead, and
the towering corn walls on either side. It was high summer in Cumberland County, time for corn, for thunderstorms, for humming air conditioners—and time for the Mifflin Fair.

After attending so many fairs where I was a stranger, it was nice to be
going to a fair at home, a fair where I knew everyone and everyone knew
me. It was even nicer to be going without a notepad and a camera.

I already knew the history of the fair. It was an offshoot of the Mifflin
Athletic Association, a yearly fund-raiser. The Athletic Association had
grown out of teenage gatherings at the Oiler farm in 1919. There was a
wagon shed on the farm, and with the addition of regulation baskets, it

became the first gymnasium. By 1920, there were both boys' and girls' basketball teams. In addition to the athletics, the association formed a singing group and orchestra, and before long the orchestra was in great demand in the surrounding community.

In 1922, Allie Brandt built a new wagon shed and offered the second floor as a gymnasium; Mr. Brandt furnished it with lights from the carbide plant at his home. There were steep stairs to the new facility, and the single dressing room under the bleachers was heated by an egg stove.

The wagon shed gymnasium was destroyed by fire in 1940. With a war in the wings, no effort was made to rebuild until 1946, when the Athletic Association was reorganized. The new gymnasium would cost between $5,000 and $7,000, but John Rolar graciously donated an acre of land for the Quonset-type building the association had planned. The farm families donated food, and the Mifflin Fair's reputation for good food, and plenty of it, grew.

In the early years there was homemade ice cream—Grapenut ice cream was a favorite then. There were ham sandwiches, and the ham was smoky and salty, cured in a Mifflin Township smokehouse. From piglet to sandwich, the donor had never been out of a five-mile radius of the fair. There were chicken sandwiches then, too, chicken corn soup, bean soup, and always, homemade pies.

Food has always been one of the main attractions at the Mifflin Fair. Although the menu has changed over the years to more pedestrian hamburger and french fry fare, and the ham in the sandwiches is more like deli lunch meat than country-smoked ham, still the faithful come each evening and line up by the concession stand windows, trays in hand. After all, at least the pies are still homemade.

The fair has changed in other subtle ways over the years. As a teenager, I spent half the evening on the rides, and when my niece was young, she and I rode the Ferris wheel together every night. The rides are gone now, and with them, many of the teenagers from the surrounding community. The crowd is older, some as old as the fair itself.

Nevertheless, come summer we have an appointment with the Mifflin Fair. It is our gathering place. One would think, living in a small community as we do, that the residents would run into each other daily, but the year may pass without contact with neighbors two or three blocks away. We run in different circles, we work in other communities, we attend different churches, we belong to different social organizations. The Mifflin Fair brings us together again, to share the triumphs and the disappointments of the year.

Wet-Bottom Shoofly Pie

$^1/_4$ cup blackstrap molasses   1 cup cold water
$^1/_4$ cup King syrup (golden)   1 cup light brown sugar
1 egg   1 scant teaspoon soda
Mix well and pour into 9-inch unbaked pie shell.
Top with crumbs:
   1 $^1/_2$ cups flour $^1/_4$ cup shortening
   $^1/_2$ cup light brown sugar
Bake at 375 degrees for 45 minutes.

—*Joan Oiler Brehm*

After I had parked my car in the apricot and lavender twilight that evening, I carried my lawn chair up the hill, located my parents, and dropped off the chair.

I ate dinner in the pavilion, carrying on a lively conversation with my friends Mike and Sam Hoover. They were setting up the sound system for the bingo game, but before I left, I had arranged for them to install a new water heater at my house and to clean my furnace. I ran into Leroy Miller on my way to the stage and ordered three loads of firewood as added insurance against the winter winds. When I relocated my folks, they were in the process of ordering sweet corn for the freezer from May Brownewell, an old family friend. I sat down and saw my high school friend Donna across the way. We spent a handful of minutes catching up. And all of this was before the evening's entertainment had begun.

The group that night was the second generation of the Jacobs Brothers, a popular gospel quartet. Drew Jacobs had been a favorite student of mine, and I felt a teacher's pride as I watched him perform. It magnified greatly when he rushed down to see me between sets.

It was late that night when I headed my car down the sweet corn alleyway toward the familiar lights of home. I thought about my evening at the Mifflin Fair a long time before I went to bed. It is indeed a small festival with no rides, only a few games, and no fancy concessions. The entertainment is homegrown, and in truth, anyone there could hear these groups in one of the churches around town on almost any Sunday morning of the year. And yet, folks still come as they have come to the Mifflin Fair for almost a century.

The need for continuity in a rapidly changing world is a strong incentive. But I suspect, more than anything, that these fairs cement our feeling of community and nurture our sense of belonging.

The earliest organizers of the Mifflin Athletic Association and its fair saw a need and fulfilled it with commitment. Their accomplishment was monumental in the early years of the twentieth century, and perhaps now, decades later, we celebrate their contribution to community with our steadfast presence at the fair.

❖ If you plan to attend, mark the second full weekend of July on your calendar. The Mifflin Fair runs Thursday through Saturday night. Bring a lawn chair. The Mifflin Athletic Association is located outside of Newville. From Route 233, turn onto the Steelstown Road. After the bridge, take the left branch of the Y and continue to the fairgrounds.

Tom Mix Roundup

Driftwood, Cameron County

The heat and humidity that had laid siege to the state for weeks harnessed its horses and pulled out under the cover of darkness. At dawn, a few tendrils of haze ran long fingers through forested ridges, lingering like smoke from a smoldering campfire or dust clouds behind a Conestoga wagon. Blue skies drifted in behind, pushing the smoky haze on its way.

My knowledge of Tom Mix was as vague as that waning haze when I left for Driftwood and the Tom Mix Roundup that morning. I knew that he was a movie cowboy in the early years of the motion picture industry, and that was about it. Before seeing advertising for the Tom Mix Roundup, I hadn't even realized that he was a Pennsylvania native.

There was little in the area around Driftwood that spoke of cowboys. Even after I passed the sign saying, "You are entering Tom Mix territory," the landscape was as Pennsylvania as William Penn. Wide patches of laurel bloomed under towering hemlocks. A whitetail jumped out onto the road, stared at me, and then moved on, unafraid. A few ruffed grouse, and I could have sent off the perfect Pennsylvania postcard. There wasn't a cactus, a branding iron, a ten-gallon hat, or a stalk of tumbleweed in sight.

I knew I was close to the Tom Mix birthplace when I saw the line of cars parked along the roadside. I walked down the hill and over the railroad tracks, following the sounds of a country-western tune. A western village with a barn, which doubles as a stage, a kitchen and picnic pavilion, a gift shop, a jail, an outhouse, and a museum now stand where Tom Mix, the legendary Hollywood cowboy, grew up in backwoods Pennsylvania. Only a root cellar and a hand-dug well remain where the Mix family raised their children.

I went first to the museum, in search of the man who inspires such a loyal following more than half a century after he died in an automobile accident in Arizona. There, with the help of Ray and Eva Flaugh's collection of Mix memorabilia, videos of his films, and a TV documentary, I was able to assemble an understanding of his life.

Born to Ed and Elizabeth Smith Mix in 1880, Tom Mix spent his early years at this homestead. He moved with his family to Dubois when he was four. In 1905 he joined the 101 Real Wild West Ranch in Oklahoma, earning $15 a month. He started playing parts in Miller Brothers Wild West Shows, and by the time he was forty, he was one of the biggest box office draws in the country, earning $17,000 a week during the Great Depression. Riding his famous horse, Tony, Mix became the first real rhinestone cowboy, crossing over from silent films to talkies. He made 350, perhaps 400, films, and Hollywood was known as Mixville.

In the late 1930s when his box office appeal began to fade, he formed the Tom Mix Circus. In Europe, he was so popular that schools and stores closed down when he appeared in town. Simultaneously, sponsored by Ralston-Purina, Mix starred in his own "Tom Mix and His Ralston Straight Shooters" show. This idol of America's youth encouraged fans of all ages to be straight shooters for life.

The Flaughs, owners and operators of the Mix property, have done a remarkable job of reassembling the man's life through their collections. There is a poignant contrast between the stack of excavated deer antlers, the remains of the Mix family's humble dinners, and the flashy Cord convertible he drove to his death. Authentic costumes, photos, movie and circus posters, boots, guns, knives, belt buckles, and Ralston-Purina sendoffs helped flesh out the man for me.

There were horses on the premises, and the sounds of their whinnying rang through the woods. Another set of country music started at the barn. I bought a cheeseburger and a Coke and spread out my notes at one of the picnic tables in the pavilion. Soon I was chatting with Ralph Steinbach and Ron Spencer from Dubois.

"Tom Mix was a reprobate," Ralph told me. "My stepdad's dad worked with him in John E. Dubois's woods. He used to tell me that if young Tom couldn't find a horse to ride out in the woods, he'd ride a cow."

Cowboy BBQ Marinade

$^1/_2$ cup chopped onion
1 $^1/_2$ tablespoons packed brown
   sugar
1 tablespoon vegetable oil
$^1/_3$ cup cider vinegar

$^1/_3$ cup catsup
1 tablespoon prepared
   horseradish
1 tablespoon water
$^1/_2$ teaspoon black pepper

Cook onion and brown sugar in oil in small saucepan over medium heat until onion is tender, about 3 minutes. Add remaining ingredients and continue cooking over medium heat 3 to 4 minutes, stirring occasionally. Remove from heat; cool thoroughly before adding to beef. Makes about $^3/_4$ cup.

Place a 3-pound chuck roast in marinade. Refrigerate 6 hours or overnight. Grill meat to desired doneness. Slice thinly on the diagonal. Serve.

Ray Flaugh joined us, and then the stories really began to fly.

"Hitler called Tom when he was in Sweden," Flaugh told us. "He wanted to know when Tom was coming to see all of his fans in Germany. Tom said, 'I'll be back to Germany to see my fans over your dead body!' and hung up on him."

Story matched story between the events on the stage. We quieted down long enough to see kids participate in a quick-draw contest using rubber-band guns, and the best western-dressed contest. One little Indian joined the little cowboys and cowgirls on the stage. Ray pointed out the little Indian boy to Chief Eagle Eye, one of the honorary emcees.

"Did you ever see an Indian like that?" Ray asked. "What tribe is he from?"

Without missing a beat, the chief replied, "Why, yes. The Wanna-be tribe!"

Ralph Steinbach resumed his story: "We had a Carlton Theatre in Dubois," he said. "Tom Mix's mother came to the movie every Saturday and sat in the center of the front row to see her boy perform."

I met S. A. Tom Darrigrand, the Tom Mix look-alike and western performer, and I watched the arrival of the Mix Run Gunman Gang. I stayed for the shootout, and I listened to some more country music. But nothing could compete with the poignant story about the little old Pennsylvania Dutch woman, wife of a lumberman and teamster, who went to the theater every Saturday to see her boy in the pictures.

❖ The Tom Mix Roundup is held in mid-July, at the Tom Mix Birth-place Park, off Route 555, 5 ¹/₂ miles from Driftwood. The roundup begins on Friday night with pickin' and grinnin' country music, and everyone is invited to bring guitars, fiddles, and banjos and jump in on the music making. Saturday starts with a Tom Mix breakfast at a local restaurant and includes a jailbreak, a shootout, and country music. Sunday features country gospel music and old-fashioned preaching on the stage, followed by storytelling, a shootout, and a western divorce. For exact dates and a schedule of events, write to Tom Mix Birthplace Park, R.D. 1, Driftwood, PA 15832, or call 814-546-2628 or 814-546-2044.

Lycoming County Fair

Hughesville, Lycoming County

As I sat in the wainscoted office of the Lycoming County Fair, the air conditioners were fighting a losing battle with the rapidly opening and closing front door. Carrying in armloads of problems, staff members arrived, unloaded their burdens on the fair secretary's desk, and then departed, greeting other heavily laden staffers in the lobby or by the open front door. As conversation moved ahead in fits and starts, I began to get a better, if halting, picture of what goes into producing a Class-A fair.

First, you need about eighty competent people who work well under pressure. And then you need Mary Anne Heydenreich, the fair secretary. A Bloomsburg resident, she spends two months each summer living in a travel trailer on the fairgrounds. During the rest of the year, she says, "There's hardly a day goes by that I don't do something for the fair."

Like fair staffers I'd met all over the state, Mary Anne has had a long association with the fair. In fact, the fair is a family tradition.

"I started here in the 1940s, ushering in the grandstand," she told me. "My father was fair secretary, and when he passed away in 1972, my husband took over the position. When he stepped down, I stepped up."

Her husband wasn't through with fairs, though. A past president of the State Association of Fairs, he still serves on the Lycoming County Fair's board of directors, as well as the Bloomsburg Fair's board. Their son and his wife run food concessions, and their grandson, the fourth generation, sells lemonade.

I'd arrived at the fairgrounds that afternoon just in time for the clown show. Dressed in checkerboard pants, a red-and-gold jacket, and a red, white, and blue stovepipe hat, Sonney Dayze shared his humor, wisdom, magic, and morality.

After the show, he walked down to where I sat taking notes. "Didn't I see you in Butler last week?" he asked. "It looks like we're on the same circuit."

I explained my writing project and we compared schedules for the coming months. Sonney Dayze appears at nine or ten fairs a season, sometimes as part of a carnival operator's package and sometimes independently. While on the road, he lives in a travel trailer. For the other nine months of the year, Art Jennings—his real name—teaches special education classes in the western part of the state. "I do this to get away from kids," he said with a laugh.

Like Mary Anne Heydenreich, Jennings has a family tradition to uphold. His father, now retired, spent fifty years as Happy Dayze, the clown. Art started in his father's act when he was four, pushing boxes and performing little illusions in the magic act.

I asked him what it was like to travel with the carnies. By the transient nature of their lives, they tend to live outside of society and create their own community; they seem as leery of townspeople as the locals are of them.

"First off," he corrected me, "we prefer to be called showmen. Come here—let me show you something."

In one corner of the fairgrounds, a fountain splashed prisms of afternoon sunlight. It was landscaped with blooming flowers and spotlighted for fair goers' nighttime pleasure. One plaque read, "Make a Wish," and another, "In Memory of Richard Chief Darrah. Your Showman Family."

"Let me tell you a story," he said. "For years a man hung around the fair. He was here all the time. He was a little slow, but he was everyone's buddy. His name was Richard Darrah, but we all called him 'Chief.' He'd hit you up for meals, or perhaps a little pocket change, but he'd do security, he'd watch your stage if you had to leave for a minute. Last year on the second night of the fair, he had a heart attack and died. The showmen took up a collection. Ride jocks don't make a lot of money, but we got seventeen hundred dollars, enough to build this fountain and to help with the funeral, too. We built this Thursday night, so that it would be ready for the fair."

Art walked back to his stage, and in a few minutes I heard him start his show. "It's showtime!" I stood by the fountain quite a while. Indeed, there was much that I didn't know about the folks who made these fairs happen.

Chocolate Thumbprint Cookies

$^1/_2$ cup butter or margarine
$^2/_3$ cup sugar
1 egg, separated
2 tablespoons milk
1 teaspoon vanilla extract
1 cup all-purpose flour
$^1/_3$ cup Hershey's cocoa

$^1/_2$ teaspoon of salt
$^1/_4$ cup chopped nuts
Vanilla Filling (recipe
    follows)
26 Hershey's Kisses, pecan
    halves, or candied
    cherry halves

In small mixer bowl, cream butter, sugar, egg yolk, milk, and vanilla. Combine flour, cocoa, and salt; blend into creamed mixture. Chill dough at least 1 hour or until firm enough to handle. Heat oven to 350 degrees. Shape dough into 1-inch balls. Beat egg white slightly. Dip each ball into egg white; roll in nuts. Place on lightly greased cookie sheet. Press thumb gently in center of each cookie. Bake 10 to 12 minutes or until set. As soon as cookies are removed from oven, spoon about $^1/_4$ teaspoon filling in thumbprint. Gently press unwrapped Kiss, pecan, or cherry half in center of each cookie. Carefully remove from cookie sheet to wire rack. Cool completely. Yields about 2 dozen cookies.

Vanilla Filling:

In small bowl, combine $^1/_2$ cup confectioners' sugar, 1 tablespoon softened butter or margarine, 2 teaspoons milk, and $^1/_4$ teaspoon vanilla extract; beat until smooth.

—*Janice Bower, Cogan Station*

I visited the harness-racing stables before I left. Clarence Martin was standing on a plastic lawn chair, hanging pots of impatiens from the roof. Several of the horses poked curious heads from their stalls; one reached out to have his head scratched. Bright green and yellow trunks and tack bags hanging by stall doors advertised Clarence Martin Jr.'s stables. A sulky, standing on end, served as coatrack for his racing silks.

When Mr. Martin got off of his chair, we talked for a few minutes. Like Art Jennings and his showmen friends, he and his wife follow the fair circuit all summer. He reeled off a list of fairs—Troy, Clearfield, Honesdale, Huntingdon, Indiana, York, Bloomsburg, Gratz . . .

"We get to a fair," he said, "clean out that big aluminum trailer with pine oil. We set up a couple of cots and we're as comfortable as we are at home."

I visited the agricultural exhibits, the home products displays, the antique farm equipment building, the 4-H livestock exhibits, and the Wild West Show that afternoon. I ate at the Heilman United Methodist Church's restaurant. At each stop around the racetrack, I saw the same elements at work. Pride, showmanship, family tradition, and dedication to community are all a part of every aspect of the fair.

The evening crowd was arriving as I said my good-byes to the folks in the fair office. The sound men were at work on the Clyde G. Kiess Memorial Stage, just across the racetrack on the infield. I left Hughesville to the sounds of "Test . . . one . . . two . . . ."

❖ The Lycoming County Fair runs ten days, from Thursday evening through the following Saturday, usually over the third week of July. It is a big Class-A fair with a full schedule of events, and yet it retains the feeling of a small, hometown fair. There are big-name entertainers in the grandstand, as well as tractor pulls, a demolition derby, a stunt show, and free stages around a large midway. There is an admission charge and a parking charge. To get there from Route 405, turn east onto Broadway, then go several blocks to parking. For more information, write to the fair office at P.O. Box 116, Hughesville, PA 17737, or call 717-584-2196.

Jefferson County Fair

Brookville, Jefferson County

Mile after mile of concrete and macadam, lined by thick forests that obscure the surrounding countryside, Interstate 80 ekes its way from New Jersey to Ohio. Although they promise food and lodging, exits seem to turn off into wilderness. And yet, in the months and miles I traveled to country celebrations, I'd learned that just off those unlikely exits, legendary Pennsylvania hospitality awaits those who have time for a friendly chat.

I was on I-80 once again as I headed west for the Jefferson County Fair. I had exhausted the tapes in my car and was ready to start over when I passed a break in the forest close to exit 14. There was a Ferris wheel next to the road, spinning away happily. A billboard assured me that this was, indeed, the Jefferson County Fair. I smiled and took Route 28 North, and in a mile I was pulling into the parking lot.

This must be a new fair, I thought. The ticket booth was portable, the fair office on skids. Some of the livestock was housed in tents. Permanent cinder-block bathrooms were still under construction. Everywhere, raw earth disclosed recent association with a bulldozer, especially in the grandstand area, where a portable stage was set against a backdrop of dirt piles, stone piles, and raw lumber.

But the Jefferson County Fair is an old fair. Beginning in the 1800s, it grew up around the racetrack in nearby Brookville. After the flood control

---

Chocolate Cake

2 cups sugar
2 cups flour
$^3/_4$ cup Hershey's cocoa
1 teaspoon salt
1 teaspoon baking powder
2 teaspoons baking soda

2 eggs, beaten
1 cup milk
$^1/_2$ cup vegetable oil
2 teaspoons vanilla extract
1 cup boiling water

Preheat oven to 350 degrees. Grease and flour two 8-inch or 9-inch square cake pans. Place all dry ingredients in large mixing bowl. In small bowl, blend eggs, milk, oil, and vanilla extract and add to dry ingredients. Beat on medium speed for 2 minutes. Add boiling water and beat by hand until well blended. Bake 30 to 40 minutes at 350 degrees or until toothpick inserted in center comes out clean. Cool completely on wire racks. Frost with Chocolate Buttercream Frosting (below) and top with pecan halves and Hershey's milk chocolate morsels.

—*Barbara Dale, Cranberry*

Chocolate Buttercream Frosting

4 $^1/_2$ cups sifted confectioners' sugar
$^1/_2$ cup Hershey's cocoa
$^3/_4$ cup softened butter or margarine

$^1/_2$ cup milk
2 teaspoons butter-flavor extract
$^1/_4$ teaspoon salt

In medium-size mixing bowl, add 2 cups confectioners' sugar, cocoa, butter or margarine, and milk. Beat until creamy. Add additional confectioners' sugar and butter extract and salt. Continue beating until smooth and creamy.

—*Barbara Dale, Cranberry*

Lemon Pie

1 cup and 3 tablespoons sugar
$^1/_2$ cup flour
$^1/_4$ teaspoon salt
2 cups boiling water
1 teaspoon butter

2 eggs, separated
juice and grated rind of
1 lemon
1 baked pie shell

Mix flour, 1 cup sugar, and salt. Blend with hot water. Add butter, lemon, and egg yolks. Stir constantly until it thickens. Pour into baked shell. Make meringue by beating the two egg whites with 3 tablespoons sugar until stiff. Spread over pie filling. Bake until light brown.

—*Dereatha Grant, Brockway*

Rhubarb Sponge Pie

3 egg yolks
1 cup sugar
1 tablespoon melted butter
2 tablespoons flour
$^1/_2$ teaspoon salt
1 cup milk

1 teaspoon lemon juice
  (optional)
1 to 2 cups rhubarb, cut into
  small pieces
3 egg whites, beaten
1 unbaked pie shell

Beat egg yolks and sugar together. Add salt, melted butter, and flour. Stir in milk and lemon juice. Put rhubarb in bottom of pie shell. Beat egg whites until stiff. Fold into the mixture above and pour all over rhubarb. Bake 45 minutes at 350 degrees.

wiped out everything, including the swinging bridge, the fair moved to downtown Sykesville. In time, it moved to the top of the Sykesville hill.

"We were in the clouds," Wes King told me. "It rained every night. Exhibitors had to park their trucks at the bottom of the hill and walk their cattle up. To make a long story short," he said, "we lost money and looked for a new location. We came here in 1991."

I had to appreciate the spunk of the Jefferson County Fair. It's tough to move a fair. Generations of families build fair week traditions that are hard to leave behind. Things like rain, mud, and a steep hill form part of that tradition, and "Do you remember the year when . . .?" became an oral history of the fair. Moving a fair is akin to moving the family homestead: difficult.

Lorraine Beck, superintendent of the general exhibits, was on hand when I arrived at the exhibit building. She's been at the job since 1987. A homemaker, Lorraine told me that it took some convincing to get her to take this job. During the week of the fair, she's in residence all day long, every day. One of her duties is hiring the exhibit judges.

While I was copying the blue-ribbon chocolate cake recipe, Lorraine rounded up Jean Kite, a two-time winner of the baking competition at the Farm Show in Harrisburg.

I wanted to know whether finalists baked their cakes at the Farm Show complex or at home. Ovens are different and can alter results dramatically. But if a baker lives far away, she would arrive in Harrisburg the night before and her cake would be a day old before the judges saw it.

Jean answered my questions in a manner that assured me she'd had to address these questions herself, long ago. "I baked the cake and made the icing here. Then I drove to Harrisburg and spent the night at my uncle's house. I got up the next morning at five, put the cake together, and delivered it to the Farm Show."

Unfortunately, Jean's entry didn't win at Jefferson.

I walked down the gravel pathway to the midway. The carnival wasn't busy in the early afternoon, but twelve rides and six games promised an exciting evening. Local and carnival food concessions offered pizza, ham barbecue, cabbage and noodles, funnel cakes, and other favorites.

Gil Martin, fair secretary, joined me as I sat on a bench eating cabbage and noodles.

"I'm trying to find the owner of a lost pair of shoes," he told me. "I just dropped them off at the 4-H building. I had them in my car, but they stunk so bad I had to get them out. Now I'll try to get an announcement on the P.A. system."

He pulled a list out of his shirt pocket, unfolded it, and studied it a moment. "I have to settle some disputes with the vendors. One is selling lemonade and shouldn't be. Another one is selling Coke and shouldn't be. It's worse than dealing with kids!"

He looked down the row at the concessions and shook his head. "To top it off, I laid a folder with seventy-five dollars in it on the back of a car and walked over to plug in the P.A. system. When I turned around, the car had left—money, folder, everything with it."

I decided that it was the wrong time to ask him if he enjoyed working the fair. Of course he loved it—there wasn't another reason in the world to put up with so much hassle.

Gil Martin directed me to the Pomona Grange pie stand. "It's the most popular stand at the fair," he said. Shortly, I understood why.

The Grange sells about 150 pies during fair week, whole and by the piece. The women staffing the booth had been on duty since 10 that morning and would stay until 10 that night. When I narrowed my choice down to lemon meringue or lemon sponge, Dereatha Grant helped me out.

"On the lemon meringue pie, the meringue is baked on the outside," she said. "It's baked on the inside in the lemon sponge."

Never big on decision making, I took a piece of each.

When I left the Jefferson County Fair that afternoon, as I looked back over the raw, new edges of what would be a permanent home for the yearly event, I thought about a poster I'd had at college. It was called "Building a Rainbow," and on it, a million stick figures were operating cranes, pullies, blocks and tackles, and all sorts of devices to construct a rainbow. On the poster, something magical was reduced to something mechanical. I thought about Gil Martin and his crew: The job that they tackled was a lot like that poster. Yet how exciting it must be to lay the cornerstone of a new tradition here in Jefferson County.

❖ The Jefferson County Fair runs the third week of July, from Sunday's afternoon princess and queen contests through the following Saturday. It is located one mile north of exit 14 of I-80 on Route 28. One admission price includes parking and admission to all fair events. Children under five are admitted free but must purchase a wristband to ride at the carnival. For more information, write to the Jefferson County Fair, Jefferson County Service Center, R.D. 5, Brookville, PA 15825.

Kimberton Community Fair

Kimberton, Chester County

It always amazes me that Chester County exists so close to Philadelphia. Brownstone farmhouses tucked into hillsides as steep as a bald man's forehead, herds of Black Angus cattle, Druid groves, and paddocks full of horses—these are Andrew Wyeth's world, far removed from the Schuylkill Expressway. The tiny Chester County village of Kimberton seems resolved to avoid urbanization. Its Class-A country fair is complete with livestock, handwork, baking contests, and produce. Only the food offered by local vendors hints at proximity to the city.

A violent thunderstorm had knocked trees down and scattered branches over the Pughtown Road on the first afternoon of the Kimberton Community Fair. By early evening, the parking lot was an obstacle course of tire-eating puddles and sneaker-swallowing mud. Judging from the line of cars jockeying for parking spaces, a little weather problem couldn't deter the crowds. I thought that the cooler weather had brought folks out, but before long, I found the real attraction.

As I was walking down the midway, the smell of doughnuts grabbed me by the nose and yanked me around the corner. I wheedled an invitation into the well-equipped Kimberton doughnut kitchen, where fifteen volunteers performed their well-practiced duties—mixing, cutting, frying, draining, glazing, bagging, and selling Kimberton's big moneymaker. There were no breaks. Production was going full speed ahead.

Helen Ash took time to talk with me. Her crew had made thirty-six batches of doughnuts the night before and would probably make that many each night, with a grand-slam finish of seventy or more batches on Saturday of fair week. Each batch makes twenty-five *dozen* doughnuts.

I asked whether she would share her recipe. She pointed to fifty-pound bags of Duncan Hines mix and chuckled.

"A woman once called from Florida to ask for our recipe," she told me. "She wanted the recipe in the worst way, and I was almost embarrassed to tell her that it was a mix."

Helen Ash started out with the fair in 1948. "I raised four kids at this fair," she said. "When they ran out of money, they'd run in here to the kitchen to get more.

"Before the war," she recollected, "this was a farming community, and we had a country fair. World War II changed that. The GIs came home, the community changed, and the fair changed with it. It became more of a carnival, with bright lights and flashy amusements. Now we're getting back to basics, to where we started."

A fair's displays of home and farm products always say a great deal about the community, its social stratum, and its economic base. A long table under the kitchen service windows held Hershey's cocoa baking contest entries in plastic containers. There were many entries in the needlework categories, and many crafts. The farm and garden entries occupied one small corner, along with the canned goods. In another corner, the Chester County Wildfowl Carvers' Association displayed its work. Glyn Jenkins, a Romansville resident, showed me a handsome wood duck decoy that had won third place in the Ward World Competition in Atlantic City. The Kimberton Community Fair may indeed be on an excursion back to its Depression days roots, but no one could deny that there is just a little city influence.

I complimented Karen Dobson, fair secretary, on the exhibition room.

"I put my heart and soul into that room," she told me. "I have five hundred exhibitors. It amazes me how it's grown over the years—and with no more help!"

Like so many committed fair staffers all over the state, Karen Dobson has a family history of fair involvement. She told me, "My grandmom, Alice Hughes, was one of the folks who rocketed and propelled the fair to Class-A status in 1970. My dad and uncle are both firemen and they work at the fair, along with my cousins. I don't remember not being at the fair!" A perfect choice for fair secretary, she knows where the fair came from and has a vision for its future.

She shared some of her ideas with me. "Our main thrust the last few years was to get the livestock building enclosed. It now generates money year-round as a rental. We've already had an antiques show, a gun show, and a car show. We've even had a caterer come in and do a Republican Party dinner there. He covered the floor with carpeting, brought in lat-

---

Oatmeal Surprise Cookies

2 cups butter	1 teaspoon salt
2 cups sugar	2 teaspoons baking powder
2 cups brown sugar	2 teaspoons soda
4 eggs	12 ounces chocolate chips
2 teaspoons vanilla	$3/4$ cup Hershey's cocoa
4 cups flour	3 cups chopped nuts
5 cups oatmeal	

Measure oatmeal and blend in a blender to a fine powder. Cream butter and both sugars. Add eggs and vanilla. Mix together with flour, oatmeal, salt, baking powder, and soda. Add chocolate chips, cocoa, and nuts.

Roll into balls and place 2 inches apart on cookie sheet. Bake 10 minutes at 375 degrees. Makes 112 cookies.

—*Judy Hewitt, Spring City*

ticework and draperies, tablecloths, floral arrangements, crystal, and china. He turned a cattle barn into a first-class banquet hall.

"The company has also started to use the building for weekly bingo games," she added. "The last Friday night before the fair I had to remind them not to come—the room would be full of goats!"

I walked down through the other side of the midway while I was there, stopping at the Holy Ghost Church's stand for pierogies and cabbage rolls. Many of the food concessions were local. The Jaycees were offering corn on the cob, city chicken, and roast beef sandwiches. There were fifteen or so rides, and many games to tempt the crowd. Compact and accessible, the Kimberton fairgrounds offered as many amusements as fairgrounds twice the size.

I walked down to a red-and-white-striped tent and watched the goat judging. One nimble goat stood up at the fence, craned his neck, and extracted the ribbons from the unsuspecting judge's back pocket. I stayed long enough to watch him lift a grooming brush, a visor, and a soda can. He was really working the crowd, and it made me wonder about his owners—were they also his trainers?

I picked up a bag of doughnuts before I left. They would make good company for the ride home, at least as long as they lasted. As I was leaving, I looked over my shoulder and then turned around and studied the fair. It glowed against an inky sky, just a country fair like any other country fair, with rides, homemade food, livestock, and community fun.

❖ The Kimberton Community Fair is held Monday through Saturday, the last week of July. There is entertainment on the free stage each night, and a softball tournament each evening. Most events begin after 6 P.M., although some of the livestock judging is held throughout the day. From Route 100 South take the Pughtown Road six miles to Kimberton. At the Y coming into town, take a left. Go one block past the Kimberton Inn and look for parking signs. There is a donation for parking. For more information, write to the Kimberton Community Fair, Kimberton Fair Grounds, Box 99F, Kimberton, PA 19442, or call 610-933-4566.

Shippensburg Fair

Shippensburg, Cumberland County

I have always gone to the Shippensburg Fair. Where I live, everyone in the county does—it's a tradition. For as long as I can remember, my cousin has even taken her summer vacation during fair week. She lives a few blocks from the fairgrounds and walks over several times a day, every day. The fair schedule is stuck to the refrigerator with magnets she picked up at the fair's crafts show.

For us teenagers in the late sixties, the fair in the neighboring town offered the opportunity to see and to be seen. Night after night, we buffed our Bass Weejun Tack penny loafers, dressed up in our best cutoffs and madras shirts, doused ourselves in quarts of English Leather, and with one last swipe at our Ivy League haircuts, took off to the fair. We were as polished and finished as the cows and sheep in the livestock barns, and for the same reasons.

My claim to fame my senior year in high school was dating the Shippensburg Fair Queen. It was quite an honor for me, in those innocent days when Fair Queen, Prom Queen, and Homecoming Queen were coveted titles. The girls in my high school class condemned me—"How can he date a foreigner, a girl from another school?" they asked. They ridiculed her, talked about her clothes, her hair, her makeup, but I knew they were jealous. They wanted to be Fair Queen themselves.

Later, I would go to the Shippensburg Fair with my sister and her family. I rode the rides with my niece, always smug when she would say, "Unc, will you get on the Ferris wheel with me? Mom and Dad won't— they're too old."

Now when the last week of July rolls around, you can still look for me at the fair. I've changed my pattern just a little. I go on Wednesday mornings, ostensibly to help my father sell his decoys at the crafts show. The midway still lures me, however, and I feel a real need to forage for the farm women's french fries. Seeing is still a big part of it, for I see the same people I saw decades ago, and I watch for them. Being seen, however, has lost some of its appeal.

So here I was, manning my father's booth while he and my mother took a break. The sun was hot, and the back of my neck was already sunburned. My parents' tent fly cast a shadow but no real shade. One of the regular customers showed up. She wanted a wood duck drake. I showed her three of them, but she wouldn't buy one from me. She wanted the carver to select it for her.

A woman with a hyperactive child came by. I'd helped out often enough to know that anyone who says, "Oh, look! Aren't they just darling!" isn't going to buy a thing. I was right. Meanwhile, her little angel began to pick up every carving, conduct decoy races, and chase other customers away. Finally, he dropped a carving. I drew in a very noisy breath. She got the point and left.

At the Shippensburg Fair crafts show, most of the two hundred exhibitors are in the same locations each year, making them easy to locate for regular customers. When Dad returned, Mom and I looked up Jean Speck, who was selling dried flowers, and then went off in search of Joanne Dietz and Jane Lerch. Before long, we were going down the midway, looking for lunch.

The foods at the Shippensburg Fair are reason enough to go there. Most of the concessions are run by local churches and civic organizations and, like the craftspeople, they occupy regular spots in the long, cinderblock buildings. The foods are homemade, and the variety is endless. Occasionally groups try out new foods, but most of them stick to home-style favorites: hoagies, ox roast sandwiches, corn on the cob, beef and pork barbecues, milkshakes, soups, ham sandwiches, ham salad sandwiches, turkey sandwiches, crab cakes, waffles with toppings, and pot pie.

Blue-Ribbon Chocolate Crunch Brownies

1 cup butter or margarine, softened
2 cups sugar
4 eggs
6 tablespoons Hershey's cocoa
1 cup all-purpose flour
2 teaspoons vanilla extract
$1/_2$ teaspoon salt
1 jar (7 ounces) marshmallow cream
1 cup creamy peanut butter
2 cups (12 ounces) Hershey's semisweet chocolate chips
3 cups crisp rice cereal

In a mixing bowl, cream butter and sugar. Add eggs. Stir in cocoa, flour, vanilla, and salt. Spread into a greased 13 x 9 x 2-inch baking pan. Bake at 350 degrees for 25 minutes or until done. Cool. Spread marshmallow cream over cooled brownies. In small saucepan, melt peanut butter; add chocolate chips over low heat, stirring constantly. Remove from heat. Stir in cereal. Spread over marshmallow. Refrigerate.

—*Amy Feeser*

We bought a crab cake, an ox roast sandwich, a pork barbecue, vegetable soup, pot pie, and corn soup, and went back to Dad's booth to divide it up. I was pleased to find that Dad had made the wood duck sale while I was gone, but more pleased when no one wanted to share the ox roast sandwich and I had it all to myself.

Later that afternoon I talked with Jean Thomas, fair secretary, and Frank Lerew, fair president.

"I was one of the original boys who started the fair," Frank said. "I was a teacher of vocational agriculture and I had held three fairs in the gymnasium of the high school. That wasn't big enough. So we moved to the borough parking lot on Byrd Street. We outgrew that the first year, so we came over here and bought nineteen acres for five thousand dollars. The second year we bought a one-acre junkyard on the hill for five thousand dollars—land had gone up in price! The twelfth year we bought nine more acres for thirty thousand dollars. Then we went across the street and bought another ten acres for fifty thousand dollars."

I walked through the fairgrounds in the early evening. I visited the livestock barns, picked up a winning recipe in the home products building, and walked through the commercial exhibits. This isn't a big fair, but it has a lot to offer: Sunday evening vespers and a town band concert, the queen contest on Monday evening, entertainment on the stage Wednesday and Thursday nights, a Friday-night tractor pull, and a horse show on Saturday. The Wednesday crafts show, incidentally, grows each year.

I walked back to my parents' booth to help them pack the remaining decoys. The flock of ducks had thinned out considerably during the day. Just as I was ready to leave, my niece, Tara, showed up. She's now a college student, so it surprised me when she said, "Hey Unc—wanna ride on the Ferris wheel? Mom and Dad won't—they're too old." Some things, blessedly, never change.

"Hey, what's that cologne you're wearing?" I asked her.

❖ The Shippensburg Fair is just off Fayette Street in Shippensburg. From I-81, take the Fayette Street exit and proceed north. Turn left at the railroad underpass. The fair is generally held Sunday through Saturday the last week of July. For exact dates and performance schedules, write to the Shippensburg Fair, 100 North Earl Street, Shippensburg, PA 17257.

Oil Heritage Week

Oil City, Venango County

Justus Park was a cool, shady haven on the Friday afternoon of Oil Heritage Week. The park smacked of neat contemporary architecture, landscaping, and sculpture, but the mood of the place was fragile and archaic, like an old bone teacup. I suspected that Oil City residents had been spending summer afternoons there since Cornplanter deeded the city to Thomas Mifflin.

A crafts show with fifty-odd quality vendors, interesting ethnic foods, and a stellar location usually brings out hordes of shoppers so intent on their purchases that they leave civility behind in the quest for the perfect grapevine wreath. But in Justus Park that lazy summer afternoon, older women congregated on park benches, children played in the concrete sculpture garden, and teenagers waded in the water and walked the rock-strewn shoals of the Allegheny. There was a dreamlike, almost drowsy air about the crafts show, one that lured its patrons to a little shopping, followed by an ice cream cone in the shade, and then a hand-in-hand walk along the riverbank. No doubt about it, I liked the serenity of the afternoon at Oil Heritage Week, and I liked Justus Park.

Oil Heritage Week seemed more than an effort to bring tourists to town, and when I picked up a schedule of events, I knew for sure that it was a celebration of heritage and achievement for the town's citizenry.

There were many sports events scheduled throughout the week: wrestling, tennis, volleyball and softball tournaments, a 2-mile and a 10K race, a raft race on the river, a bicycle rodeo for kids, and free pool parties for youngsters.

For those more interested in history and heritage, the festival offered a Heritage Day on the first Saturday featuring music, contests, and a huge sampler of ethnic foods. There were also caravans to historic sites and a walking tour of the cemetery.

Music was a big part of Heritage Week. For a week, the park by the river would echo with a polka fest, the Pennzoil Big Band Concert, the Country Night Concern with its Three Rivers Band, the Mellon Bank Jazz Concert, an a cappella group, a female soloist, and a rock concert featuring local groups.

Libby Williams at the chamber of commerce information booth on the river's edge encouraged me to stay for Thursday night's jazz concert, one of the big attractions of the week, which features local musicians and

Cabbage and Noodles

1 10-ounce package wide egg
   noodles
1 large head cabbage
1 tablespoon salt
1 medium onion, chopped
$^1/_4$ cup butter

1 teaspoon paprika
$^1/_2$ teaspoon coarse black
   pepper
$^1/_4$ cup snipped parsley
salt to taste

Boil noodles, following package directions, and drain. Finely chop
cabbage and wash in colander. Sprinkle tablespoon of salt over cabbage, mix, and let stand 10 minutes. Sauté onion in butter until
golden and sprinkle with paprika. Squeeze cabbage with hands
until dry. Add to onion mixture. Mix and cook over medium heat
15 minutes, stirring to prevent scorching. Stir in noodles and seasonings until well blended.

The addition of a pound of browned bulk country sausage is
nice.

former students of Rex Mitchell, a retired Clarion University professor.

Phil Runzo, an eighty-two-year-old pianist and trombonist, the
retired music department head at Oil City High, still performs alongside
other retired and active local teachers.

If you have only one day to spend, the first Sunday may be your best
bet, with the ethnic food fest, entertainment, and raft race, ending with
the prayer service at 8.

For a long weekend, you might arrive in town on Thursday night of
festival week for the jazz concert; bring a lawn chair. The Holiday Inn on
Justus Park's border is convenient to Friday's crafts show the second weekend. You could also reserve a space on Friday night's Wine and Cheese
Party Train Ride that leaves from Rynd Farm Station, then take in the
rock concert. After a long brunch on Saturday, you could enjoy the
parade.

❖ Oil Heritage Week is held the last week of July from Saturday
through the following Sunday. Events are held continually all over the
city. To plan your visit with the schedule of events, write to the Oil City
Chamber of Commerce, Center Street, Oil City, PA 16301, or call 814-
676-6296.

Fayette County Fair

Dunbar, Fayette County

Many years ago I stood on the observation deck of the art museum at Cornell University, looking out over the campus for the first time. "It's amazing! It's a city!" I said aloud.

I said the same words when I looked out over the Fayette County Fair from the second floor of the fair office. Paved streets with road signs made neat city blocks. Permanent buildings clustered in neighborhoods. There were landscaped areas, park benches, streetlights, and even "neighborhood" restaurants with colorful awnings and sidewalk seating. Beyond the colorful center of the city, the livestock barns of rural America edged the busy community.

I was talking with Rolland Herring, the only member of the board of directors who's been with the fair since its 1954 beginnings. A former fair secretary, he's now superintendent. If the fairgrounds really were a city, he would be mayor.

"We have four miles of paved roads," he said matter-of-factly, "and all the roads in our sixty-acre parking lot are either paved or graveled. There are thirty-two permanent buildings; the Old Time Fiddlers' Association building is heated.

"You see Williams Street, leading from the main gate? That's the dividing line between the fair and the carnival. If you want the fair, come in the gate and go to the left. If you want the carnival, come in the gate and go to the right. From day one, we've never mixed the carnival and the fair."

So many of the big county fairs I'd attended were so long in the tooth that tales of their earliest days were largely speculation and supposition liberally sprinkled with fable and legend. Here was an opportunity to talk with one of the founding fathers of a showcase fair. I was pleased when we settled into sodas and his story.

"Rex Carter was a County Agricultural Agent in Fayette County. He wanted a fair, so he started out with a couple of field days in 1951. He got a group of men together to sponsor a fall foliage festival in '52 and '53. Incidentally, the Fayette County Agricultural Improvement Association still sponsors the fair, its one function, and for $20 you can become a life member. Anyhow, he organized the foliage festival for them. He had a show of animals and brought some exhibits into a garage.

"We held the first Fayette County Fair in 1954. It was a tent fair at the county home. Hurricane Agnes came that weekend. O. W. Rittenhouse, the first fair president, called me at five A.M. and said, 'Get over here, Rolland,' and as he was talking, the tent he was in blew over. It was so muddy, I came in four-buckle arctics.

"Then we moved to a place called Swaney Farm. We had a tent fair, and it rained both years. We figured we were doomed.

"We had two county commissioners who were farmers. They bought this eighty-acre farm in 1956, and they paid Mr. Swaney—he was in the construction business—thirty-two thousand dollars to level this fairground. A group of taxpayers took these two commissioners to court for squandering tax money. The commissioners won, and before the 1957 fair, they fenced in twenty acres in chain link and built the cement-block restrooms. In 1957, they leased the fairgrounds to the Fayette County Agricultural Improvement Association for thirty years at a time at a dollar a year. The current lease runs till 2023.

"Aside from running city water onto the grounds—we'd outgrown our well—this fairground hasn't cost the county a cent. All the money we make is put back into the fair for buildings, maintenance, and improvements. The fair is now the biggest moneymaker in the county."

I repeated something that Art "Sonney Dayze the Clown" Jennings had told me in Hughesville, that fairs are a good entertainment buy.

Rolland agreed. "There's definitely a renewed interest in fairs. Ten years ago, the average age of the board of directors for this fair was sixty-nine. It was a little scary. Today, the oldest fair director, myself excluded, is fifty-two."

We walked down Carter Street to the Bethel Brethren in Christ Church's food booth, where Rolland treated me to one of their famous roast beef sandwiches. A sign advertised 125,000 sandwiches sold. The beef was pit roasted, juicy and tender, and the brewed iced tea was wonderful.

I used the street map Rolland Herring had given me and visited the livestock barns, the exhibit buildings, and the free stage areas. I even tried a pepperoni roll at one of the food stands.

The free stage areas featured a lion tamer's show, a skateboard half pipe show, pig races, and a clown show, all on the fair side of the grounds. The home ec building was overflowing with home products, including a blue-ribbon needlepoint picture of a house and barn that I coveted terribly. The Fayette County Fair was the only fair I'd seen thus far that had a fine-arts building. Everywhere, the clean grounds, clean bathrooms, and adequate security impressed me.

I walked over to the carnival area and on the way stopped by the

Pepperoni Rolls

2 packages dry yeast
1 tablespoon sugar
1 cup lukewarm water
1 cup milk
6 tablespoons oleo or butter
$^1/_2$ cup sugar

1 tablespoon salt
5 to 6 cups flour
3 eggs, beaten
Hormel sandwich
   pepperoni, unsliced

Dissolve yeast and 1 tablespoon sugar in lukewarm water. Scald milk; add shortening, $^1/_2$ cup of sugar, and salt and cool to lukewarm. Add 2 cups flour to make a batter. Add yeast and beaten eggs. Beat well. Add remaining flour to make soft dough. Knead lightly and place in greased bowl. Let rise until doubled in bulk. Roll out to $^1/_4$ inch; cut in rectangles. Place pepperoni, cut in 2-inch sections, on rectangles and roll up. Let rise. Bake 20 minutes at 370 to 400 degrees.

tractor pull in the outdoor arena. The carnival included thirty rides, eighteen games of chance, and about ten good concessions. I had a feeling that Rolland Herring kept the number of carnival food stands down to support the fair-side local concessions run by churches, Lions Clubs, Easter Seals, and the 4-H Club. I'd learned enough about Rolland Herring to know that he'd lend these charities a hand if he could.

❖ The Fayette County Fair runs ten days, Thursday through the next Saturday. The Monday of the fair is always five Mondays before Labor Day. Like any really big fair, it offers big-name entertainment indoors and a full schedule of events in the outdoor arena. The fairgrounds is along Route 119, south of the Pennsylvania Turnpike. For more information, write to the Fayette County Fair, Box 2, R.D. 1, Dunbar, PA 15430, or call 412-628-3360.

August

Lebanon Area Fair

Lebanon, Lebanon County

After spending a year at country fairs and festivals all over the state, it was getting difficult to impress me. I'd visited fairs as vast as cities and small-town festivals in friendly little hamlets. And everywhere I went, I met people who were dedicated, ambitious, and visionary. But I was beginning to think I could no longer write excited, illegible notes on my legal pad, to be translated and deciphered as soon as I got home.

There were surprises still in store, however. The main building at the Lebanon Area Fair is a monument to vision and determination and a model for other fairs' aspirations. One wing of the L-shaped building is a large, well-lighted exhibition hall, the other a massive auditorium. In between is a spacious corridor that leads to the fairgrounds beyond. A display area runs along the auditorium entrance, making standing in line, one of the pastimes of most fairs, comfortable and interesting.

Ben Bow, fair chairperson, showed me through the complex, proud as any parent. A vo-ag teacher, he'd wrapped up his school year at the end of June and spent a month fulfilling his duties for the National Guard. He'd arrived home the night before, gone to the fair at 6 that morning, and planned to stay until midnight—a routine he would follow each day of the fair. For me, that kind of dedication was both commendable and impressive, and yet he shunned my accolades and praised his colleagues instead. To him, it was the community's efforts that deserved the praise.

Ben introduced me to Kristi Wright, the newly crowned fair queen. I asked her about the pageant.

"I was nervous when I had to do my speech and impromptu questions," she said, "but once I started, everything went okay. We had to do an essay." (As an English teacher, I was liking this fair better and better.) "I did mine on my trip to Ireland. Our band marched in the St. Patrick's Day parade in Dublin. Our trip money came from fund-raisers the band sponsored.

"We flew into Heathrow the week it was bombed. I prayed we'd make it safely. When I looked out my window over the Irish Sea, there were two rainbows. God had heard me and I was safe.

"I had only one regret. In fourth grade I had a teacher named Glenn Swavely. He was my favorite teacher. I was Ireland-nuts, even then. Mr. Swavely made me promise that I would let him know when I went. I wish he had lived to know, but he was killed in an auto accident. He really made a difference."

Moist Chocolate Cake

2 cups flour   2 teaspoons baking soda
1 teaspoon salt $^3/_4$ cup Hershey's cocoa
1 teaspoon baking powder   2 cups sugar
Mix above ingredients in large bowl.
Add to mixture and beat for 2 minutes:
1 cup oil   1 cup milk
1 cup hot coffee
Add:
2 eggs   1 teaspoon vanilla
Beat mixture 2 more minutes.
Pour batter into prepared 9 x 13-inch pan. Bake 25 to 30 minutes at 325 degrees till done. Cool and frost as desired.

—Lois J. Meyer, Annville

We talked about Ireland for a long time, comparing notes and sharing "must do's" for our next trips. We talked about schools, about her plans, and we talked about Ireland some more.

The Lebanon Area Fair wasn't a big fair by any means, but it had wonderful country flavor. For youngsters, there were a little garden tractor train ride around the grounds and a small Ferris wheel, among other rides. There were ten games on the midway, and a nice selection of professional carnival concession foods. A long line snaked from a little red barn around telephone cable spools that functioned as stand-up tables, and as I waited, the woman behind me said, "This is one of the things you think about during those winter storms—fair french fries. The thought keeps you going through all of that snow!"

The fries *were* fantastic, and I stood in line all over again.

A seniors' polka group performed in one end of the pavilion while I ate. Before I left, I walked over to the bird show where cockatoos danced disco and performed magic tricks. I also watched an alligator wrestle with his handler.

I ran into Ben Bow again in the exhibition hall.

"Did you get enough to eat?" he asked. "We try to make sure that we have good food all day long. We have a lot of kids who stay over with their livestock, and they should have quality food at reasonable prices.

"You should try one of the breakfasts here," he continued. "They make the best eggs. They're mixed up with green pepper and onions.

They do potatoes the same way. I call them hunky eggs and hunky pota-toes. I don't know what they're really called."

According to Ben Bow, anything with wheels—tractor pulls, monster trucks, and even antique farm equipment—will draw Lebanon folks out to the fair. The real pleasures to me were the livestock, good food, local entertainment, produce displays, and a hall full of premium entries in many categories.

❖ The fair runs from the end of July into the first week of August, from Saturday to Saturday. The fairgrounds is located 2 miles south of Lebanon off Route 72, at the intersection of Cornwall and Evergreen Roads. There is a full schedule of daily events, many of them agricultural. For exact dates and schedules, call 717-273-3795.

Shade Gap Picnic

Shade Gap, Huntingdon County

Before I left for the Shade Gap Picnic, I called my friend Deb to tell her where I was going.

"I haven't thought about Shade Gap in years!" she said. "I wonder what ever happened to Peggy Ann Bradnick?"

Deb and I grew up next door to each other. We were in every class together, from first grade through high school graduation, and then we went to the same university. One memory stands out. In May during our freshman year of high school, we'd met on my back porch every evening. Not far away, just over two mountains, a seventeen-year-old girl had been kidnapped by a mountain man. For ten days, while he dragged her around the mountainside, we followed her progress. Deb's father was one of the state policemen assigned to the case. Occasionally he dropped some inside information when he came home, things the public didn't know, and so we spoke in whispers, mouth to ear and ear to mouth. We were uneasy. Our safe world had been violated.

The whole nation held its breath through Peggy Ann's ordeal. Every newspaper carried the story, and soon the tabloids grabbed it up and sea-soned it with titillating fiction. A song found its way to the radio—"The Ballad of Peggy Ann." Movies followed, including the 1991 film *A Cry in the Dark*. Like Deb, I wanted to know what had happened to Peggy Ann Bradnick *after* her ordeal.

When I drove up the lane beside the Shade Gap Fire Company to

Harper's Memorial Park that Sunday evening, I found the carnival rides with their heads tucked under their wings, obviously roosting for the night. I backed up. The sign at the firehouse notwithstanding, it looked like I'd wasted a drive. Then I saw some people in a pavilion and decided that at least I could find out when the picnic really opened.

As it turned out, I'd walked right into a family reunion. Mrs. Ralph Locke, from Fayetteville, answered my questions. The only activity for the Shade Gap Picnic that Sunday evening was the vesper service. The fair really opened the next night, after the parade. Despite my intrusion, everyone was more than gracious, and so I asked my final question.

"What ever happened to Peggy Ann Bradnick?"

The air froze, hung there for a while, and then shattered over the table.

"She's sitting right over there."

I talked to Peggy Ann for a long time that evening. Still pretty, she's married and has a grown daughter. She has a ready smile and talks about her ordeal with an ease that shows she worked through the horror long ago.

As soon as I got home, I called Deb.

"You'll never guess whom I met!"

I went back to Shade Gap on the following Tuesday night, just in time for the Little Miss Shade Gap pageant. Comfortable benches were lined up in rows down the sloping dirt floor of the rustic theater. Yellow light bulbs cut the darkness of evening.

The pageant was utterly enjoyable. Dressed as mice, two little girls from Orbisonia sang "Somewhere Out There." Katie Peck, the queen, was introduced, along with the Little Miss Princess from the year before. The announcer had just begun introducing the contestants when I heard an ominous peal of thunder and saw lightning snake across the sky in the valley behind the stage. I knew that I had to get moving if I wanted to see the rest of the fair, so I gathered up and walked down the midway.

The first exhibit building I went into was made of sheet metal. It was well lighted and had beautiful hardwood floors. An odd conglomeration of things was for sale there, ranging from Princess House crystal to cowboy hats and clothing.

The second building, much newer than the first, had more clothing, T-shirts, and a tombstone display. I thought that was a little odd, but I'd seen the exhibitor before and I'd see him again. Apparently he did pretty well at fairs.

A collection of early fair posters, simply tacked up to the wooden frames of the metal building, told a little of the history of the park. One advertised the appearance of Don Reno, Red Smiley, and the Tennessee Cut-ups at Soldiers Memorial Picnic Grounds. Another promised Hawkshaw Hawkins in person at Soldiers Memorial Park. Still another advertised Bud Messner and the Skyliners, but by this time the park had become Harper's Memorial Park. Then I saw one that advertised the sixty-second annual picnic at Harper's Memorial Park. That would have been 1932.

I was still trying to place the posters in chronological order when a blast of thunder shook the ground. I took off down the midway, noting the bingo building in the center strip, the rides at either end, the first-aid building, and the variety of carnival concessions available, as well as local foods.

I stopped at the Lions Club stand and bought a home-cured fried ham sandwich and a cup of coffee. While I sat in the picnic pavilion, the liner of the sky ripped open and rain fell out. The rides stopped and folks stampeded the parking lot. When it became clear that the storm intended to outstay me, I let it have its way and walked out to my car.

Lightning skulked around the mountains of Shade Gap like a fugitive, scurrying here and there. As each flash illuminated another ridge or hollow, I thought about the frightened seventeen-year-old girl who spent ten days on these same hillsides with a mountain man, and I had to admire the strength that enabled her to come through the horror still able to smile. Meeting Peggy Ann was a remarkable experience for me.

❖ The Shade Gap Picnic is usually held the first week of August, Monday through Saturday. The fairgrounds is on the hill behind the Shade Gap Volunteer Fire Company on Route 641, just south of town. Admission is free some nights, but on the nights when there is entertainment on the stage, there is a small gate charge. For more information, call the Shade Gap Volunteer Fire Company at 814-259-3252 or 814-259-3454.

Jacktown Fair

Wind Ridge, Greene County

There are circles worn into the grounds of the Jacktown Fair. The years have most certainly softened their contours. Winter snows have piled up in them, summer rains have turned them to circular puddles, and each storm tries to erase them, for Nature always struggles to reclaim her own. Yet they linger there like the ghostly shadows of a front porch that's been removed from an old house. Buck Burns knows knows what pounded those circles into the hilltop years ago.

"This is where the merry-go-round stood," he said. "The horses and oxen that once pulled it around made those rings."

It was hard to think that a fair had existed on the same site since 1865. The Civil War ended in 1865. Lincoln was assassinated in April that year. The country hadn't celebrated its first centennial yet, and the Transcontinental Railroad was four years and miles away from completion. Houses built that year have fallen in on themselves and been forgotten. And yet tiny Wind Ridge threw a fair that year and has done so every year since. Amazing.

"It started out as a picnic get-together," Buck Burns told me. "There, right at the base of the hill, the old-timers would bring their horses and trade them at the trading alley. I remember the trading alley," he went on. "They quit it forty-four years ago. And I was seven years old when they ran the last horse race."

The Jacktown Fairgrounds needs a keeper, a curator to protect it and to preserve it for future generations when memories are second- and third-hand tales, and Buck is doing a fine job of it.

"My grandfather was president of this fair," he told me, "and then my great-uncle. Now me and my brother are involved and our families. My son is assistant superintendent of the livestock barns. My youngest brother's second boy and my grandson—those boys have been working like mad all week. My son is assistant superintendent of the livestock barns. It just keeps filtering down."

We walked around the grounds that evening while he pointed out other landmarks. The two early exhibition buildings resemble one-room schoolhouses. Built of clapboard with wooden shutters at the shop pane windows, their double doors at each end let in both light and patrons. One was filled with flea market vendors selling T-shirts, tube socks, and jewelry. The other one, wearing the date 1865 over its doorway, housed a noisy, busy arcade. A kitchen was attached to one side, its shutters thrown open for business and for air.

"We're trying to have the one building restored," Buck told me, "but it's expensive. The estimate was around thirty thousand dollars. I don't know what'll happen yet."

A much-patched stone structure next to it also looked very old. Its ground level housed another local food concession. Steps led to a para-pet-lined flat rooftop. Buck referred to the building as the bandstand, but I wondered, given its position in the center of the grounds, whether it might have been the judges' tower for the horse races.

The new exhibition hall, overlooking one of the stadiums, held neat displays of flowers, vegetables, fruits, grains, chocolate cakes, and cookies. Photography and needlework adorned the walls. In one corner, the folks at the Jacktown Fair have started a small museum. There were old fair programs in the case: "Jacktown Fair, August 17, 18, 19, 1915"; "Nineteenth Annual Exhibition, Richhill Agricultural Society." An 1865 coin was found by one of the workers helping to build the barn. There were also six-pointed stars worn by early fair policemen. A scrapbook and photo album contained shots of former queens, displays at the state convention, scenes around earlier fairs, and floats from parades.

Oil paintings of the fair hung on the wall behind the museum display case. The fair has a competition each year, and the first-place prize is $75, but the fair keeps the winning painting. Buck plans to use the paintings for a Jacktown Fair calendar.

"Why is this called the Jacktown Fair?" I asked. "The town is Wind Ridge, isn't it?"

Jacktown Fair Chocolate Applesauce Cookies

$^1/_2$ cup applesauce	$^1/_2$ teaspoon baking powder
1 cup sugar	1 $^1/_2$ teaspoon baking soda
1 egg	$^1/_2$ teaspoon salt
1 teaspoon vanilla	$^1/_2$ cup Hershey's cocoa
1 cup milk	$^3/_4$ cup nuts
2 cups flour	$^3/_4$ cup raisins

Mix all ingredients together. Drop on cookie sheets and bake 7 minutes at 400 degrees.

Yield: 4 dozen.

—*Jennifer Crouse, Youth Division under 10*

"Used to be called Elk Ridge," Buck said. "Then some folks called it Jacksonville. Later on, they shortened it to Jacktown and the fair kept that name, even though its real name is the Richhill Agricultural Society. The town is now Wind Ridge."

I pretended to follow the logic. At least "Wind Ridge" described the one-street mountaintop village.

And indeed, when a rainstorm came up, winds lashed the hilltop and rain sandblasted the buildings of the Jacktown Fairgrounds. I sat out the worst of it in the arcade, watching the storm bully the valley through the shop pane windows, and there were quite a few exhibits and attractions that I never explored that night. There were five rides for adults, carnival concession fast foods, an extensive agricultural display area, and a respectable book of premiums in a wide variety of areas.

❖ The Jacktown Fair is worth seeing; the fairgrounds merits a serious preservation effort. The fair opens with a Sunday-morning church service the first week in August. Tuesday, the first day of the fair, is highlighted by the crowning of the fair queen and the parade through town. There is entertainment at the two grandstands nightly, and features vary from professional wrestling to pony pulls, demolition derbies, and tractor pulls. The music on the stages is mostly country.

The fairgrounds is located on Route 21 just west of town. For more information, write to the Jacktown Fair, Wind Ridge, PA 15380.

Mercer County Grange Fair

Mercer, Mercer County

As fairs go, the Mercer County Grange Fair isn't very old. It was started by the youth organization of the Pomona Granges of Mercer County in 1965. Fair secretary Ginny Richardson chaired the committee. Among a display of old fair programs in the exhibit building is a program from that first event. Its purple mimeograph ink has faded to gray and the paper has yellowed, but in bold print the program still proudly announces, "1st Mercer County Grange Farm Show, September 16, 17, 18, 1965, sponsored by Grange Youth."

For the first five or six years, the fair was held at different Granges. Then the organization purchased twenty-five acres and formed a fair board with representatives from each of the county's fifteen Granges.

Somehow the fairground seems older—better seasoned, perhaps. At first impression, the buildings come off as 1930s-vintage country fair architecture. Only after looking more closely does one discover that they are of modern construction, built of sheet metal and concrete blocks and firmly planted on cement floors. It is the design that is misleading, and the way that they hug the hilltop, clustered like the outbuildings of a Pennsylvania farm.

Inside, the auditorium is sheathed in modern wood paneling that manages to come off as later improvement to something older and more rustic. The stage has a farm scene handpainted on a canvas backdrop. Slat-back wooden folding chairs, their varnish worn to a cinnamon patina, stand in rows facing the stage. A battle-scarred turn-of-the-century upright piano is in the pit.

The 1994 fair season carried on the illusion of age with the theme "The Good Old Times." Elaborate displays of antiques, nostalgia, and memorabilia lined one wall of the exhibit building. The display of agricultural produce included more grains in competition than I'd seen at much larger fairs. The produce spoke well of the farming community, and the canned and baked goods harked back to a simpler, more self-sufficient era. The needlework recalled long winter nights when farm wives brightened their homes with their toil and talent.

The dining hall, too, seemed to have seen many seasons. Old-timers sat at the picnic tables and looked like they'd been there since Lindbergh flew over—the perfect props for the masquerade. I wouldn't have been surprised to find a poster advertising War Bonds.

The dining hall was bright, and with double screen doors at each end, it was pleasant and breezy. Red, white, and blue bunting decorated the walls, and in keeping with the fair's theme, there were displays of antique china and glass on one side. Six tables would accommodate the 150 diners the cooks planned on feeding each evening.

The kitchen was just inside the door. It had a cozy, homey atmosphere. A pie safe on one wall held a dozen pies and at least thirty slices, already cut and on plates. There were also two whole cakes.

Although it was early afternoon, six aproned cooks were already at work on dinner. The menu for the night was braised steak, mashed potatoes and gravy, green beans, tossed salad, and applesauce. They had already peeled fifty pounds of potatoes.

"For the salad alone we use eight heads of lettuce, two large onions, two pounds of radishes, a large stalk of celery, three tomatoes, three large cucumbers, and one package of carrots," Clara Mansel told me.

Sarah Gault, who co-heads the kitchen with Frances Steese, explained a few of the intricacies of operating the cafeteria. She's been at

Toasted Butter Pecan Cake and Frosting

1 $^1/_3$ cups pecans (chopped)   2 cups sugar
1 $^1/_4$ cups butter   4 eggs, unbeaten
3 cups sifted enriched flour   1 cup milk
2 teaspoons baking powder   1 teaspoon vanilla
$^1/_2$ teaspoon salt

Grease and flour three round cake pans.

Toast pecans in $^1/_4$ cup butter for 20 to 25 minutes at 350 degrees.

Sift together flour, baking powder, and salt. Cream 1 cup butter and gradually add sugar, creaming well. Blend in eggs one at a time, beating after each addition. Add dry ingredients alternately with the milk. Add vanilla and pecans. Bake at 350 degrees for 20 to 30 minutes. Makes three layers; serves 16 to 18.

Frosting:

$^1/_4$ cup butter   4 to 6 tablespoons cream
1 pound confectioners' sugar $^2/_3$ cup pecans
1 teaspoon vanilla

Cream butter, confectioners' sugar, and vanilla. Add cream. Add pecans. Will frost a three-layer cake.

the job for ten years, and in addition to all the responsibilities of purchasing, organizing, and cooking, she also trains the volunteers.

"Each Grange is responsible for five pies and a cake," she told me. "I made a butter pecan cake."

Aside from hot dogs and hot sausages, daytime offerings from the kitchen were homemade: potato salad, macaroni salad, barbecue, ham barbecue, and that pie cupboard full of delights and pleasures.

I bought a ham barbecue and coffee and sat down to work on my notes in the breezy building. The wind was kicking up, so I put my notes away and went back for a piece of cherry pie. The crust crumbled like Marc Antony at Cleopatra's feet.

A medic rushed in looking for Ginny Richardson and blurted out his bad news as he ran. "A storm is coming!" he gasped. "Lightning, hail, heavy rains, possible tornadoes—winds up to seventy miles per hour. We're a sure target!"

"Button the tents," Ginny replied calmly. "Close the buildings. Make sure you tell the retail people. Let the cement-block building open so we have someplace safe to go."

I said a hasty good-bye to Ginny and the cooks. I needed to get a look at the rest of the fair before we all landed in Munchkinland.

There were no rides at the Mercer County Fair when I visited. Ginny told me that a nearby fair running simultaneously had lured her company away. She'd already begun the search for a company that wanted to grow with the folks at Mercer.

I didn't miss the smell of diesel fuel exhaust, myself. There were plenty of activities throughout the week to suit everyone's taste. With all the four-legged and four-wheeled pulls in the arena, the music, the Tuesday-night card party, the Wednesday parade, and the "Saturday Afternoon on the Farm" games, the fair had much to offer. And I suspected that many folks came for the nightly dinners and the chance to see old friends—perhaps the most old-fashioned and enduring aspect of the fair. To me, Mercer County Grange Fair was as endearing as an old Hoosier cabinet.

❖ The Mercer County Grange Fair always ends on the first Saturday in August. It starts the Sunday evening before with a vesper service, and runs through the week. There is no admission charge, but there is a minimal bleacher charge for some events. The fairgrounds is east of Mercer on Route 58. For information, write to the Mercer County Grange Fair, 34 Grange Fair Road, Mercer, PA 16137.

Blueberry Festival

Montrose, Susquehanna County

Whenever my upstate New York friend, Sabra Kopec, speaks of Montrose, she withdraws into that curious room of memory. She speaks of her family's store, of the wonderful homes on Lake Street. She speaks of her neighbor's pony, Good Boy, and of the village happenings and personalities as if it were only yesterday that she left home—though I suspect that in some ways she's never left at all.

The Blueberry Festival's advance flier advertised the event as "small town life at its finest," but the same could be said of the town itself. As small towns in Pennsylvania go, Montrose is country elegant, but like any great hostess, she aims to put guests at ease, not to impress. Grand old white Federal and Greek revival homes with green shutters stand back from tree-lined streets. Broad, shady porches full of green wicker rockers invite quiet conversation and cool, summer afternoon drinks.

Though the little shopping district may be the heart of the village, it is the village green that gives Montrose heart. There is a gazebo there, and a fountain. A Civil War–era monument reads, "The Union Shall and Must Be Preserved." The courthouse stands by, stately and imposing, and the brick Victorian firehouse is there, too. The library is also on the green, and one can easily imagine the pleasure of finding a wonderful book and spending a summer afternoon on a bench in the welcoming shade.

Although it was only the first weekend in August when my friend Deb and I turned off I-81 and headed toward the Blueberry Festival, autumn had already begun to bully summer in the northern tier of the state. Along the way, sumac was raising auburn heads along the roadsides. The sunlight had thickened. Most telling, however, was the temperature—fifty-seven degrees when we entered Montrose.

Not surprisingly, the first thing we did when we got to the green was eat breakfast. It would have been impossible to do anything else. The big griddles set up in the center of the festival sent out missionaries on the breeze, and the savory smells pulled converts from all over town directly to the altar.

We ate blueberry pancakes and sausage and drank steaming cups of coffee that morning, with fresh fruit on the side. There must have been fifty card tables, each covered in blue-and-white-checked oilcloth and decorated with a mason jar of wildflowers. Tables in the sunlight were in most demand. We brazenly carried an empty table from the yellow-and-white-striped tent to a patch of sunlight. Other people liked our idea and soon the tables were being carted around like TV trays, but no one minded.

When we finished eating, we walked up the hill to another tent. A used book and record sale was attracting quite a bit of attention. With crates, tables, and boxes full of books and records, and bumper-to-bumper traffic in the aisles, it was almost impossible to get from one end of the tent to the other. When I finally managed to edge my way in, I could see the attraction—variety and quality, teamed with low prices. I bought six albums from the sixties for $3.

A silent auction was set up on the street. I'd never seen one before, and I was surprised by its simplicity. Each article had a notebook with it. Interested buyers wrote their names, addresses, and bid amounts. Seeing the previous bids encouraged bidders to part with more money. Some of

Blueberry Delight

3 cups flour   1 $1/2$ teaspoons baking
1 cup sugar   powder
1 cup butter or margarine

Mix dry ingredients and then add butter.

Add 1 egg and mix. Pat half of mixture in bottom of 9 x 13-inch pan.

3 cups berries   2 to 3 tablespoons
$1/2$ cup sugar   cornstarch

Cook together for filling.

Pour on top of crust. Sprinkle remaining crumb mixture on top. Bake 30 to 35 minutes at 350 degrees.

Blueberry Sauce

4 cups blueberries   1 cup water
$2/3$ cup sugar   1 rounded tablespoon
1 tablespoon lemon juice   cornstarch
$1/2$ teaspoon vanilla

Wash and crush blueberries. Add sugar and lemon juice. Mix cornstarch with water and stir into mixture. Bring to boil. Boil 1 to 2 minutes. Chill. Makes 1 quart.

—*Roxanne Connelly*

the merchandise was very nice, and if I were staying around town, I would have bid on a fine nineteenth-century writing box. That we were leaving didn't deter Deb. She took one look at the quilt that was being raffled and bought a ticket.

There was a booth devoted to blueberry pies, another to jams and jellies. There was no reason to resist either, and between us, Deb and I carried four jars of jam and two pies to the car. We also stopped by the children's game corner and by the library and historical society, where I talked with Gladys Bennett, who chairs the Blueberry Festival.

Deb and I agreed to drive around Montrose before we left. And then, simultaneously, we said, "Let's go back!" Before long we were seated at an oilcloth-covered card table eating huge helpings of blueberry delight, covered with French vanilla ice cream and drowning in blueberry sauce.

Roxanne Connelly sent the recipes along, but I'm not certain they'll taste as good without the gentle folk music in the background or the village green spread out before me.

I called Sabra to tell her about my adventure that day. "Now do you see what I mean?" she asked. For the record, yes, I do.

❖ The Blueberry Festival Kick-off Dinner is held the Thursday evening before the festival. The festival itself, held on the first Friday and Saturday in August, runs from 9 A.M. till 4 P.M. each day on the village green in the center of town. All proceeds, including the sale of T-shirts, foods, and commemorative items, benefit the town library. For more information, call 717-278-1881.

Watermelon Festival

Shartlesville, Berks County

Unless someone has been born, died, or moved away, Shartlesville has a population of 322 people. Just off exit 8 of busy Interstate 78, Shartlesville's Main Street parallels the four-lane highway for three blocks before petering out into farmland at each end of town. Yet the town manages to support two rather famous Pennsylvania Dutch restaurants, the miniature village called Roadside America, several quaint and charming shops, and each year, since 1989, the Painted Ladies' Watermelon Festival.

My friend Jo and I parked beside the famous Shartlesville Hotel, long renowned for its fine Pennsylvania Dutch fare, the seven sweets and seven sours of the culinary world. We started down the street but returned to the car within ten minutes, carrying a long wicker porch basket from the 1920s. Jo had found it at an antiques shop across the street on the corner of First and Main. After a little rummaging around, the dealer had even managed to find the two tin liners. From the start, that Sunday morning, Jo felt that our mission was a success.

The town had really dressed up for the occasion. Like most small towns with a festival in the offing, the citizens take advantage of the out-of-town traffic, and yard sales pop up like mushrooms after a rainstorm. I found a blue granite double boiler in wonderful shape; that necessitated another trip to the car. Along the way, we bought two dozen gladioli from buckets on a front porch, begged two mayonnaise jars and enough water to hold them, and added them to the rapidly growing backseat collection.

I warned Jo, "This has got to stop. Remember—this is a VW."

We stopped in a pink building with a sign advertising "The Shirt Factory Shops." We didn't buy anything, but the clerk gave us tickets for free watermelon. Around back, about twenty-five people were gathered, bending over in typical watermelon-eating posture. While pink juice ran down their arms, seeds were flying like machine-gun fire. It was a regular watermelon seed battlefield.

A sign on the side of the shop gave the day's schedule.

10–5	Free watermelon
10–5	Watermelon sculpture
10–5	Craft booths open
10–5	Museum of watermelons
10–11	Watermelon carving demonstration
11:30, 1:00, 3:30	Seed spitting contest
12:00, 2:30	Music at jailhouse
12:30	Watermelon rolling relays
2:00	Egg and spoon race
4–5	Carving display
10–5	Picnic, play area town park

We walked down the street, looking at crafts. The Melon Patch, owned by Tammy and Mike Smith from Mechanicsburg, offered an amazing collection of watermelon items: watermelon trash cans, tables, wooden baskets, salad bowls, umbrellas, placemats, pillows, door decorations, and wedges of wood painted like watermelon slices. Other vendors offered hats, flowerpots, T-shirts, and signs.

We stopped at another shop farther down to view the watermelon sculptures. There were birds, baskets, palm trees, and a pond with a watermelon swan. One had "I Love You" carved in the side. I had to admit that they would be interesting centerpieces for a summer dinner party.

Food vendors offered breakfast, hamburgers, hot dogs, and strawberry daiquiris. There was also a bake sale in progress. We decided to go to the Shartlesville Hotel and weren't disappointed.

Dinner there is served family style, and we were seated with a family from the Philadelphia area. Our first course consisted of tapioca pudding, chow chow, beets, applesauce, pepper slaw, apple butter, and rhubarb sauce. We'd scarcely finished that round when the main course appeared. There was chicken, sausage, potato filling, ham, ham and chicken croquettes, chicken pot pie, corn, peas, barbecued lima beans, mashed potatoes and gravy, and string beans. I passed on dessert, but my tablemates were served generous slices of homemade pie while I talked with the hotel owner, Dona Bowman.

"I came here because I've enjoyed this restaurant all of my life," she said. "Six years ago a friend of mine told me it was for sale. I came and looked around, thought about it, went back to Jersey, and promptly forgot about it. I found out the next spring that it was still for sale. I bought it."

I looked around the dining room. It's an extremely cozy place, a little like grandmothers' kitchens all over the state. Homey antiques and warm wainscoting add to its country charm.

"This has been a hotel since 1740. We have a ghost here. Lights go on and off all night long. The minute I walk out the door strange things happen. But when I'm here everything runs smoothly. My boyfriend once saw the apparition, at three in the morning. He came down to get a sandwich, looked up, and there was a very animated woman with her hair piled up."

Before we left town, we went back to Sweet Heritage Antiques. Jo bought an early washstand, and the only way to get it into the car was to put the top down. This wasn't a problem until we decided to stop at Roadside America. We had to move the washstand to the front seat to put the top up.

I hadn't been to Roadside America since I was twelve, when my Scout troop came in our old school bus. I suspect that nostalgia may have contributed to my enjoyment that Sunday afternoon, but the display can impress even the most jaded tourist. Oil wells pump, farm animals move around barnyards, waterfalls gush water, trains move through tiny towns, and airplanes fly overhead. When the house lights go down for the grand finale, the villages sparkle with nighttime lights, and Kate Smith belts "God Bless America" against an American flag, it's truly Americana at its finest.

Watermelon Punch

6 cups pureed watermelon
2 cups pineapple juice
1 12-ounce can frozen cranberry juice
6 ounces frozen orange juice concentrate
$1/4$ cup lemon juice
1 liter club soda

Combine all ingredients except club soda. Chill; add soda before serving.

When we left Shartlesville, there were cloud shadows on the distant blue mountainsides. It had been a very full day, and I was surprised when Jo said, "I have only one regret."

"What's that?"

"We never did eat any watermelon!" And she was right.

❖ The Watermelon Festival is usually held on the first Saturday and Sunday of August. Events are scheduled from 10 A.M. to 5 P.M. both days. If you are planning to spend a full day in Shartlesville, you may want to visit Roadside America and eat at the Shartlesville Hotel. Shartlesville is forty-five miles east of Harrisburg off exit 8 of I-78. For more information, send a stamped, self-addressed envelope to Watermelons, P.O. Box 212, Shartlesville, PA 19554, or call 610-488-7792.

Wayne County Fair

Honesdale, Wayne County

Before I began researching this book, I knew more about the history and geography of Ireland than I did about my own state. As I traveled the carnival circuit, bits and pieces of Pennsylvania history remembered from junior high social studies classes began to come together. New place names and stories snapped into place, forming whole pictures from jigsaw pieces. Still, I was always happiest going to a fair or festival in a town I was familiar with, a place with a name that meant something to me, and even more so if the town was hometown to a friend.

Honesdale meant something to me. Years ago I'd visited the town briefly. I was on the road with my high school pal Jim. We were headed for Albany to move him and all his worldly chattel to a new corporate position in Philadelphia. We'd been best buddies since his family had moved from Honesdale to my hometown in our freshman year.

"Do you mind if we take a little side trip?" Jim asked. "I'd really like to see Honesdale again."

And so we went. We drove up and down the streets that night. He showed me his father's church and the parsonage, and he showed me his elementary school. We stopped at a diner for coffee, and all the while he talked about Honesdale, about growing up there. And that's my experience with the town: a handful of dusty stories, all forgotten, and an hour-long nighttime visit.

It was spritzing rain and cool enough for a sweatshirt when my friend

Kay and I visited Honesdale for the Wayne County Fair. I had timed my arrival so that I could attend the harness races that afternoon, but after the long drive, both Kay and I were ready for lunch. From the many vendors, we chose one that offered smoked pork chop dinners served with red cabbage and German potato salad, as well as bratwurst, knockwurst, and smoked sausages.

"Think this is German?" Kay asked as we ordered our sandwiches.

Behind the dining tent, a staccato patter from the track peppered our lunch. Across the macadam pathway in front of the tent, an organist from National Music's piano and organ sale serenaded us with "As Time Goes By" and other old standards.

"And you say I never take you nice places for dinner!" I teased. "Here we are at the track, live music playing . . . what more do you want?"

Like the grandstand at Clarion County, this grandstand was also an old one, only much larger. The wooden structure was painted red and white with a green roof. We took upper seats, but then I saw the yellow-and-green silks of Clarence Martin Jr.'s stables, and we moved down to cheer the horses of the man I'd met at the Lycoming County Fair. Once again that day, a little familiarity had bred a great deal of enthusiasm. I was a cheering maniac, and I suspect that Kay thought I'd been on the road too long.

We stayed for the rest of the races that afternoon, then walked through the fair. The commercial exhibits were housed under the stadium, and we visited them first. The vendors there were attracting the crowd's attention with T-shirts, sun catchers, and maple products. Outside, along the back of the stadium, were food stands manned by local groups. We stopped at Nina's spaghetti stand for a piece of warm apple pie and struck up a conversation with James Rosengrant. He told us that the pies were made at the Cortez Methodist Church at Lake Ariel, just down the road. On that chilly, drizzly day, the old-fashioned apple pie really hit the spot.

The midway was packed tightly between the back of the grandstand and the hillside that jutted up behind it. Local and carnival food concessions vied for business. A whole alley was given to carnival games. There were a freak show and a few other sideshow attractions, plus an act on the free stage.

We walked over to the livestock area for the 4-H sheep show. The barns and the arena make up one of the best livestock-showing facilities on the Pennsylvania fair circuit. The barns, more elegant than the grandstand, opened into a large, roofed arena surrounded by bleachers. The area was landscaped, and there was no doubt about the agricultural community's importance in Wayne County.

Oatmeal Pocket Treat

$1/_2$ cup honey   1 cup nonfat dry milk
$1/_2$ cup peanut butter   1 cup rolled oats
Mix together and wrap in bite-size pieces in plastic wrap.
                                                    —*Amber Kovaleski, age 13*

We continued around the outside of the track to the horse barns. We said hello to Mr. Martin and his horses before moving on down the line to the poultry building. There, a display of exotic fowl in a chicken-wire cage commanded the front of the building. The little showgirls and chorus boys of the poultry world would no doubt attract more spectators than the egg and meat producers inside.

Before we left we went over to the long red display building to view cookies, cakes, jams, jellies, produce, needlework, and the lot of home and farm products. Donna Branning was hovering around the apple pie display.

"In addition to the ordinary apple pie contest," she said, "we run a grand prix pie contest. It's the best of the best, and it requires creativity. I've won for three years."

Before we left Honesdale, I stopped in town and bought a postcard for my high school buddy. That night, I called his mother to tell her where I had spent the day. She told me about the fire that destroyed the original barns, and about Jim's boyhood. When we said good-bye, I put the postcard in an envelope along with a fair schedule and mailed it to Philadelphia, hoping that it would bring the same smile I had heard in his mother's voice when she talked about Honesdale.

❖ The Wayne County Fair runs nine days, from the first Friday in August through the following Saturday night. Except for sideshows and an occasional grandstand event, the admission price covers everything, including tractor pulls, stunt shows, and concerts. The fairgrounds is located one mile north of Honesdale on Route 191. For more information, write to the Wayne County Fair, Wayne County Agricultural Society, Honesdale, PA 18431.

Blain Picnic and Homecoming

Blain, Perry County

There are small nooks and crannies all over Pennsylvania where time has had no more lasting effect than an August afternoon thunderstorm. There may be telephone poles, electric lines, and television antennas, yet in stubborn defiance of progress, cistern pumps stand patiently beside kitchen doorways, outhouses wait at the ends of backyards, and kerosene lamps, wicks intact, sleep in dusty garrets under two-hundred-year-old roofs. In these drowsy communities, blue granite kettles are more likely on the stove than on display.

Blain is one of these timeless places. Established in 1763, this three-street hamlet nestles in a corner of western Perry County, surrounded by fields of rolling corn. The tiny village supports the nine-room Blain Hotel, renowned for its Sunday buffet and enormous breakfasts, as well as Book's Market, with personnel so helpful and friendly, one feels like a native son stopping by for dinner fixings.

For almost a century and a half, the town has also supported its annual festival, the Blain Picnic and Homecoming. Fifth-generation resident Barry Sheaffer told me, "In the early days, families held their reunions down here by Sherman's Creek each summer. They built picnic tables to use and left them standing all year long. Eventually they all decided to hold their reunions on the same day, the second Saturday in August. That was the first Blain Picnic and Homecoming—in 1852."

Another resident, Rob Neidigh, with roots four generations deep in Blain's soil, added, "By the turn of the century, railroad tracks ran along Sherman's Creek. On the day of the picnic, many people would arrive by train and walk across the bridge, carrying their picnics with them."

And then I remembered, faint as a whisper in the wind, my grandmother's stories of walking over the mountain with her parents from McCrea in Cumberland County to attend the Blain Picnic. It could only have been early in the first decade of this century.

The Blain Picnic and Homecoming has changed more than the village. It's no longer a one-day event. Fortune tellers, try-your-luck games, a dunking booth, clothing vendors, picnic pavilions, and flea market tables line gravel pathways. Food stands feature the usual offerings of fries, hot dogs, and pizza, as well as homemade pies, ham and bean soup, chicken corn soup, and the Lions Club chicken barbecue. Several organizations offer chances on tractors and trucks, and there are amusement rides for both children and adults. There is nightly entertainment.

Ginger Cakes

1 cup dark molasses	1 tablespoon soda
1 ¹/₂ cups brown sugar	1 cup boiling water
1 cup lard	5 cups flour
1 tablespoon ginger	2 eggs

Mix all ingredients.

Drop by tablespoon on greased and floured cookie sheet. Beat one whole egg and spread on top of cookies to glaze. Bake for 10 minutes at 350 degrees.

With all of the changes, the word *homecoming* still figures largely in Blain's yearly festival. For locals and former residents, Saturday is an all-day affair, as it must have been in 1852. Breakfast is served from 7 to 9, and by the time I arrived at 10, multigenerational families had already staked claims to coveted shady areas along the midway. All day long, as the crowd increased, folding lawn chairs multiplied like field mice. Although the rides ran full tilt and a home-grown gospel group performed in the afternoon, conversation seemed to be the primary activity. Ignoring the temptations of the midway, members of the younger generation played on the banks of Sherman's Creek, defying both parents and heat. The Blain Picnic and Homecoming still feels like a large, happy family reunion.

Late in the afternoon, I walked down to the creek myself. I think that I was hoping to catch a glimpse of a phantom train unloading passengers in white lawn dresses, skimmers, and knickers, carrying picnic baskets across a shadowy footbridge. The Blain Picnic does that to you.

❖ The Blain Picnic and Homecoming is held the second week of August, Wednesday through Friday evenings and all day Saturday. Take Route 274 to Blain and turn onto SR 3006-100. In a mile, turn left onto Picnic Road. Campsites are available on the grounds. For reservations, call 717-789-3907. For rooms at the Blain Hotel, call 717-536-3322.

Moscow Country Fair

Moscow, Lackawanna County

Saying that Moscow has a country fair is a little like saying that the Vanderbilts built a cottage in Newport. Both understatements mislead while promising a most pleasant surprise to the unsuspecting tourist headed to either location.

Although it was drizzling rain in Moscow, the town of fifteen hundred residents was abustle on the first night of the fair. Groups of patrons huddled by parking lot edges all over town waiting for the busy yellow school buses to transport them to the fair. A traffic policeman directed me to Harmony Hills, a new housing development where even more patrons gathered under umbrellas at three stops. I didn't know exactly where the fair was being held, who was holding it, or what I should expect when I got there.

We exited our buses at the North Pocono Middle School, where two cutout elephants were pulling a plywood circus wagon with a giraffe. In the lobby of the school, a pianist was playing classical music, and a well-dressed teenager directed me to the juried art show in the gymnasium.

I met Bob and June Blasko, co-chairs for the visual arts exhibit, just inside the door. They walked through the exhibit with me, pointing out favorite works and winners. There were seven categories with four winners in each class: paintings, water soluble, crafts, sculpture, black-and-white photography, color photography, and drawing, each represented by many contestants.

Mr. Blasko told me, "We give cash prizes to the kids to stimulate their interest. A ribbon is nice, but five bucks is nicer. One of our judges, William Tietsworth, wanted to buy one of the kids' drawings. He offered five dollars, but the little guy said firmly that the price was two dollars. Finally, Tietsworth won out and gave him the five dollars!"

Most of the works were for sale, and the terms were 10 percent down with the balance due at the end of the show.

Mike Butash of Scranton, along with several other circus enthusiasts, had taken over two rooms down the hall. Elephants marched along one table, and a trainload of lions and tigers and bears chugged across another table. There were circus posters across the chalkboard, memorabilia, and miniatures everywhere.

In the cafeteria, quilts were displayed open for potential buyers.

"I call quilters the jocks of the art field," Blasko said. "They're very competitive!"

In the lobby, as if to prove his point, two quilters were arguing over a bolt of material.

A long flight of steps led down from the parking lot to the athletic fields, which had been transformed by a sea of red-, white-, and yellow-striped tents. The art show in the lobby had been the hors d'oeuvres. Here was the main course!

"There are no rides," Mr. Blasko said, "so it's not a carnival and we have no hoodlums. This is what a country fair used to be, this is what a fair should be. This fair profits the school arts programs as well as the community arts programs."

Mr. Blasko introduced me to Mark Gaughan. Like many of the fair organizers I had met all over the state, Mark Gaughan is a teacher. Obviously well rehearsed as spokesperson for the Moscow Fair, he knew what I needed to know for the book and he shared it with me.

"This is a very small community," he began. "We are the center of the North Pocono area. We will draw about fifty thousand people before the weekend is over.

"All our games are done by nonprofit groups, and many of the games are homemade. It keeps the fair noncommercial. Olympus Camera underwrites the balloon rally, but they must stay outside the grounds. Local businesses also underwrite many aspects of the fair. They can't actually participate, but they want to help.

"A lot of people are surprised—they expect animals and a carnival. Instead, once they get used to the idea, they enjoy the slow pace, sitting under a tent listening to music, watching a potter.

"We take only eighty-five crafters from the hundreds who apply. We have them from fifteen states, from all over the East Coast to as far west as Indiana."

I walked through the tents, amazed at the quality of the merchandise there. This was not a crafts show like so many I had seen, where true art was a rare commodity among the ducks on a stick. Nor was the work offered for sale out of someone's pattern book. This was gallery-quality artwork.

The foods were also a cut above. Caterers—not vendors or concessionaires—offered steak and cheese subs, hamburgers, cheeseburgers, fried vegetables, cheesecake, barbecued chicken and ribs, buffalo burgers, salads, blickies, pasties, corned beef and crab stews, tacos, kielbasa, spiedies, grilled Welsh cookies, funnel cakes, strawberry smoothies, fresh lemonade, white pizza, candy apples, all sorts of fresh pasta, potato pancakes, clam chowder, Belgian waffles, Italian sausage, roast beef sandwiches,

Potato Pancakes

3 medium potatoes, peeled
   and grated
1 medium onion, chopped
   finely
1 egg

1 teaspoon baking powder
$1/4$ cup flour
1 teaspoon salt
generous amount of oil
   for frying

Combine potatoes and onion. Put half in blender and process until pureed. Add egg, baking powder, flour, and salt. Blend well. Add reserved grated potato and onion. Drop by tablespoonfuls onto greased, heated griddle. Fry on both sides over medium heat until brown; drain on paper towels. Serve with sour cream or applesauce.

Author's note: When I asked if the cook would share her recipe, she replied, "No way!" This is close.

---

fries, pierogies, pita hoagies, popcorn, wings, ice cream, brownies, nachos, shrimp and ham jambalaya, blackened chicken, bread pudding, hot dogs, Texas dogs, Italian pastries, Greek gyros, spinach pies, and homemade fudge.

The entertainment was just as impressive. The acts were carefully chosen for variety and appeal. I sat in on Mary Bernard's cabaret show, captivated by her music and her comedy act. Jim Weiss, a traditional folk singer, and John Sebastian, from the sixties group The Lovin' Spoonful, followed. Other performers scheduled throughout the weekend offered 1940s swing, big band music, jazz, country rock, and bluegrass. Also on the performance schedule were cloggers, the cast of *Beatlemania*, a clown, and a mime.

Two of the biggest events of the weekend would undoubtedly be the hot air balloon rally and the street rod show. Each day of the fair, the famous Olympus hot air balloons would launch from the outer field. A special appearance by the *Forbes* magazine Giant Macaw would highlight the balloon display. Sunday's schedule included the Pocono Mountain Street Rod Show, and more than three hundred classic muscle cars were expected between 9 A.M. and 4 P.M.

The Moscow Country Fair certainly exceeded my expectations. Every detail was flawlessly executed, and the atmosphere was one of a garden party on a large estate.

❖ The fair is held the second weekend of August every year at the

North Pocono School campus in Moscow. Take exit 4 east on I-380 or 6 west. Follow signs to free shuttle bus parking. Events are scheduled for Thursday and Friday evenings, Saturday from noon, and Sunday from 9. For more information, write to the Moscow Country Fair, P.O. Box 315, Moscow, PA 18444.

Clinton County Fair

Mackeyville, Clinton County

At the gates of the Clinton County Fair, I told the ticket taker that I had called ahead and talked to Martha Munro, the fair manager, and that she had promised press passes for Kay and me. To no avail.

Then I broke into the second stanza of my little ditty, the one about writing a book on country fairs and festivals. It looked like this might fail too and I'd have to pay admission, but it was worth a shot, and I was not about to tell anyone how easily I capitulated. So I talked some more.

The man at the gate sprouted a smile and said, "You have a great line, buddy. I don't know anything about press passes, but it's worth the four bucks just to listen to you. Enjoy yourself!" With that he motioned me on.

We entered just in time to hear the post horn for the pig races.

"Let's stay and watch," Kay said.

Robinson's Racing Pigs had a 150-foot sawdust track. Four Yorkshire pigs, just three months old and small enough to be cute, were given Oreo cookies at the gate. Their handler made a big production of placing additional treats at the finish line. When the gate opened, the little porkers took off like they had seen a butcher. The race was over momentarily.

The announcer introduced the next heat. These four contestants were Florida wild pigs, and like the first group to the gate, they were also youngsters. They had names like Oinkle Sam and Rush Limhog. While the handler was lining them up, the announcer explained that the piglets run 150 feet in six to seven seconds. Pigs are the fifth most intelligent animals, he said, much smarter than dogs and horses, and they were trained with the cookie treats.

Kay nudged me and pointed to the neighboring food concession. It was steaming and smoking in the afternoon sunlight. The sign read, "Pork Rinds." "Think that has anything to do with their track records?" she asked.

The fairground buildings were neat, well built, and modern: a nice exhibition building and a functional livestock area.

The midway, in keeping with this agricultural fair, was midsize, with eight rides and eight games. Virtually all the food offered was concession food, contracted by the carnival company, although one church offered ham and roast beef sandwiches, and the band boosters from the local high school were selling baked potatoes.

One might consider packing a picnic, for the most appealing part of the Clinton County Fair was the spectacular view from the picnic pavilion on the hill, just above the main gate. We sat there quite a while just staring at the mountains across Interstate 80. A handful of other folks, probably livestock exhibitors, had also found the quiet retreat and were savoring the afternoon shade with us.

When I met fair manager Martha Munro that afternoon, I complimented her on the fair's beautiful location.

"We're a young fair," she said. "We were founded in 1972. The good Lord had this property planned for us. We were looking at other properties, and then someone approached us and told us that their property—and this view—was for sale. We bought it in 1983.

"Thanks to a lot of faithful volunteers, we've made a lot of headway in a short time. I've always said, 'Show me a fair person—they're lovely people, they're giving people.' We had a small horseshoe-pitching area and now, thanks to our volunteers, we have a much larger one."

I asked her about the activity around the first-aid station. There was medical staff on duty when I passed it, and a child was getting an injection, something I had never associated with a fair.

"Today is Kiddies' Day," she explained. "The Rotary Club, the State Nurses' Association, the fair, and local doctors give free immunization and booster shots. Any child who receives shots gets to ride free this afternoon."

The Clinton County Fair is indeed a family fair. "If a family can bring their children here and enjoy it and make memories," Martha said, "all of our efforts are worth it."

Tuesday at Clinton County Fair was Senior Day, with the Sizzlin' Seniors Talent Show of homespun entertainment. The Susque Valley Sticky Buns Kitchen Band had performed, playing everything but the kitchen sink. Ethel Yearick had taken a second place with her "Old Gray Mule," and first-place finisher Peg Rhine had read "When I Am an Old Woman, I Shall Wear Purple." There were soloists, instrumentalists, comics, and vocal duets. Some of the performers had simply told stories from their wheelchairs.

Variety Apple-Orange Pie

Crust:

Cut 2 cups flour and 1 teaspoon salt into $1/3$ cup shortening and $1/3$ cup butter. Continue blending until mixture resembles corn-meal, then sprinkle 5 tablespoons cold water over and toss with fork. Roll out half the dough, carefully placing in pie pan. After filling, cover with top crust and decorate with bits of dough.

Apple Filling:

8 cups sliced apples—mix 2 cups Golden Delicious, 2 cups McIntosh, 2 cups Rome, and 2 cups Granny Smith (other varia-tions can be used, but be careful to keep a balance between sweet and tart)

zest of 1 orange	1 teaspoon cinnamon
$1/2$ cup brown sugar	$1/2$ teaspoon salt
$1/2$ cup sugar	$1/4$ teaspoon nutmeg

Mix well and put half the mixture into shell and sprinkle with $1/4$ cup flour.

Pour remaining apple mixture in. Top with additional $1/4$ cup flour and dot with 1 tablespoon butter.

Bake for 55 minutes at 400 degrees—check often. If it's brown-ing too fast, cover with foil.

The Clinton County Fair is big on family fun and big on community involvement. There are performances by local groups, high school bands, and community bands. There are also rodeos, horse shows, car races, and chicken barbecues. This is a country fair, the way country fairs used to be, and for all the same reasons.

❖ The fair runs Sunday through Saturday the first full week of August and is located on Route 200 near Mackeyville, just off exit 26 of I-80. For the schedule of theme days, write to the Clinton County Fair, P.O. Box 174, Mackeyville, PA 17750, or call 717-726-4148.

Goschenhoppen Folk Festival

East Greenville, Montgomery County

At the Goschenhoppen Historians' book stand I asked the question that had undoubtedly already been answered a hundred times that day.

"What is Goschenhoppen?"

"No one is quite sure," Evan Snyder said as he settled into his explanation. "One theory is that it was an Indian word that the early Pennsylvania Dutch settlers interpreted as Goschenhoppen. Another theory is that there is a location in Germany—no one knows where—with the name Goschenhoppen. Today one man walked up very authoritatively and said that it means 'Land of Tubers.'

"As early as 1728, the name was being used for two areas, one close to Philadelphia and the other one in Montgomery County. The Philadelphia area was known as Goschenhoppen, and this area was known as New Goschenhoppen."

Whatever the origin, by the time I left East Greenville that afternoon, I was quite certain what Goschenhoppen meant to me: the best folk festival I had ever attended. All the elements—the park itself, the quality, selection, and authenticity of the demonstrations, the staff, the music, the foods—worked together. The Folk Festival is sponsored by the Goschenhoppen Historians, an educational society dedicated to the learning and teaching of local folk culture. Among its goals are the identification, preservation, and restoration of historic sites, buildings, bridges, dam breasts, and fences.

At Goschenhoppen Park the historians practice what they preach. The tree-studded knoll boasts a Victorian band shell, unsurpassed in the state. The stage is a half dome built of beaded boards, its curved walls and ceiling rising thirty feet above the pit, its crisp red, white, and blue paint draped in bunting. Seating is under roof and the slanted floor of the open-air theater assures every patron a good seat. There is also a tiny glen on the grounds that provides a natural stage and seating.

The scope and variety of the demonstrations were amazing. I counted more than ninety stations, each well stocked with authentic equipment.

Howie Landis was demonstrating sausage making close to the main gate. "I use only carbon steel knives," he told me. "Stainless steel would not be appropriate. At Goschenhoppen, everything must be to the era."

For a heat source, the Goschenhoppen Historians set up cookstoves. Stovepipes belched all over the park, and the smoke hung under the trees, another reminder of life a century ago. Studying the cookstoves alone would have kept the curators at Winterthur busy for weeks.

For ice, a horse-drawn wagon was making deliveries. A youngster jumped out and lugged large blocks of ice to the lemonade and home-made ice cream stands, using ice tongs and no doubt saying prayers of thanks for modern child labor laws.

There were wooden washtubs and washrubbers for laundry day. A copper wash boiler cooked whites on the cookstove. Clothing was hung to dry, but the linens were spread out on the grass. Not surprisingly, clothes and linens were either old or meticulous reproductions. Old slaw cutters were in service for sauerkraut making. Crocks were covered with tea towels rather than plastic wrap.

For the early settlers, food was a constant concern, especially during the winter months. Many of the demonstrations reflected that preoccupa-tion: dried food, pig stomach, jellies, chicken waffles, potato candy, apple butter, sauerkraut, fruit pies, potato cultures for baking bread, fritters, pot pie, chowchow, fastnaughts, cookies, main dish pies, cakes, homemade ice cream, root beer, corn pie, sausage, lard, and scrapple. There was also a working smokehouse, set conveniently close to the butchering in the little glen.

The butchering attracted a large audience when the star of the show arrived in a horse-drawn cart. It was scalded in a black cast-iron pot, and then the hair was scraped off. The audience watched attentively, chatting happily. Then workers incised the pig's stomach and intestines poured out. Silence preceded an exodus from the butchering, the crowd scatter-ing like cockroaches when the light switches on.

"Guess they're not farm folks," I heard one man say as I hurried off.

The staff at Goschenhoppen was helpful and friendly. Lorin and David Tuttle were cutting straw for a chaff tick when I stopped and exam-ined a handsome old bed, roped and waiting for its mattress. I confessed that I owned several rope beds fitted with box springs and mattresses. They dropped everything for my lesson.

"You need a hundred twenty to a hundred thirty feet of rope," David said. "Three-eighths-inch sisal rope. Tie the rope to the top peg on the right side of the headboard and bring it down to the footboard. Go around two pegs and take it back to the headboard. Go around two pegs there and continue until you come to the corner. Take the rope across to the first peg on the left side of the rail. Then go back and forth two pegs at a time. Don't weave the ropes. When you come to the last peg, take the rope diagonally across two ropes and tie. Then to tighten, push down one rope at a time, starting with the second rope, continuing around the

United Church of Christ Pickled Cabbage

2 $^1/_2$ cups finely shredded cabbage, $^1/_2$ red pepper, diced
    packed $^1/_2$ green pepper, diced
$^1/_2$ teaspoon salt $^1/_2$ teaspoon celery seed
a little pepper $^3/_4$ cup sugar
1 stalk celery (optional) $^1/_2$ cup vinegar
a little chopped carrot

Mix all ingredients. Let stand 1 hour to flavor before serving.
Serves 6.

—*Women's Fellowship of New Goschenhoppen Church*

Corn Pie

Crust: Pie Filling:
(Makes three double crusts for   (For one 8-inch pie)
    8-inch pies)   2 cups corn
3 cups flour   1 teaspoon salt
1 cup lard ($^1/_2$ pound)   1 teaspoon sugar
$^3/_4$ cup water $^1/_4$ cup milk (or
1 teaspoon salt   use corn juice)
                                            1 hard-boiled egg

Bake at 400 degrees for 35 minutes. Serve with hot buttered milk.
—*Women's Fellowship of New Goschenhoppen Church*

corner and up the bed. Retie your final knot." He demonstrated, then had
me tighten ropes to make certain I understood.

As Lorin reappeared with a diagram and written directions, a frightful
noise rent the air. "It's the serenading!" Lorin cried, and we followed the
crowd to the commotion. A dozen people were using all manner of ingenious noisemaking devices to torment a newly married Pennsylvania
Dutch couple. Lorin handed me a conch shell with the pointy end cut off.
I produced a sound somewhere between a foghorn and an elephant's mat-
ing call, but it was lost in the din. The noisiest device was a three-foot-
square wooden box. Two men pushed a two-by-four back and forth across
the open top. A little boy perched on the board provided the right amount
of resistance to get the box singing. Other participants beat on pans with
soup ladles and banged pot lids together. We had a wonderful time.

For dinner that evening, the dining hall was serving ham, potato filling,

Aunt Goldie's Corn Pie

crust for a deep-dish casserole,
   top and bottom
2 cups corn, fresh, canned,
   or frozen
4 hard-cooked eggs, sliced
3 potatoes, peeled, boiled,
   and sliced thin

chopped celery (to taste)
chopped green pepper
   (to taste)
enough milk to fill the pie
   to top

Layer ingredients in order listed; repeat until used up. Add milk to top of vegetables and eggs. Dot with butter. Add top crust. Bake at 350 degrees for 1 hour. Serve with chicken gravy.

This is an old Pennsylvania Dutch recipe that I sometimes vary by adding chopped, cooked chicken as the center layer. Then it truly is a meal in one dish.

Apple Sausage

25 pounds pork shoulder
12 peeled, cored apples,
   chopped

cinnamon, salt, and pepper
   to taste

Cut pork into 1-inch cubes. Chill. Toss with apple chunks, add seasonings, and grind. Chill again and grind once more. Shape into patties or fill pork casings. Freeze.

dried corn, pickled cabbage, string beans, bread, butter, and a beverage, but I had filled up on the many samples offered at the cooking demonstrations. And I ran out of time before I could see the cooper, the wheelwright, the gunsmith, and the stonecutter. Without a doubt, though, this would not be my only visit to Goschenhoppen.

❖ The Goschenhoppen Folk Festival is held each year on the second Friday and Saturday in August at New Goschenhoppen Park, East Greenville. From Route 29, turn onto Third Street. The park is a few blocks down on the right. For more information, write to Goschenhoppen Historians Inc., Box 476 Red Men's Hall, Green Lane, PA 18054.

Schuylkill County Fair

Schuylkill Haven, Schuylkill County

Christmas trees in August? That would be as incongruous as snow on a hot day . . . and just as welcome. On the day I attended the Schuylkill County Fair, the air was as thick as the plot of a soap opera. A thunderstorm was waiting in the wings, ready to make its appearance at the right cue line. Without a doubt, it would upstage the entertainment that night, if not sooner.

Despite the scowling, grumbling skies, a hefty crowd was milling around the fairgrounds that morning. Temporary landscaping on the grounds brightened corners with flowers, ornamental shrubs, and small trees. Some gardens served to break up areas of macadam while gently directing traffic. Pots of plants filled empty spots. All over the fairgrounds, the cheerful red-, yellow-, and green-striped tents reflected the colors of the flowers.

By the main gate were a campfire, a tepee, and a display of Native American objects: a living history encampment. One poor soul in a long dress was cooking over the open fire, and I could only imagine how hot she must have been.

I stopped by the poultry tent and watched several fancy pigeons open their tails, puff up, and preen for their audience. At the commercial tent, I tried my luck at the Schuylkill Symphony Orchestra's Diamond Dig. I scooped, the clerk sifted, and I walked away a dollar poorer. I also visited the petting zoo, and although the baby animals were cute, the little kids petting them were cuter. I stopped by a farm equipment display and priced snowblowers. The convenient arrangement of the fairgrounds invited these stops—no one would have walked very far in that heat and humidity.

Even with snowblowers on my mind, I was not prepared for the exhibits in the large metal hall close to the nature center. When I stepped inside the doorway, I stopped, momentarily startled. The tangy, spicy smell of pine, exaggerated by the heat and humidity, filled the building. It was the smell of the Christmas-tree lot, sharp and brittle, the smell that I anticipate all day long at work as Christmas nears, the one that greets me when I open my front door during the last month of the year.

Trees were hanging from the rafters. I could not stop myself from spinning them around, looking for imperfections.

"Where are these guys, come December?" a voice behind me asked. "Did you ever see such perfect trees?"

Blue-Ribbon Coconut Cake
....

Blend together:
    2 cups sugar $^1/_2$ cup butter or margarine
Add:
    1 cup milk $^1/_2$ cup shredded coconut
    2 cups sifted flour   7 egg whites, beaten stiff
    2 teaspoons baking powder   and folded in last
    1 teaspoon coconut flavoring
Bake at 350 degrees for about 30 minutes.
    Cool and frost with buttercream frosting. Top with shredded coconut.

                                       —*Ina Evanchalk*

The smell of pine was a cool hand on my forehead, even in the closed building, and it made the humidity less oppressive. When I walked outside, the smell lingered on my clothing.

I had lunch at the fair's restaurant, seated at a picnic table under the porch roof. Wisely, I chose the roast pork sandwich. The Schuylkill County Fair is famous for its roast pork sandwiches. The pork shoulders are trimmed and roasted right on the fairgrounds. The sandwich I ate that day was filled with juicy, tender roast pork—the kind that melts in your mouth, as simple and savory as the morsels your grandmother sneaked to you before Sunday dinner, just beyond your mother's range of vision. I shared the table with Joan Mingione and her father, Robert Hand, who lives just down the road from the fairgrounds.

"Last year," Joan said, "the fair was so crowded they had to stop letting people in."

"It must have been crowded last night," her father said. "There was a lot of traffic going by my house."

We were joined by Patty and Dave Meese, fair directors. Dave confirmed Mr. Hand's speculation. "We had sixteen thousand Friday night."

Ina Evanchalk, Patty's mother, arrived a few minutes later and offered her blue-ribbon coconut cake recipe. When the cake was auctioned, it brought $52. It was an old recipe from her mother, she told me in her Pennsylvania Dutch accent.

I walked around the rest of the fairgrounds before I left. The food vendors offered many choices, and quite a few were featuring sit-down dinners. The homemade clam chowder, vegetable, chicken corn, and bean soups looked delicious. There were baked potatoes, hot beef sandwiches, sausage, barbecued ribs, apple and corn fritters, chicken barbecued over charcoal, homemade ice cream, fresh peach sundaes, shrimp, crab cakes, and fried oysters, all from local organizations and restaurants.

The carnival was separate from the fair, with a dozen rides and as many carnival games. Among the twenty acts scheduled for the two stages during the week were big band music, folk music, and gospel music. The Mudflaps were setting up as I left, and Connie Smith had been there the night before. Concert goers should take lawn chairs.

❖ The Schuylkill County Fairgrounds, originally the Happy Holiday Park, is on Route 895, 1 $^1/_2$ miles east of Route 183. If you are coming from Route 61, take Route 895 West. The fair is usually held the first full week of August from Sunday through Saturday. For more information, write to the Schuylkill County Fair Association, P.O. Box 445, Schuylkill Haven, PA 17972, or call 717-429-1744.

Huntingdon County Fair

Huntingdon, Huntingdon County

When I arrived at the rustic gate of the Huntingdon County Fair, I explained that fair director Betty Grove was waiting for me and asked the attendant to direct me to the office.

"Follow that road to the left," he said, pointing.

He didn't tell me to park first and walk, so I drove—and found myself motoring down the midway. The fair was crowded, and pedestrians looked at me with scorn and disbelief as they begrudgingly parted. I motored along, puttering in first gear, waving and smiling like Mr. America and feeling like an idiot.

Fair secretary George Fitzgerald invited me into his office. Yes, Huntingdon is a Class-A fair . . . owns sixty-nine acres and rents five more . . . most of the food concessions are fair-run or local . . . big-name entertainment at the grandstand . . . Monday- and Friday-night demolition derbies . . . harness racing. We were moving through the vital statistics in record time.

I had learned that the history of a community fair reflects the history of the entire community, and the Huntingdon County Fair did not disappoint me.

"Our fair started in 1831," Fitzgerald said. "We've moved five times over the years and for four years we didn't have a fair. We missed two years during the war"—that would be World War I—"and then another two for smallpox epidemics. The local historians say we can't claim those years. But if you were married and your husband went overseas to war, you were still married, weren't you?"

Soon director Betty Grove joined us. "We're not a big fair," she said, "but we're a big *country* fair.

"The building we call the Art House was part of the East Broadtop Railroad. Another part of the same building is down at the horse barn. By the way, I brought you one of my apple rolls. And the recipe."

"Here's my recipe for chocolate cake," George said, not to be out-done. "We both cook, and this is a competition between us.

"Two years ago I won with my apple pie and I went to state competition. The pie had a vanilla pudding bottom and was topped with apples I'd cooked in lemon juice with just a hint of nutmeg. I cooked them until they were fork tender. I arranged them overtop and glazed it with apricot jam. I was disqualified at the state level because I used another fruit."

Apple Rolls

Put in a 13 x 9-inch pan:

1 1/2 cups sugar	2 cups water

Boil for 5 minutes.

Sift together in a bowl:

2 cups flour	2 tablespoons sugar
3 teaspoons baking powder	1 teaspoon salt

Cut in with a pastry blender:
   6 tablespoons shortening
Stir in to make soft dough:

2/3 cup milk	4 tablespoons melted butter

Roll out dough and spread with 3 to 4 cups of sliced apples.

Sprinkle with 1/2 cup sugar and some cinnamon.

Roll like a jelly roll and cut in 1 1/2-inch slices (divide so that it makes 12 slices).

Put the slices in the hot syrup.

Bake at 350 degrees till golden brown, about 45 minutes.

—*Betty Grove*

Chocolate Cake

$^3/_4$ cup Hershey's cocoa   2 eggs
$^1/_2$ cup boiling water   2 $^3/_4$ cups all-purpose flour
1 $^2/_3$ cups margarine or butter   1 $^1/_2$ cups sour milk
1 $^3/_4$ cups sugar   1 teaspoon baking powder
1 teaspoon vanilla   1 teaspoon soda

Preheat oven to 350 degrees.

In bowl, add water to cocoa and stir until smooth and set aside.

In separate large bowl, cream sugar and butter, add eggs, and beat all together. Add vanilla and cocoa mixture. Mix all together well.

Alternately add flour and milk, mixing well after each addition. Add baking powder and soda.

Beat by hand three hundred strokes, and pour into two greased 9-inch pans.

Bake cake 30 to 40 minutes or until cake springs back at light touch.

—*George Fitzgerald*

While we were talking about food, I mentioned Junior Bush, whose roast turkey sandwiches had earned praise from my sister's in-laws, Huntingdon natives.

"Oh, *John* Bush?" Betty asked. "He's been in business at this fair for fifty years selling turkey sandwiches and turkey dinners. You can't leave Huntingdon County Fair without stopping by for a sandwich."

"When I have visitors," George said, "I always take them to Bush's. His turkey is legendary. I had the secretary of agriculture here, the state Grange master, the state farm bureau president—and we all ate at Bush's. It's an institution."

On my way to Bush's, I walked through the carnival and counted fourteen rides and as many games. In square feet, however, the whole carnival area was smaller than the livestock barns, which seemed to go on forever.

Owens Hall, a long, turquoise exhibition building, had Grange exhibits in one end and horses and goats in the other. One pony, named Rainbow's Butterscotch, had a sign proclaiming her age as fifty-five. In her career she had been shown hunter seat, saddle, cart, and then halter.

I moved through the dairy barn, the sheep barn, the horse barn, and the longhorn stables. Everywhere there was evidence of 4-H involvement and everywhere the buildings were neat, airy, clean, and well maintained.

After the livestock area, I visited the two commercial buildings, Laney and Neary Halls. Folks in the halls were selling everything from organs to water heaters to gravestones. Lobbying groups had also found their way into these buildings. The Democrats were on one side of the hall while the Republicans occupied the other. Crafts vendors flowed out the door and around the edge of the track to the stadium gates.

I hurried over to the farm museum close to the main gate to see a variety of artifacts from all periods of rural life in Huntingdon County. It was a bit like sorting through the contents of the outbuildings of a five-generation farm. From vehicles to farm equipment to toys and kitchen items, the museum covered the broad scope of rural life.

Finally, I reached Junior Bush's turkey restaurant. He remembered Hazel and John Houser, my sister's in-laws, even knew that Hazel was an Eisenberg. I had a turkey barbecue sandwich and a bowl of snapper soup. He had caught the snappers himself. Everything was delicious, down to the zucchini bread and sticky roll he handed me as I was leaving. "For the road," he said.

The food would not survive the drive, but I had greetings from Junior and a package of Huntingdon County notecards for Hazel and John.

❖ The Huntingdon County Fair runs from Sunday through Saturday the third week of August. From Route 22 North, turn right at the second light. At the first stop, go left onto Fairground Road. The main entrance is one mile on the left. For additional information, write to the Huntingdon County Fair, Huntingdon, PA 16652.

Path Valley
Picnic and Homecoming

Spring Run, Juniata County

Spring Run is a quiet, almost forgotten country town, I thought as I counted the few houses hanging tenaciously on to the four corners at the intersection of Routes 75 and 641. The narrow borders of the town, however, are deceiving. Like so many villages in rural, mountainous sections of our state, town businesses, churches, and social functions are supported by the population from the surrounding woods and farmland, and the community extends far beyond the village borders.

I was returning from another mission when I saw signs advertising the forthcoming Path Valley Picnic and drove up the country lane into Hammonds Grove. I found a simple fairgrounds, a few cinder-block buildings under the shade trees. There had been no effort to landscape, to level the ground, or to alter the charming hilltop.

I walked over the little hilltop and sat for a while that evening while the old grove spoke to me of years of country fairs, picnics, and quiet family reunions. I knew from the facility itself that the Path Valley Picnic would be small yet deeply ingrained in the fabric of life in the Path Valley. I knew that this would be one of the fairs that folks attend each evening for fair food and leisurely conversation.

My quiet reverie that afternoon had not prepared me for the actuality of the fair. When I arrived two weeks later, I barely recognized Spring Run. From the village the whole way up to the fairgrounds, every inch of roadside real estate was occupied by pickup trucks, cars, and vans. There were lawn chairs, coolers, hampers, and even a charcoal grill or two smoking by parking spots. The less fortunate latecomers, and I was one of them, parked in the field beside the lane.

I was not sure what we were all awaiting. Was the president coming? Lady Godiva? I walked up to the top of the lane and took a spot behind six rows of lawn chairs. By 7:30 I had my answer. Far below, seemingly in HO scale from our vantage point, the VFW led the parade, followed by the school band and the Fannett-Metal fire trucks. Slowly, no faster than an eighth-grade bully walks to the principal's office, they crawled down Route 75 and rounded the turn to the fairgrounds.

The parade lasted more than an hour. There were at least a hundred entries: bands, percussion bands, fire companies, antique cars and tractors, floats, twirling units, dance schools, kids on ponies, tractor trailer trucks, new cars and trucks, a Shriners' unit in midget cars, a log truck, beauty queens, a World War II–vintage Jeep.

The floats ranged from clever to ingenious to funny. There was a harvest scene with the caption, "Let Us Give Thanks." Two old people getting a loan from the Orrstown Bank advertised the longevity of the business. A church had mounted Daniel in the lions' den, and on another float Fred Flintstone put the cat out repeatedly. Smokey the Bear waved from the Rosenberry Lumber Company's float, and a live calf advertised a local dairy. There was even a Christmas tree from Elliott's Nursery. Each float had taken a great deal of effort, and the crowd cheered, waved, and applauded its appreciation.

Evening shifted into twilight, and as the last entries rounded the bend at the top of the hill, night settled over Path Valley. Lights from the

Montgomery Pie

Top Part:

1 cup flour	1 cup sugar
1 teaspoon baking powder	1 egg
dash salt	$^1/_2$ cup milk
$^1/_4$ cup butter	

Sift flour, baking powder, and salt together and set aside. Cream butter in a large mixing bowl. Gradually add sugar; beat well until light and fluffy. Add egg, beating well. Add sifted ingredients alternately with milk. Once all is mixed, set aside.

Bottom Part:

1 cup sugar	$^1/_2$ cup hot water
grated rind and juice of 1 lemon	$^1/_2$ cup light molasses
dash salt	unbaked 9-inch pie shell
1 egg	

Combine lemon rind, lemon juice, and sugar. Add egg, then molasses and hot water; blend well. Cool. Pour into pie shell. Drop top part onto bottom layer by spoonfuls. Bake for 50 to 55 minutes at 350 degrees.

—*Adapted from Fannett-Metal Volunteer Fire Company #12 cookbook*

rides and concessions snapped on, luring the crowds to the attractions in the grove of trees. The music on the stage began as soon as the parade disbanded. A popular local group was performing, and many of the lawn chairs along the parade route moved in that direction as the last fire truck passed the bend.

Violet Cowan, a Fannettsburg resident, took me on a tour of the picnic.

"I usually come to the picnic," she told me. "It's like a homecoming. You see everyone you haven't seen all year long. In the olden days, everyone brought a picnic basket from home and this is where they gathered—I guess it hasn't changed all that much, has it?"

There was definitely a homecoming atmosphere that night in Hammonds Grove. Judging from the crowd, everyone who ever lived there, been related to someone who lived there, or passed through town once or twice had come. There was hardly room to walk.

I bought a barbecued chicken dinner from the fire company after a long wait. As soon as I finished eating, I vacated my seat at the picnic table, embarrassed to have monopolized one seat so long.

There were six rides. Other than the Ferris wheel, most of them were for younger kids. The picnic also featured twenty games, many of them homemade by local civic organizations. In addition to the fire company's chicken dinners, the Fannett-Metal Fire Police were selling funnel cakes, and the Booster club was running a french fry booth. There were also peanuts, sandwiches, and ice cream. It was refreshing to think that the profits would funnel back into the community.

I walked through the flea market before I left. When I rounded the bend onto Route 75 that night, I looked back to the Path Valley Picnic and chuckled at my mistaken speculations. Spring Run had never been a forgotten town after all, and like the cactus flower, it blooms spectacularly once a year.

❖ The Path Valley Picnic and Homecoming is held the third Wednesday, Thursday, Friday, and Saturday of August. With the exception of Saturday, when events begin at 8 A.M., events are scheduled for evenings only. In addition to Thursday night's parade and barbecued chicken, there is an ox roast on Friday night, and both chicken and ox sandwiches on Saturday night. There is entertainment each night. The picnic is held at Hammonds Grove on Route 75 one mile north of Route 641. Admission, parking, and entertainment are free, but there is a fee for rides. For more information, call the Fannett-Metal Fire Company at 717-349-2212.

Montour DeLong Community Fair

Washingtonville, Montour County

I arrived in Washingtonville on a dreamy late-summer afternoon. Aside from the gingerbread trim remaining on a few houses, the town was nondescript, just a dusty little byway indistinguishable from scores of other rural communities across the state. It seemed the kind of town whose residents say they are from the closest large town. In truth, I had no desire to relocate there, myself.

I had called my friend and colleague Mark Hagenbuch, a Washingtonville native, before my trip. Mark had told me about Frank DeLong, inventor of the bobby pin. In the 1920s, when fashion turned to bobbed hair, his invention held shorter coiffs in place better than hairpins, those

U-shaped wires suitable for mountains of Victorian-era hair. In the 1890s DeLong had also improved the hook-and-eye clothing fastener.

There was, Mark told me, a DeLong museum in town that owned the flight helmet Charles Lindbergh wore on his trans-Atlantic flight. Lindbergh had thrown it out to the crowd when he arrived in France and DeLong had purchased it from the man who had caught it, at an enormous price.

In twenty minutes I located DeLong's home, his museum, and the school that he built for the town. At each stop, I photographed the building, and then I drove to the fair.

It was at the fair that I began to feel just a little envious of the folks who lived there on the surrounding hills, just a little homesick for a less complicated life. There were a few folks sitting in the picnic pavilion and a few more with their sheep and cattle in the livestock barns. The rides were still and silent; the food stands and games were shuttered. Ponies were grazing on the hillside. Only an occasional bleat from the sheep or the gentle grumble of the cattle interrupted the afternoon hush.

I walked through one display building, unhurried and unheeded. Then, with time in my pocket, I visited the two barns, nodding hellos to the exhibitors. I noted the menus at the various food stands. There were the expected hot dogs, hamburgers, fries, and hot sausages, plus potato pancakes and ice cream. Finally, I walked into the firehouse, where the baked goods and crafts were displayed. I started looking for prize winners, but the noisy activity in the kitchen distracted me. While the rest of the Montour DeLong Community Fair enjoyed its afternoon siesta, Virginia Klein, head cook, had the kitchen staff hopping.

She wiped her hands on a tea towel and dropped her apron on the counter as she came out to chat.

"I've lived here all my life," she told me. "Do you want my address? Jacksonville, Florida. I'm down there seven months of the year. My oldest daughter lives there and I live with her. I come back for the fair. I have five children here I like to come back to see. Plus, I see so many people I know—people I ordinarily don't get to see. I drove school bus for twenty-five years. I know most everyone."

We talked about the exhibits. "Only people in parts of northern Northumberland County, the lower part of Columbia County, and all of Montour County may exhibit here. I entered twenty items and I won with every one of them, not first prize on every one, but I did have seven firsts.

"I entered eight pies—all different kinds. I took a first for a peach, blueberry, and cherry pie. When I was done baking, I had raisin filling,

Sticky Buns

1 yellow Duncan Hines cake
   mix (no pudding, no butter)
2 packets Fleischman's yeast
   (rapid rise)

5 cups flour
1 $^1/_2$ cups hot water

Mix together and let rise until double in a greased bowl. Roll it out. Spread with butter, brown sugar, and cinnamon. Roll up, jelly-roll style. Slice about 1 $^1/_2$ to 2 inches thick. Lay down flat in a pan so that they do not touch. Let rise till double. Meanwhile, melt one stick of butter, 4 tablespoons brown sugar, and 4 tablespoons white Karo. Spoon over buns.

   Bake at 375 degrees for 25 minutes.

—*Virginia Klein*

cherry filling, and the mixed-fruit filling left. I mixed them all together and won a first for a mixed-fruit, two-crust pie.

"We take all of the Hershey's cocoa entries, the apple pie entries, and the decorated cake entries and auction them off to benefit Camp Drozd, a camp for kids who have serious health problems.

"I'll give you the recipe for my sticky buns. I must have made about a million by now. I've sent them all over the country. This morning I made two batches for the help."

She disappeared for a moment and returned with a fat sticky bun and a cup of coffee for each of us.

Soon it was suppertime. Although the kitchen's menu that night was fish, baked macaroni and cheese, and stewed tomatoes, the roast beef dinner the night before had been rained out and Virginia was featuring a second choice, hot beef sandwiches, mashed potatoes, and gravy, with pepper slaw and applesauce on the side. I chose the alternate, but Virginia also loaded my plate with macaroni and cheese and threw in a piece of pie as well. Ken and Jeannette Hauck joined me at my table. At thirty or so, they were the youngest people in the crowd.

"They're mostly local, these people," Ken said. "Most of them come to the fair every night, eat dinner, sit around and chew the fat, and then go home to their farms."

The snatches of conversation I overheard around me confirmed what he told me.

"Do you need any sweet corn?"

"I canned thirty quarts of tomatoes today."

"You find out what was wrong with that cow of yours?"

"How much hay did you get in?"

It was the talk of good people—honest, hard-working people—and the web of conversation drew me in. I lingered a long time at the Montour DeLong Community Fair that evening. The sapphire sky turned to heathery lavender and then to smoky gray. Lights from neighboring farms twinkled on the hillsides. The carnival came to life and the Mud Flaps began their show down at the tractor-pull track, and still I stayed on, reluctant to leave.

❖ The Montour DeLong Community Fair is as simple and quaint as a DeLong bobby pin. It is held from Saturday to Saturday, the third week of August, but the first Saturday is a 4-H function and Sunday is a 7 P.M. vesper service. Dinners are served beginning at 4, Monday through Saturday. There is entertainment every night. Admission, parking, and entertainment are free.

From I-80, take 54 West 8 miles to the blinker. Take Route 254 West and go .7 mile to fair on left. For more information, write to the Montour DeLong Community Fair, P.O. Box 11, Washingtonville, PA 17884, or call 717-437-2178.

Middletown Grange Fair

Wrightstown, Bucks County

The Middletown Grange Fair is not held in Middletown. Instead, it is held fifteen miles away in Wrightstown. At one time the fair had been held on a farm in Middletown. When the Grange finally bought a property in Wrightstown in the 1960s, no one felt the need to change the fair's name, and the old name stuck, just as houses are often known by the names of the families who occupied them years earlier rather than by the names of their present owners.

At first it seemed a little odd to be going to a Grange fair in Bucks County, so close to Philadelphia. The fair, however, though not an ancient one, predated the condos and housing developments that now dominate the landscape. I had also underestimated Bucks County's recalcitrant hold on the countryside and country lifestyle. Anything that had tradition or country roots in an area sharing an uneasy alliance with the growing city would be preserved.

To my surprise, the Middletown Grange Fair, though compact, held all of the attractions of any other country fair. I had expected a large carnival area with a token sampling of country exhibits, produce, home products, and livestock. Instead, there were two large exhibit halls containing produce and home products. The first hall I entered had vegetables displayed on long tables. There was a huge display of fine needlework, the best I had seen anywhere. Tiffany's window "View from Oyster Bay" was recreated in counted cross-stitch. There were needlework house portraits, landscapes, oriental art, samplers, a carousel horse, and a World War II B-17 fighter plane. In the Christmas crafts exhibits, one of the blue-ribbon entries was a needlepoint crèche, delicate and beautifully detailed. All these shared the hall with canned foods, baked goods, and fine art. At the end of the hall, Grange members were selling sugar cookies to benefit the scholarship fund.

At noon that day, twelve women were sitting in front of the Charles D. Lownes Dining Hall shucking corn for the barbecued chicken dinners that evening. The chicken barbecue, served with sweet corn, potatoes, tomatoes, cranberry jelly, a roll, butter, and a choice of beverages, was advertised as "a favorite for 40 years!"

Inside, head cook Marian Lownes from Newtown was sitting with her feet propped up.

"I'm the woman who died yesterday!" she said as she introduced herself. "We serve about fourteen hundred a night for three nights. I made bags out of lace curtains, and we put the corn in them and drop them into the water. After the water boils it's about ten minutes' cooking time. The girls keep rotating the bags.

"We have a commercial potato peeler—that's the foaming thing over there at the end. Then we eye them and cut them up by hand. We use about five hundred pounds of potatoes a night. That's why I have tape on my finger—I'll get a blister if I don't. By the end of the day, the tape wears off.

"I use about thirty pounds of butter a day for the potatoes and the chicken. I have eight big pots to cook the potatoes in, so I do them in shifts."

When I asked her about her staff she said, "All volunteer. What some folks will do for a free chicken dinner is beyond me."

From Marian I heard the now-familiar story of family involvement.

"You'll see my grandfather's name on the dining room. He was the fair chairman until he passed away. Uncle Charlie is in charge of the chickens—ordering, bringing them in, barbecuing them, and organizing his crew. Uncle Bill wires and lights the tents. My dad, Harold, is in

Blue-Ribbon Tomato Marmalade

1 quart tomatoes   1 good-size lemon
1 pound sugar (2 cups)

Use large tomatoes that are red and firm but not so ripe as to be soft. To a quart of tomatoes use 1 pound of white sugar (1 $^1/_2$ pounds if small tomatoes). Peel and quarter tomatoes and remove seeds, put tomatoes and lemon on to boil slowly until the mixture begins to thicken, then add sugar and boil to the consistency of jam. Seal while hot.

—*Dorothy Gabel, Perkasie*

Barbecued Chicken Sauce

2 quarts water   1 $^1/_2$ pounds butter
2 quarts cider vinegar $^1/_4$ cup salt

Cook until the butter is melted. Put it in sprayers and spray it on the chicken as it cooks.

—*Middletown Grange Fair*

charge of the livestock buildings and the paperwork. All three brothers are retired dairy farmers. They sold the farm and raised a crop of houses, the best cash crop we ever had."

She reeled off the chicken barbecue recipe before we said good-bye.

The five commercial tents were a little more upscale than those tents at rural fairs. Vendors displayed furniture, computers, jewelry, dried fruits, T-shirts, and candy. They also advertised private schools, nursery schools, and private nursing organizations. Other tents contained automobiles, farm equipment, potbellied pigs, herb vinegars, iron works, and children's crafts. There were several tents advertising haunted hayrides, one of them with a clever maze built of hay bales.

In many of the country fairs I had attended, the livestock was of interest mostly to the exhibitors themselves and their families. Here, young couples and their small children paid rapt attention to the livestock competition. Fathers carried three-year-olds through the barns, stopping to pet cattle and sheep. The children were fascinated by the displays so alien to their suburban lives.

The carnival area, with ten rides and three games, did not draw as big a crowd as the pedal-power tractor pull. Folks at Wrightstown, it seemed, had come to see country.

The fair was lovely and festive and, I realized, served a purpose just a little different from the country fairs in more rural areas. For urban and suburban families, it was a learning experience, a chance to visit the country in an easy day's outing. Although not the gathering place that many country fairs have always been, the Middletown Grange Fair is also important to the community it serves. One could not help but say "Bravo!" to the Bucks County farmers.

❖ The Middletown Grange Fair runs from Thursday to Saturday the third week of August. From Route 413 turn onto Penns Park Road. The fairgrounds is about two hundred yards on the left. For more information, write to the Middletown Grange Fair, Penns Park Road, Wrightstown, PA 18940.

Harford Fair

Harford, Susquehanna County

I had neglected to pack my duck boots. Although the rain stopped before I got off I-81 at the Harford exit, the parking lot was a swamp, and soon I wished I had boots for the VW as well. She sashayed sweetly toward a van and when I stopped to back up, the tires spun and sang happy little foul-weather songs. Like it or not, she was staying where she was, the back end a little skewed toward the van. My first foot out of the car door was swallowed up to the ankle. Water rushed into my sneaker. With no other choice, the second foot followed the first to the same fate.

At my first stop, the fair office, president Kenneth Adams directed me to Prudence Clark, fair historian, in the log cabin nearby. Miss Clark, a retired teacher, was presiding over an extensive collection of fair artifacts and memorabilia when I arrived. We had just gotten through introductions when one of her former students appeared.

"Do you remember me, Miss Clark?" he asked.

She did, and after a little catching up, the middle-aged man departed. She called after him, "Keep your feet dry. Do you have your boots on?"

He lifted one foot obligingly. "Yes I do. That's one thing you learn as a farmer, when to wear your boots!"

Miss Clark turned to me, averting her eyes from the two mudballs at the ends of my legs. Just a half hour earlier, they had been a new pair of Nikes.

"We never cancel for the weather. In Harford this is typical fair weather. Look over here," she said, leading me to a case where six carved, wooden boots were displayed. A sign by the carvings proclaimed, "I survived the mud—1990."

"The weather was terrible in 1990," she explained. "Cars got stuck in the mud and had to be pulled out. Terrible! Mr. Adams got a hundred thirty loads of gravel and all of the sawdust the mills could give us. People keep coming—in new sneakers.

"These wooden boots, carved from a piece of the log cabin built on the fairgrounds in 1890, commemorate not only the bicentennial of the town, but also the year of the mud."

Listening to Miss Clark, one learns pretty quickly that in Harford, the history of the fair is considered an important part of the larger history of the community. Rather than an isolated patch in the quilt top of town history, it is a thread that runs the length of the fabric. When Miss Clark tells her history, she skillfully weaves the two together, town and fair, using artifacts from the museum to illustrate her talk.

Through her, I learned of the Nine Partners ("Capital N, capital P, and genuflect when you say it") who came to the wilderness from Massachusetts in 1790 to found this community. I learned that until the school built an auditorium in 1936, the only stage in town belonged to the Independent Order of the Odd Fellows—all school and town productions were held in the Odd Fellows' Hall. I also learned that when the fair started in 1858, nineteen states had not yet joined the Union, and that the Republican booth close to the center of the fairground had begun life as the fair's band shell. The earliest fair photographs, 1870, show the band shell. Prudence Clark showed me the canvas backdrop from the Odd Fellows' Hall, a black iron pot formerly owned by one of the Nine Partners, original fair china, and a friendship quilt completed in 1924. Before I left, she wrote down her name and address in her fine copperplate hand and asked for a copy of the book. As I was leaving, she called after me, "Good luck! Stay dry!"

There was a great deal to see at the Harford Fair. In addition to the large carnival area featuring a dozen rides and thirty-five games, there was a large agricultural exhibit area. One building was shared by the homemaking exhibits and the fine-arts displays. In the huge arena a draft horse show was in progress. Entertainment was scheduled throughout the week.

I visited a schoolhouse on the grounds filled with children's art. I also visited a church bazaar held in the centennial log cabin. There, an embroidered sign above the fireplace read, "May this cabin stand a hun-

New England Clam Chowder

3 7-ounce cans minced clams   2 cups raw potatoes, cubed
$1/4$ pound salt pork or bacon,   3 tablespoons butter
   minced   2 cups cream
1 chopped onion   2 cups milk
3 tablespoons flour   parsley, salt, black pepper,
1 cup of water   herbs to taste

Dice pork or bacon and sauté over low heat until crisp. Add onion
and cook until transparent. Sprinkle flour over mixture. Add juice
from clams and 1 cup water. Add potatoes; simmer until tender.
Add clams and butter, and heat to boiling. Add milk and cream
and reheat, but do not boil. Add seasonings. Remove from heat and
let sit $1/2$ to 1 hour. Reheat to serve.

dred years. May the tempest spare it, the lightning not strike it. To the
memory of the Nine let it stand, and pass down into history, to live
through all time. Dedication ceremony 1890."

I kept that thought and savored it over dinner at the fair dining hall.
The Congregationalists featured a pasta buffet that night, and other
churches would serve meals throughout the week. I looked up while I was
eating and noted the original cedar shake roof under the tin and thought
about the days of monogrammed Harford Fair China, and the days long
before when the Nine Partners blazed a trail into the wilderness.

I drove into the village of Harford that afternoon before I left the
area. It is a tiny village, as New England in flavor as a bowl of clam chowder. Tiny white story-and-a-half Capes line the streets. The Odd Fellows
hall still stands in the center of things, though it looks a little down in
the heels. There is a magnificent Greek revival mansion by the Odd Fellows hall, and an open house that afternoon allowed me to appease my
curiosity about the interior. I ended my visit at the beautiful Congrega-
tional church on the hill with its mossy graveyard.

❖ The Harford Fair is held Monday through Saturday, the third week
of August. Harford is off exit 65 of I-81. Take Route 547 South 1 mile to
the stop sign. Turn right on Fair Hill Road, .4 mile to the fairgrounds. For
more information, write to the Harford Fair, R.R. 1, Box 4, Kingsley, PA
18826, or call 717-289-4405 year-round or 717-434-2655 during fair
week.

Centre County Grange Fair and Encampment

Centre Hall, Centre County

Beatrice and Willard Weber were sitting on the front porch visiting with their daughter, Barbara Forbes from Pottstown, when my mother and I stopped to say hello that summer evening. It was not long before Willard offered us chairs on the porch and we were conversing like old friends. The whole neighborhood seemed to be out that evening. Passersby hollered hellos from the street and greetings were exchanged warmly. A few stragglers like us ended up on the porch with the Weber family looking for a breather on the hot August evening, a little gossip, or simply the pleasantries of good friends and neighbors. The woman next door came over to borrow a cup of flour, and Beatrice went to her kitchen. It could have been any summer evening in any small town across the state, but it was the Centre Hall Grange Fair and Encampment and we were sitting in front of a fourteen-by-fourteen-foot green army tent.

"The fair began in 1874," Beatrice told me. "It was a basket picnic on the Centre Hall Mountain, a one-day affair. Then Leonard Rhone established the Grange, and the picnickers came down off the mountain. Then families started to bring tents. They brought cookstoves. From there, it just kept growing."

Now, deep into its second century, the week-long Centre Hall Grange Fair, thought to be the last tent encampment fair surviving in this country, sprawls out on a 212-acre fairground surrounded by grazing cattle from the Penns Valley's many farms. A crop of white exhibition buildings and livestock barns has grown up under the grove of trees, and once a year about a thousand tents appear surrounded by as many campers and trailers.

Landing a tent site at Centre Hall is not an easy thing. Spots on the list are jealously guarded, handed down through families, generation after generation.

"We've had a tent here since 1952," Beatrice told us. "We haven't always had this location, but you can get the same location each year if you want it. As long as I can remember, we've come to the fair. I came with my parents."

Pointing to his daughter, Willard said, "She came here first when she was five weeks old. For her first fair, she slept in her grandmother's clothes basket."

Although cherished by their tenants, the tents are far from elaborate. In recent years underground wiring has improved the standard of living, and Willard pointed out a four-outlet electrical box behind the refrigerator. One might be lucky enough to be camped next to a water spigot, but there are no showers on the grounds.

The Centre Hall Grange campers customize their dwellings with surprising results. For an additional fee, campers can have asphalt front porches laid. Tarps soon follow, then ingenious riggings and trimmings. Porch posts, latticework, strings of lanterns, and hanging plants finish off the new additions. Occasionally campers add a smaller tent in the back for a kitchen.

The furnishings vary from Spartan to elaborate, mostly the latter. We saw tents outfitted with oriental rugs, antique brass beds, wicker rockers. There were hide-a-beds galore, some fine drop-leaf tables, and more than a few sets of plank-bottomed chairs.

When I wondered aloud about the inconvenience of moving all this paraphernalia in for a little more than a week, Willard explained, "They have buildings here to store things for the campers from year to year. We don't take our fair refrigerator home with us; we leave it here. You'll hear the campers talk about their fair refrigerators, their fair beds, their fair stoves, and so on. What they mean is that they have this stuff for use only during the fair, and it's left here all winter."

"That becomes part of the tradition," Beatrice added. "Your fair bed may have been used by your grandparents at the fair."

Since this is a Grange fair and Granges are local farming organizations, many of the campers are from nearby. They leave to do farm chores, returning in the evening after the milking is done and the cattle fed and bedded down for the night. For many, this is the family vacation. For the younger set, it means a never-ending carnival at the front door, new friendships, visits with friends from years before, a safe place to wander just a little freer of parental scrutiny than usual, and no chores.

It is a big fair with agricultural exhibits, livestock, produce, and home products on display. There is entertainment each night in the grandstand, and so many food choices that even the most jaded gourmand would be satisfied. Restaurants are set up all over the grounds, serving fries and burgers, homemade soups in bread bowls, and Pennsylvania Dutch favorites like ham pot pie and pig stomach. A huge carnival area with fifteen rides and countless games draws all age groups.

As evening falls on the tent village, lights come on and residents move to their porches. Grandparents watch pajama-clad toddlers while

Beatrice Weber's Heartsafe Pie Crust

2 cups flour   2 tablespoons milk
$^2/_3$ cup corn oil or olive oil $^1/_4$ cup ice water

Mix together and roll out between two sheets of wax paper. The dough will be hard to work with. For bottom crust remove top wax paper. Invert the pie pan over the crust and flip over. For the top crust, remove top wax paper. Pick up the bottom paper. Flip over onto top of pie.

Mock Pig Stomach

1 $^1/_2$ pounds bulk pork sausage   1 cup dried cabbage
6 potatoes, diced $^1/_2$ teaspoon salt
2 slices bread, cubed   dash pepper
1 stem celery, diced

Toss together with hands. Place in casserole dish. Bake at 350 degrees for 1 hour and 15 minutes.

parents visit the midway or take in the grandstand entertainment. There is hushed conversation and muted laughter. From somewhere deep in the village the smell of brewing coffee finds its way between the rows of tents and mingles with the carnival smells beyond.

Here and there, a family reunion is held around a tent. Parents greet family members arriving for the weekend and wave good-bye to the departing shift. In the tent encampment at Centre Hall, family tradition glows as brightly as the strings of lanterns hanging over the tent flap doorways.

❖ The Centre Hall Grange Fair and Encampment begins the weekend before Labor Day and runs through the Friday of Labor Day Weekend. Centre Hall is located midway between I-80 and Route 322. The fair is a block west of the main drag. For more information, write to Centre County Grange Fair, P.O. Box 271, Centre Hall, PA 16828.

Buchanan Valley Picnic

Orrtanna, Adams County

Adams County is as pretty as a Currier and Ives print. Here and there a stone farmhouse shares a hilltop with a red barn, but most of the rolling hills and quiet valleys are covered by rows of fruit trees. This is orchard country.

In Adams County, autumn tucks the hills in for their winter sleep under a Victorian crazy quilt pieced from russet, scarlet, and amber velvet. Winter follows, the rows of trees embroidered in black on a white down comforter. In spring, the orchards awaken in an explosion of pinks and greens, and summer follows, rich and wanton in waxy foliage and a progression of fruit.

On the fourth Saturday of August, the apples of Adams County were ripening in the sun as I drove to the historic St. Ignatius Loyola Catholic Church, the White Squaw Mission, for the Buchanan Valley Picnic. The little church sits in one of the prettiest spots in the county, a hillside overlooking a tiny valley. The church itself is country-elegant. Built in 1817, it was altered later with a Gothic bell tower, and again with a modern addition. None of that mars its charm. It is an architectural jewel. The other buildings on the property—the rectory, the shingled activities hall, and the kitchen and screened dining hall—sparkle under fresh yellow paint.

There is a statue of a young woman in the courtyard. Dressed simply, a cloak or blanket around her shoulders, her hair in braids, she stares out across the valley, across the years. She is Mary Jemison, the White Woman of the Genesee. Born at sea in 1743 to Irish immigrants, she settled with her family on a farm close to the church. In 1758, a raiding party of French soldiers and Shawnee braves attacked the family. Two boys escaped; Mary watched the Indians clean and dry the scalps of the rest of her family.

A Seneca family adopted the young girl and took her to their home on the Ohio River. She was treated well, and in time she married a brave from the Delaware tribe. Upon his death, she married a chief and raised a family in the Genesee Valley of Western New York. Her wealth grew, and eventually she became one of the most considerable landowners in the state. Although she lived in a log cabin most of her years, she refused to adopt other white customs and never returned to white civilization.

Two and a half centuries had passed between the day of the Jemison massacre and the one when I arrived at the Buchanan Valley Picnic. The only shrieks I heard that day were shrieks of delight, and any pain was quickly relieved by unloosening the belt a notch or two.

"The picnic began about a hundred years ago as a way to make money for the parish," Paul Hall, general chairman, told me. "It was harvest season, and people brought what they could spare.

Bread and Butter Pickles

2 or 3 dozen pickling cucumbers	1 teaspoon celery seed
5 or 6 onions	1 teaspoon mustard seed
salt	pinch black pepper
1 ¹/₂ cups vinegar	1 tablespoon turmeric
2 cups white sugar	pinch alum

Slice cukes and onions, combine, and add salt and work through; allow to stand for ¹/₂ hour. Combine vinegar and sugar; boil for 5 minutes. Add remaining ingredients to vinegar and sugar. Drain pickles and onions and add to liquid. Boil for 10 minutes or until you can run a broom splint into them.

—*Mary Ellen Hall*

Potato Salad

24 potatoes	10 hard-boiled eggs,
4 cups chopped celery	chopped
3 cups chopped onion	2 tablespoons parsley flakes

Peel potatoes. Cook in salted water till done, but not soft. Do not overcook. When cool, dice potatoes. Add chopped celery, onions, and eggs. Add parsley flakes. Salt and pepper to taste.
Mix with dressing:

4 cups sugar	6 cups water
1 cup flour	¹/₂ pound margarine,
6 eggs	melted
1 cup prepared mustard	2 tablespoons salt
2 cups vinegar	

Mix sugar, flour, and salt together. Add eggs and mustard. Stir together. Add vinegar and water. Mix till well blended. Cook on medium heat till thick. Can be stored in refrigerator for later use.

—*Anna Hall*

Cucumbers and Onions

24 cucumbers   3 tablespoons salt
4 large onions
Wash cucumbers. Slice on slicers; also slice the onions. Sprinkle
with salt. Put into containers. Cover with dressing:
2 cups water   4 cups vinegar
8 cups sugar
Mix together until sugar is dissolved. Pour over cucumbers.

—Anna Hall

Pepper Slaw

6 large heads cabbage   5 cups chopped red and
3 tablespoons salt   green peppers
2 tablespoons celery seed
Grate cabbage and sprinkle with salt. Mix and squeeze cabbage
with hands. Add celery seed and chopped peppers. Mix all
together. Add dressing:
12 cups sugar   4 cups water
8 cups white vinegar
Mix all together in large cook pot. Bring to boil. Then simmer 5
minutes. Cool. Store in refrigerator till ready for use.

—Anna Hall

"We serve about sixteen hundred to eighteen hundred meals. We come over here Thursday morning at two and put gas under the chicken kettles. We did one thousand two hundred and thirty-five pounds of chicken this year. We cook it, cool it, and pick it off the bone. Our ham we slice and serve cold. Our corn is fresh, just cut off the cob. Most of our vegetables are fresh, except the butter beans. The potatoes are fresh. We peeled them last night. Six hundred pounds should feed seventeen hundred people. My sister and I go over our list of donors to see what we have to buy. We buy the pie filling and take it to volunteers to bake the pies. This is all from scratch. All the pickles, relishes, coleslaw, potato salad, pickled eggs, and macaroni salad are from volunteers, too."

The screened dining pavilion seats about 140 guests. Folks are seated by table after a short wait in line. The food is served family style, and the meal is huge. Our table was served heaping plates and bowls of ham, chicken, corn, butter beans, pepper slaw, sliced tomatoes, mashed pota-toes and gravy, potato salad, macaroni salad, applesauce, pickled eggs, bread-and-butter pickles, fresh cucumbers and onions, cranberry sauce, green beans, and bread and butter. There was a choice of beverages. When our table quieted down and plates were unloaded and forks uncocked, the attentive serving staff offered a choice of desserts.

I was seated with Jeanie Troxell and George Cole and Violet and Ray Flickinger. Talk turned to Jeanie and George's pending wedding.

Ray told them, "Well, I hope you make out as well as we did. This is fifty years for us. The day I got married I baled hay in the morning, washed two cars that afternoon."

"It was so hot," Violet chimed in, "that the knot in his tie was soaked through."

Our conversation turned to building homes, redoing old houses, fruit farming, and piano lessons. Such is the way of a family-style dinner. The conversation is the best sauce for the meal.

There were other foods offered on the grounds, but I felt that only a fool would forgo the chicken dinner. Six games were set up, including ring toss, a paddle wheel, bingo, and a fish bowl. Most of the games had cash prizes, but prizes for one were baskets of fresh fruits and vegetables donated by farmers. Later, I was told, pies and cakes left over from the kitchen would be used as prizes too.

There were kids on swings, folks sitting on benches in the shade. Other groups of people stood around talking. The pace was leisurely, the feeling inviting.

I walked over to the church and sat for a while in the quiet sanctuary. The afternoon sunlight on the stained glass windows set the room on fire, and I watched the shadows move along the wall as evening matured.

Before I left, I visited the statue of Mary Jemison, the white squaw, trying to see the valley through her eyes. And then I drove off through Adams County, taking every side road I could find, thankful for the opportunity to live in such a beautiful area, so richly steeped in history.

❖ The Buchanan Valley Picnic is held the fourth Saturday of August. It is halfway between Chambersburg and Gettysburg. Follow signs off Route 30 at Route 234. For more information, write to the St. Ignatius Loyola Church, 1095 Church Road, Orrtanna, PA 17353-9766, or call 717-677-8012.

Perry County Fair

Newport, Perry County

There are few places more pleasant than a country fairgrounds early on a summer morning, especially at summer's crest, before it ebbs toward autumn. There is a gentle hush and an unruffled calm before the crowds arrive, before the sun turns morning mist to scalding steam.

When I arrived at the Perry County Fair just outside of Newport, the sun had already caught the mist, lighting it with the soft glow of a frosted shade on a kerosene lamp. Man and beast alike moved in slow motion that morning. The lowing of the cattle, the bleating of the sheep, and the metallic clink of horseshoes hitting stakes at the horseshoe pit on the hill above the entrance gate marred the silence, but they were far off and muted.

The smells of the fair had barely awakened when I slung my daypack over my shoulder and went out to explore. From somewhere deep in the fair a hint of coffee joined hands with the ghostly promise of frying bacon and wandered about the fairgrounds. The savor of simmering beef and tomatoes and onion joined them and then ambled off on its own, appearing and reappearing around corners of buildings. The smells of the livestock barns, of cattle and sheep and horses and hay and burnished leather, sent out emissaries and, finding no resistance, returned to the barns. Dew and dust danced and whirled over the empty grounds.

I walked over to the carnival area that morning. It was more than respectable, with thirteen rides for all ages and as many games. In the early morning light, however, the rides were closed and the games were shuttered. A carnival is a nocturnal creature. Though glittering, glamorous, and gay at night, seen in the uncompromising light of morning it is pallid and threadbare, a little like stage costumes without the support of theatrical lighting.

I was working on my notes at a picnic table when Annie Campbell, fair secretary, sat down and put a cup of coffee in front of me. "So, what are you writing?" she asked. I liked her immediately. Her practical, no-nonsense manner appealed to my own Perry County heritage. After all, my great-great-grandfather was Alexander T. Kennedy, who settled Kennedy's Valley, just over the hill from the fairgrounds.

From her I learned that the original Perry County Fair had disbanded after World War II. The Pomona Grange picked up the pieces in 1970 and reestablished the Perry County tradition. This did not surprise me.

Although only eight fairs in the state retained the Grange in their names, I had found in my travels that the Granges of Pennsylvania carried much of the burden of fair making silently and without due respect. Find a fair, look for a Grange.

She explained the term *Pomona Grange*. Six subordinate Granges make up a Pomona. A Pomona contains all of the Granges in a county. When counties do not have enough Granges to make a Pomona, several counties may go together. That explained the Pomona Grange at Jefferson County Fair, at Huntingdon County Fair, and here in Perry County.

While we talked that morning, I learned that the Perry County Fair owns thirty-one acres and leases ten more for parking. It is a Class-A fair, subsidized by the state Department of Agriculture.

Then Annie interviewed me. When she found out where I taught, she said, "I thought I'd heard your name before. You had my great-nephew, Tommy Hand, in class."

I had lunch at the Oliver Grange's stand that day. The beef and tomato and onion smell that morning materialized into Jerry Gabel's Swiss steak, rice pilaf, and succotash dinner, served with a roll and butter and beverage.

I walked through the agricultural and home products displays before I

Whoopie Pies

1 cup shortening	4 cups flour
2 cups sugar	2 teaspoons baking soda
2 egg yolks	2 teaspoons vanilla
2 whole eggs	1 cup sour milk
1 cup cocoa	1 cup hot water
$1/2$ teaspoon salt	

Mix first four ingredients. Add other ingredients. Drop by spoonfuls on cookie sheets. Bake at 450 degrees for 5 minutes.

Filling:

2 egg whites, unbeaten	4 teaspoons milk
1 teaspoon vanilla	$1 1/2$ cups shortening
4 teaspoons flour	1 box powdered sugar
2 teaspoons powdered sugar	

Beat first six ingredients until smooth and fluffy. Add box of powdered sugar and beat. Spread between two cookies.

—*Annie Campbell*

Swiss Steak

....

2 pounds round steak, 1 inch thick	2 small sliced onions
$^1/_3$ cup flour	1-pound can tomatoes or sauce
1 $^1/_2$ teaspoons salt	1 teaspoon Worcestershire sauce
$^1/_4$ teaspoon pepper	
$^1/_4$ cup oil	

Trim fat from meat and cut into serving-size pieces. Mix flour, salt, and pepper together and pound into both sides of steak. Brown both sides in oil in a skillet. Place in a baking dish, cover with onion slices and tomatoes or sauce mixed with Worcestershire sauce, and bake 2 to 2 $^1/_2$ hours at 325 to 350 degrees, until fork tender.

—*Jerry Gabel*

---

left. Though not as large as some of the really big county fairs, the Perry County Fair has nothing to be ashamed of. It is country at its most honest. There are pony races, a horse show of some consequence, and many agricultural entries. The nightly entertainment on the stage is mostly homegrown.

❖ The Perry County Fair runs during the third full week of August. From the intersection of Routes 849 and 34 in Newport, take Fourth Street north 1.2 miles to Fairground Road. Go left. The fairgrounds is a stone's throw on the right. For more information, write to the Perry County Community Fair, Perry County Extension Office, P.O. Box 127, New Bloomfield, PA 17068.

Corn Festival

Shippensburg, Cumberland County

By 10 on the morning of Shippensburg's Corn Festival, temperatures had sailed into the nineties. The sun had evaporated the haze that hung over the valley earlier that morning, adding its moisture to a humidity level that was already cresting at flood stage. At the intersection of King and Prince Streets, a dike of yellow sawhorses and two jovial police officers protected the town from a surging tidal wave of Corn Festival shoppers,

---

Corn Fritters

1 $1/_2$ cups flour   2 eggs
1 $1/_2$ teaspoons baking powder   2 teaspoons Crisco, melted
$1/_2$ teaspoon salt   1 cup drained canned corn
$1/_2$ cup milk
Mix dry ingredients; also milk, eggs, and corn. Mix well. Fry on hot
griddle.

—*Elma Shunk*

---

continually fed from all directions into the center of town. Before I could
reconsider, I took a deep breath and plunged into the churning crowd.

For two and a half blocks down both sides of the street, more than
250 juried craftspeople hawked their goods from elaborate stalls and back-
drops: pottery, baskets, dried flowers, wooden cutouts, prints, quilts, carvings, woven goods, lamp shades, jewelry, and leather goods.

The crowd was in a feeding frenzy, and it was impossible to get close
to some of the more popular stands. I walked down the center of the
street, bumping shoulders with folks who had the same idea but were
headed in the opposite direction. Halfway down the first block I pulled
out of the mainstream and came up for air in a vacant lot holding a display of antique cars.

This established the pattern for the rest of my morning at the Corn
Festival. At half-block intervals, I would drift over to the side to enjoy
the entertainment, indulge in corn fritters, or chat with friends. On one
of my forays into calmer water, I headed off to the working craft demonstration behind the library. In the shady driveway, I saw cabinetmaker Jim
Small. His nine-year-old son, Tyler, was selling his wares: tiny wooden
boxes whose swivel lids bore the carefully printed inscription "Three
Piece Chicken Dinner." Inside were three kernels of corn. A "Three Piece
Chicken Dinner" went into my pocket and $1.50 went into Tyler's.

Jim and I sat in the shade and discussed the festival. "Who would
have thought that this country thing would have lasted this long?" he
asked. "It's been twenty years."

I knew what he meant—a decorating trend that became a way of life.
Nevertheless, I couldn't help saying, "Beats the heck out of the foil wall-
papers and chrome-and-glass furniture of the seventies." Even Jim agreed
with me on that point.

I left the shady driveway reluctantly and plunged back into the swiftly flowing current on King Street. The whole way up the street I tried to find the Corn Festival's place in the scheme of country festivals. And then it hit me—market day—a custom older than Pennsylvania itself. Our immigrant ancestors brought this custom with them from all over Europe. Once a week, farmers and artisans brought their goods to town. There was entertainment, food, and opportunity to meet friends and catch up on the news. And much like Jim Small, artisans trained their children early in production and salesmanship. This was as much a part of our Pennsylvania heritage as stone farmhouses and red barns.

From the top of King Street, I stood and watched as the Old Guard parted the crowd with the sound of fife and drum. "We're not so far from our roots, after all," I thought to myself.

❖ The Corn Festival is held the last Saturday of August from 8 A.M. to 6 P.M. Along with the crafts, the festival features a variety of foods, including corn on the cob. Entertainment is offered at half-block intervals along King Street throughout the day. Strolling musicians fill in the gaps. There is a children's petting zoo as well as entertainment for kids.

To get to the Corn Festival from I-81, take the King Street exit (exit 10) and follow PA 174 into town. Turn left onto King Street and pray for a parking space. For more information, contact the Shippensburg Chamber of Commerce, Shippensburg, PA 17257.

Williams Grove Historical Steam Engine Association Show

Mechanicsburg, Cumberland County

The Williams Grove Historical Steam Engine Association Show always starts on the last Sunday of August, with a horse and buggy parade. That much of the schedule is certain, but the rest of it is variable.

"We have a micro-mini tractor pull on the first Sunday, too," Glenn Morningstar told me. "They are toys with gas engines. That starts whenever the horse and buggy parade is over. We also have a micro-mini pull on the second Sunday of the fair. We have no time on that—whenever they come in here and decide to run.

"We have a sawmill that runs every day at one. That's this year. Next year it may change. See, all of these things are volunteer. It depends on how much help we can get to run them.

"We have a fodder cutter. You take corn that they used to put into the silo for feed for winter. We have a stone crusher, too. They haven't come down and said anything about running that yet.

"Oh!" he exclaimed, finally arriving at something I could see in operation. "The shingle mill. They're going to run every day this year at two."

Lee Burgett jumped in to help out.

"We have thrashing and baling and a dynamometer, a machine that measures how much horsepower your engine is putting out. We have a tractor pull, a parade, a horse-pulling contest. We also have a pedal tractor pull for the children on weekends. That'll probably be Saturday or Sunday this year. We also have a train ride that's pulled by an authentic steam locomotive."

"You can pretty much count on that weekends," Glenn interjected, "and we have a huge flea market, when there's a crowd."

"We do have a consignment sale on Saturday of the show," Lee added hopefully. "Antiques, tractors, gas engines, garden tractors, mostly farm-related items. When does that start, Glenn?"

One thing is certain. There is a huge display of antique steam equipment, some of the machinery quite rare. Lee pointed out an oil pull, a machine that burned kerosene and water. He told me that Bud Stambaugh, an expert on oil pulls, went to Missouri and had one of the old machines pulled out of a riverbank. It had been put there to stop erosion.

There is another given at Williams Grove: the Country Butcher Shop. During the nine days of the fair, this shop is in continual production. It offers sweet bologna, pork chops, sausage, ham steaks, tenderloins, ribs, and scrapple. I was fortunate to be there as the volunteers were finishing a batch of four hundred two-pound pans of scrapple. One pan went home with me.

Richard Arnold from Franklintown was in charge of the scrapple-producing operation.

"We buy four 4-H hogs and about thirty other hogs," he said. "We make twelve to sixteen hundred pounds before the week is out."

Bob Carpenter, another butcher, told me, "Just about all of us have another trade. I'm a computer analyst. I take the whole week off to work here."

You can also count on good food at Williams Grove. Though the menu is not extensive, the meals are tasty, and the prices are affordable. I bought a roast beef dinner, which included mashed potatoes, filling, gravy, a vegetable, applesauce, and bread and butter. While I ate in the picnic pavilion, I tried to make sense of the schedule and the theme of this festival.

I stopped at the museum before I left. It had a Victorian parlor display, a bedroom with a rope bed, and a turn-of-the-century kitchen. The rest of the items had no unifying theme or time period. There were sleds, old farm tools, a wagon jack, crosscut saws, a bag wagon, a sod cutter, a sleigh, and push plows. At the end of the building was a model railroad.

I wandered around the grounds awhile, looking at the small engines, bantering with antiques dealers at the flea market, and studying the advertisements for the nightly entertainment. I sat on the sidelines of the horse pull, still wondering about a unifying theme or a purpose.

Finally on the way home I understood. The Williams Grove Historical Steam Engine Association is interested in preserving the past, especially farm life; hence, the country butcher, the museum relics, the old train, and of course, the steam engines that built the nation. I had to admit they had done a wonderful job of collecting. They had everything—except a schedule.

❖ The Williams Grove Historical Steam Engine Association Show begins on the last Sunday of August and runs nine days. Demonstrations are by chance and availability of volunteers. It is located ten miles south of Harrisburg, off Route 15 or Route 74. The fairgrounds is annexed to Williams Grove Amusement Park, and for an additional fee there are rides available for the whole family. The Williams Grove Speedway is across the street. For more information, write to the Williams Grove Historical Steam Engine Association, P.O. Box 509, Mechanicsburg, PA 17055.

Wyoming County Fair

Tunkhannock, Wyoming County

Route 6 is one of the prettiest roads in the state. From Clarks Summit, it meanders west, climbing mountains, plummeting into valleys, hanging on to cliff sides. The towns along the way are pretty and charming and far enough north to have a little drop of New England in their bloodlines. Village greens appear, and white churches with spires so tall they snag the clouds.

I had stumbled upon Route 6 looking for an alternate route home from upstate New York during graduate school years. Long after, I found excuses to drive that stretch, exposing countless rolls of film at the scenic overlooks and in the towns along its miles.

When I read the advertisement for the Wyoming County Fair, eleven miles west of Tunkhannock, I marked the dates on my calendar. I knew what to expect—an old fairgrounds with whitewashed buildings, probably trimmed in green. I anticipated a white clapboard fair office with shutters at the windows. Undoubtedly there would be an old grandstand with gingerbread bracketing the columns. I set a Victorian band shell in the center, and I trimmed my imaginary fairgrounds with big evergreens. I could not have been more wrong.

When I turned at the Wyoming County Fairground sign, I thought I had made a mistake and driven into someone's dairy farm. There was a cattle barn the size of a football field, and two silos towered over it where my hemlocks should have been.

"That silo says Wyoming County Fair," my friend Ken Swomley said to me, and sure enough, a respectable fair was sprawled around it. In the fair office, Phil Broadhead explained.

"This building was on the grounds when our Kiwanis Club bought it in 1991. A big dairy barn—four hundred cattle. It was fully automated with feeders, manure removal, the works. We added the three livestock barns in the back, and now this is our exhibit hall."

Fair president Jim Dillon went farther back. "This fair started in 1857 and ran until 1942. You know what happened in 1942. They tried to activate it again after 1946, but they were not successful. In 1986, the Tunkhannock Kiwanis Club, which sponsored a dozen projects a year, decided to make it a baker's dozen.

"We started out in town, but we ran out of space. There was a bankruptcy sale here in 1990 and the Kiwanis bid $247,000 on 231 acres of land. We had $5,000 in the treasury at the time. To raise the money, we decided to sell ten-year non-interest-bearing subvention certificates. We sold 252 of them. We'll sell 300 and that's it. The buyers will end up being part owners."

Ken and I gathered up premium books and schedules of events and then walked through the former cattle barn. One side was devoted to agricultural exhibits, home products, and handcraft entries. I copied an interesting recipe before going to the other side of the building to see the 4-H exhibits.

Outside is the grandstand area of the Kiwanis Club's fairgrounds. Called the Pit, it is a big hole in the ground with slanted sides. The stage was set up at the bottom, and spectators would sit on the banks for the evening show. "Ingenious," I said to Ken. "Very practical."

"Craig, I can tell where you grew up, and it wasn't on a farm. This was the liquid manure pit."

One exhibit held our attention far longer than the baked goods inside the barn. Lined up outside, almost as an afterthought, was a row of scarecrows. There were only six entries, but each was a work of art, far transcending the stuffed-blue-jeans-and-flannel-shirt species. There was an old farm woman, an Indian woman passing the afternoon in a chair, and a hula dancer with a palm tree behind her. My favorite was a seven-foot cowboy, fresh from the shower with a barrel guarding his nether regions. In my photo album now Ken and I pose forever with these masterpieces, but I shall never share them with anyone.

There was a lot of entertainment that afternoon. We stopped by the horse show before watching a high-wire act on the free stage. We also took in a comedy show that afternoon and listened to a folk singer perform for youngsters. A local town band played in the band shell.

The food at the Wyoming County Fair was interesting and varied, with many local concessions. We enjoyed the Kiwanis Club's corn and potato chowder and Buffalo shrimp. Chris Hamlon's roast beef sandwiches were wonderful, and the rice pudding in a waffle cone was more refreshing than ice cream.

The carnival area offered many rides and games, and it was busy that afternoon.

It wasn't until that night, at home, that I had time to read the materials I'd picked up in the fair office. In the winter of 1993–94, snow and ice brought down the roof of the main exhibition building. The roof caved in, taking one wall with it. The damages exceeded $100,000. The Kiwanis had not insured the building because of the enormous cost, and

---

Blue-Ribbon Honey Muffins

1 cup butter   1 teaspoon soda
1 $1/2$ cups honey $1/2$ teaspoon salt
2 cups flour   1 egg
1 cup sour cream   jelly or jam

Stir all ingredients except jelly together. Fill muffin cups (with papers) one-third full. Put $3/4$ teaspoon jelly or jam in each cup. Fill cups with batter. Bake at 375 degrees for 15 to 20 minutes.

—*Susie Robinson*

---

the loss was devastating. Volunteers had made the repair. That said a good deal about the fair and the community that supports it.

❖ The Wyoming County Fair is held from the Wednesday before until Labor Day. For more information, write to the Kiwanis Club Wyoming County Fair, R.R. 1, Box 259A, Tunkhannock, PA 18657. Do not go home without a pound of Wyoming County Fair cheese, made from the milk collected during fair week.

Germania Old Home Day

Germania, Potter County

The lawns were freshly cut, the porches swept, the windows washed all over tiny Germania. The entire town had readied itself for Old Home Day and the Firemen's Parade. Yard sales lined the streets, displaying anything and everything, from a porch rocker with no seat to a pink fiberglass shower stall. On the corner of the town's main intersection a house, itself for sale, had a yard sale in the shade of its magnificent spruce trees. Two nieces of the deceased owner hopefully invited all yard sale customers to tour the old manse. It was a beauty. I heard several people say they wished it were closer to home, and that was my feeling, too, as I thanked the heirs for their time and drove up the hill to Germania's firemen's celebration.

That hilltop is one of the many reasons Potter Countians refer to their home as God's Country. Chicory and goldenrod danced in the breeze that afternoon, and a few trees were sporting autumn highlights in their tresses. There was a 360-degree view of fields, valleys, hills, forests, and distant blue mountain ridges. Cloud shadows chased each other across the rolling landscape. I would not have been surprised to hear Julie Andrews singing "The Sound of Music."

The main parking lot at the Germania Fire Company is terraced. Three or four rows of cars face down on the firehouse, a reproduction of an earlier firehouse, and a gazebo. On the day of the festival, festivities began in the parking lot and flowed down the hill. Country music poured from open doors and windows of pickup trucks, and tailgate parties were in progress, fueled from coolers on truck beds. More than a few picnics were spread out on the terraces. Several older couples sat in lawn chairs by their cars, content to watch the activities below from a distance.

On the main level of the festival, the firemen were competing with other fire companies in firemen's games, many of them repeats from the other fire company fairs and festivals I had visited along the northern tier of the state. They were not attracting much attention despite the size of the crowd. A country-western band in the gazebo was cranking out its rendition of a Hank Williams song, but it was merely background music.

I walked over to the gingerbread Victorian building with the tower and read the sign: "This replica was built and presented to the public September 1, 1991. It was constructed as close as possible to the original building that was located on the south end of Germania. The high tower was used to house the fire bell and also to hoist up the wet fire hose so that it would dry." Inside the building, I discovered, was one of the big attractions at Germania Old Home Day.

A cash drawing was in progress. Pink tickets had been sold in advance for $20 apiece. The first name drawn from the tumbler received $100. Ninety-eight more names were drawn. The hundredth name drawn also won $100. Every hundredth name drawn thereafter was also a $100 winner, and the last two tickets drawn received $1,000 and $10,000. Another drawing earlier that day had awarded eight cash prizes. For $2 a ticket or three for $5, buyers had a chance at a $1,000 prize, a $100 prize, two $50 prizes, and three $25 prizes.

The dining hall was another big draw at Germania. The menu featured a roast pork sandwich with sauerkraut and applesauce, and half a barbecued chicken with macaroni salad, baked beans, and a roll and butter. There were also burgers, hot dogs, sausages, and fries, but the dinners seemed to be more popular. There was plenty of seating inside the firehouse.

There was a line in front of Bud's Saloon. Signs advertised Genesee Beer and encouraged patrons to buy from the Germania Fire Company and the Ladies Auxiliary.

Whole Wheat Bread

Combine in large mixer bowl:
3 cups whole-wheat flour	2 tablespoons salt
$^1/_2$ cup sugar	3 packages dry yeast

Heat in saucepan until very warm:
1 $^1/_2$ cups water	$^1/_2$ cup oil
2 $^1/_2$ cups milk	

Add to dry ingredients:
warmed liquids	2 eggs

Blend at low speed until moistened. Beat 3 minutes at medium speed. Stir in by hand enough white flour (5 to 6 cups) to form a stiff batter. Cover and let rise until double. Stir down and spoon into two greased 9 x 5-inch bread pans. Let rise 20 to 30 minutes. Bake at 375 degrees for 35 to 40 minutes.

—*Adapted from the* Germania Newsletter

Activities at Germania that day included a pig race for women and kids and a dance. Most people, it seemed, had come to drink a couple of beers, lie around on blankets, and celebrate a leisurely end of summer.

The horseshoe pit was busy throughout the afternoon. There was a steady clink of horseshoe against stake coming from the woods just below the firehouse. I ran into my cousins Bill and Tom Kennedy at the horseshoe pit and learned that there were ten teams from Mount Holly Springs, 180 miles away.

Did they know about the house I had toured that morning?

"That belonged to old man Braun," Tom said. "He was principal at Coudersport Schools for years and years. He donated this land to the fire company. I didn't know he'd died."

He paused for a moment and then added, "Maybe that's why they didn't have a parade this year. He was always grand marshal."

❖ Germania Old Home Day is held the first Sunday in September. Coming into Germania on Route 44–144 North, turn right at the stop sign and go up the hill a half mile. At the Y take the right branch. For more information, call 814-435-8881.

York Interstate Fair

York, York County

"During fair week," my friend Beth said, "the fairgrounds becomes a city within a city." And so it seemed on that Sunday morning when we began to walk the 120 acres of the York Fair. Although it was only 10 A.M., already the well-oiled gears and cogs of the fair hummed with life and activity.

Fair director Creston Ottemiller had told me that despite persistent rumors that agricultural exhibits would disappear from the fair, agriculture was maintaining its hold on York. The 1993 fair registered a record number of entries in all categories, with as much interest in horticulture as in agriculture. With this in mind, we made the livestock barns our first stop.

Activities there had begun much earlier that morning. A fine current of tension ran through the frenzy of activity in the sheep barns as the Open Class Market Lamb judging gathered steam and began to roll. Between the long barns, half-grown sheep, chins secured in metal stands like nineteenth-century photographers' models, stood patiently while their masters applied last-minute spit shine to their snowy coats. Some wore spandex suits to tighten muscles; others, already groomed and ready for the ring, looked for all the world like medieval chargers in their protective coats and hoods.

As we walked through the barns, chatting with livestock owners, I quickly began to realize that during fair week, the life of the exhibitors isn't an easy one. Traveling at night, most had arrived in the wee hours Friday morning to make the 8 A.M. registration cutoff. Since it takes a day for the animals to settle in to the environment, there had been little sleep for competitors on Friday night, either—the animals come first, after all. Exhibitors are on call to answer the public's many questions about breed or farm. Quite a few, on the fair circuit, had shown animals at the Allentown Fair the week before and were headed for the Reading Fair following this show.

Eighteen-year-old Richard Kerper of Fleetwood told me, "You don't get much sleep here at the fair. At home, all you have to do is feed and water the animals and clean their pens. Here, they require almost constant attention. I wash them every day. Of course, it's fun," he added. "It doesn't pay well enough not to be fun."

And indeed, it does seem like fun. All the competitors know each other, and an air of festivity and good-natured camaraderie smiles over the barns. Some exhibitors sleep in trucks and trailers; others bunk down in unoccupied boxes in the cattle barns. Impromptu kitchens, furnished with folding chairs and equipped with steaming Crockpots and coffee makers, spring up in empty stalls. Some tables even have tablecloths and vases of fresh flowers—all the comforts of home.

Unlike at home, however, livestock competitors at the fair walk out the barn door into a dazzling, high-tech carnival world of rides, concessionaires offering a wide array of international food choices, countless games, and the obligatory freak shows of the interstate fair. A short walk takes them to big-name entertainment each night or harness racing Monday through Wednesday afternoons. As Beth said, the fairgrounds had become a big, noisy city, complete with neighborhoods.

It is impossible to see all of the attractions at the York Fair in one day. I cruised through the poultry, horticulture, and homemaking and crafts buildings, barely doing justice to the displays. I did catch the pig races, shake hands with the organ grinder's monkey, and pay a visit to a lethargic grizzly bear, but I missed the Budweiser Clydesdales and the woman with two bodies. Still, I felt that I had gotten my money's worth.

❖ The week-long York Interstate Fair runs the second week of September, from Friday through the following Saturday. There is a full schedule of activities from morning to night for the eight days of the fair. From Harrisburg, take Interstate 83 south to the Route 30 bypass. Head west on Route 30 to Route 74. Turn left on 74. Go through one traffic light and proceed two blocks to the fairgrounds. For information, call 717-848-3596.

McClure Bean Soup

McClure, Snyder County

When I think of the McClure Bean Soup, I will always think of Erman Lepley. Although his official title at McClure's annual festival is assistant cook, he is the Bean Soup's oral historian and spinner of tales, as well as its foremost goodwill ambassador. He can season your evening with stories and laughter as rich as the soup itself.

When I drove to McClure, the trees that line Route 522 were sporting their first colored leaves. Wild asters and black-eyed Susans danced at their feet. Far back from the road, barns with faded Mail Pouch Tobacco signs stood sentry over their acreage. Cattle waded through meadows

slathered with sunlight as thick as butterscotch pudding. It was the perfect setting for a country celebration.

The path to the Bean Soup would have been easy to follow even if
the Ferris wheel and the bungee-jumping crane hadn't been etched in
sunlight against the mountainside that forms McClure's backdrop. As a
matter of fact, the directions might have read, "Take Route 522 to
McClure, then follow the wood smoke to the Bean Soup." The same
directions will lead you to Erman Lepley in Cold Spring Grove's kitchen.
From the moment he sat down and settled into his tale, I could tell he
liked not only his subject matter but also the many folks with whom he
has shared his stories over the years.

"The first official Bean Soup was held in 1891," he started out. "That
was the first year the public was invited. Beginning in 1865, after the
Civil War ended, the Grand Army of the Republic held reunions for the
vets in the area. They served bean soup and hardtack because that's what
the vets ate in the army. They wore their uniforms and even staged mock
battles in the early years. There were always political speeches and usually
entertainment of some sort. Then, when the vets got too old to do it,
their children took over for them—that's when the public was invited.

"The bean soup recipe is pretty much what they used in the Civil
War. I take twenty-five pounds of navy beans and soak them for a half
hour in a tub of hot water. Well, sometimes I do and sometimes I don't. It
depends how busy it is. Sometimes I just throw them in the kettle and put
them on the fire. Anyhow, add enough water to almost fill the kettle. We
used to use the water right from the Cold Spring, but the DER put a cap
on it in the sixties—now we just use town water. Bring the beans to boiling and boil them for half an hour. Then add fifteen pounds of ground
beef, six ounces of salt, and six pounds of suet. Boil for two hours, stirring
all the time to break up the beans."

Erman excused himself to check on the kitchen crew. I watched him
peering into the fires beneath the nine thirty-five-gallon cast-iron kettles,
adding a log or two, and stopping to chat with the crew. Two cooks were
delivering a soup cauldron via pulleys and an overhead track to servers
dressed in Civil War uniforms. When Erman returned, his story turned to
a more personal level.

"I got dragged into this when I was working for PennDOT," he
recalled. "My supervisor was on the committee, and they needed help for
the 1963 Bean Soup. Been doing it ever since."

Throughout his narrative, a steady line of customers came, ate their
soup, and went from the pavilion. Another cauldron of soup was brought

out, and then another, and still he talked. He told me about the folks he's met over the years, people from faraway places like California and England, people who heard the legend of the McClure Bean Soup and came to see and taste it for themselves. He told me about the record crowd the night the Hagers from "Hee Haw" performed in the 1970s—fifteen thousand people filled the grove for that show.

While he talked, the light went out of the sky and neon lit the concession stands along the rambling midway. The lighted Ferris wheel spun like a jeweled necklace against the black velvet sky. Shelly West's second show of the evening filled the Cold Spring Grove with country music as I closed my notebook and headed for home.

❖ The McClure Bean Soup generally runs the second week of September, Tuesday through Friday evenings and all day Saturday. Soup is available from noon each day, in single servings or by the quart. Concession stands offer a variety of other foods. There is quality entertainment each evening in the band shell. Admission is free, but bring lawn chairs. Saturday afternoon is the rally, and a fireworks display closes the Bean Soup that evening. McClure is located on Route 522 midway between Lewistown and Selinsgrove. The Bean Soup can be seen from Route 522. For more information, call 800-338-7389 or 717-658-8425. And when you get there, look for Erman and tell him I send my best.

Harvest Festival

Schaefferstown, Lebanon County

Zinnias were blooming and cockscomb waved red heads against the September sky in Alexander Schaeffer's kitchen garden. Two fat pigs gobbled their slops noisily in their pigsty, then grunted contentedly. Wood smoke filtering from the cookstove and the drying house joined the enticing smells of chicken pot pie and apple schnitz, sharp, sweet, and spicy.

A group of neighbors sat under the porch roof of an outbuilding peeling apples, chuckling and talking as they peeled and brushed yellow jackets aside. Two draft horses cooled their feet in the stream by the springhouse while a flotilla of ducks held formation, treading water nearby. "Gee!" and "Haw!" from the surrounding fields announced the location of the oxen team.

It could have been any late-summer afternoon in the eighteenth century at Alexander Schaeffer's farm, but it was two and a half centuries after the farm was built and it was Historic Schaefferstown's Harvest Festival.

When I arrived in Schaefferstown that morning, the horse-drawn plowing contest was already under way. I was fortunate to take a seat on an old wagon with Paul Egan from Leesport and George Schlappich from Bernville. The two old farmers recognized a greenhorn and began explaining what the judges were looking for in the competition.

"You have to lift your plow a little bit so it doesn't wear the handle off. See how he's doing it," Paul explained patiently.

"And you have to plow a straight furrow," George said. "No holes in it, either. You don't want to plant potatoes in your furrow.

"This is one-furrow plowing," he continued. "They have plows that throw up a right furrow or a left furrow. That's a left furrow plow."

"That one's doing pretty good." Paul pointed. "They're judged on how they start out, how straight the furrow is, how deep it is, and how they stop at the ends. Neatness and evenness, especially at the ends, are important. There are also sulky plows that you sit on. I never liked them, myself.

"I was raised on a farm and I live on a farm now," he went on. "My pop was fussy. Milk at four-thirty in the morning and four-thirty in the afternoon. Not four and not five. I quit school the April I was thirteen. In May I got fourteen and Pop told me, 'Now you gotta work.' For thirty-five years I worked for Agway at daytime and I farmed at night."

"In those days," George reminisced, "if a farmer had a pair of horses and ten or twelve dairy cattle, he was set. They thought more of their livestock then than they did of their wives."

When the horse-drawn plowing contest ended, I walked over to see the oxen perform. Rob Flory from Howell Farm, a living history museum in Titusville, New Jersey, was taking Jesse and Frank, two chocolate oxen, through their paces.

"Frank, haw! Frank, haw!" he hollered.

"Haw means left and gee means right," Pam Horsley, his companion, explained. "You see, Frank walks a little slower than Jesse, so they pull to one side."

I asked her how they had become involved with oxen, and Pam's answer surprised me a little.

"I was heading to the Peace Corps when I heard about Howell Farm. Rob runs a program there to prepare folks for work in Third World countries. I took the eleven-week program and stayed on for a few months. From there I went overseas. When I came back, I returned to Howell Farm."

I walked over the farm that afternoon, as enchanted by the September sunshine as I was by the setting. Alexander Schaeffer's house is in a state of arrested decay. It is not a restoration and that is fortunate, for the missing plaster here and there allows guests to see the methods of colonial

Dried String Beans with Ham

Simmer an end of a ham, several smoked ham hocks, or at least a ham bone with some meat left on it.

Meanwhile, soak dried beans in water for about an hour. Drain off the water and add the beans to the ham. Cook until ham and beans are almost tender, then add one potato for each person to be served. Cook until potatoes are soft. Sometimes vinegar is served with this.

Dried Corn and Sausage Stew

1 cup dried corn   salt and pepper to taste
1 pound fresh sausage   milk
4 medium potatoes, diced

Soak corn overnight or use leftover corn from a previous meal. Cook corn seasoned with salt until soft, about 1 hour. Cut sausage in 1- to 2-inch pieces and add to corn together with the diced potatoes. Cook until potatoes are soft. Add milk to cover. Season with pepper.

—Boyertown Cookery

Corn Pone

1 cup sugar   1 $^1/_2$ cups white flour
2 eggs   1 $^1/_2$ cups cornmeal
$^1/_2$ cup shortening   3 teaspoons baking powder
1 $^1/_2$ cups milk   1 teaspoon salt

Mix sugar, eggs, and shortening. Beat well.

Add milk and dry ingredients. Beat well again. Bake in 8 x 8-inch pan at 325 degrees about 40 minutes.

—Lester Spitler

Recipes used courtesy of Historic Schaefferstown Inc.

construction. There were cooking demonstrations on the hearth in the kitchen and a winemaking demonstration in the basement.

The springhouse is a three-story log structure. The first floor houses the spring. On the main floor, a trap door hides an ingenious set of shelves on a pulley system that raises and lowers food to the cooling area above the spring. A narrow staircase around the fireplace leads to a sleeping loft.

"This building predates the main house," said Bill Miller, the docent in the springhouse. "It was built around 1730. When settlers came to a new area, the first thing they did was find water. They built a house over it for shelter and then set about to clear the land. Eventually they started building the main house."

He directed me to the summerhouse, where corn pone was baking in the beehive oven. "I was raised on it. When we didn't have anything else, we'd break it up in a bowl, pour milk over it, and sprinkle it with sugar. That was supper many nights when I was growing up." The authentic summerhouse, not original to the farm, was moved in from another location. It is a charming little building, filled with sunlight and fresh air.

I had lunch in the dining hall that afternoon. The menu was strictly old Pennsylvania Dutch: schnitz and knepp, chicken pot pie, pork and sauerkraut, ham with green beans and potatoes, baked ham, and roast turkey. The side dishes included corn, baked beans, potato filling, mashed potatoes, and lettuce with hot bacon dressing.

The woman in front of me ordered the ham with green beans and potatoes. "Could I pass on the potatoes?" she asked. "Just give me the ham and extra green beans."

"I can't," the server explained. "It's a meal in a pot, like stew."

"Oh," she said, a little perplexed.

"Where are you from?" I asked her.

"New Jersey."

Figures, I thought to myself. Maybe you have to have a little Dutch in you to understand these things. I chose schnitz and knepp.

After lunch I continued my tour of the grounds. There were at least forty demonstrations in progress, many in original buildings, all of them from the era of Alexander Schaeffer's farm. There were a tobacco shed, a sawmill, a stone crusher, a smokehouse, hay forks, vinegar making, beekeeping, pot pie making, and rug hooking, to name a few.

Eventually I found a shady spot and sat listening to the musicians on the stage. You may want to do that, too, when you visit, and watch the Schaeffer farm from a distance.

❖ The Harvest Festival is held the second weekend in September, on Saturday and Sunday. Historic Schaefferstown Inc. is on Route 501, north of Lancaster at the intersection with Route 897. For exact dates, write to Alexander Schaeffer Farm Museum, Box 307, Schaefferstown, PA 17088, or call 717-272-8555, 717-949-3235, or 717-949-2374

Flax Scutching Festival

Stahlstown, Westmoreland County

Buckwheat pancakes still sizzling from the griddle were drowning in butter and maple syrup on my plate that Sunday morning. Two pieces of
whole-hog sausage, browned to a turn, lay beside them, spicy and juicy. A
cup of coffee on the side was steaming in the brisk September air, and a
fiddler played a country jig in the background while sunlight played
checkers with patches of shade. "It does not get much better than this," I
thought to myself at the Stahlstown Flax Scutching Festival.

Started in 1911, Stahlstown's Flax Scutching Festival is said to be the
second oldest flax-scutching celebration in the world. Today the flax
scutching at Stahlstown consists of twenty-minute demonstrations
throughout the day, and one wonders whether the original scutchings in
Monticue Grove were not less entertaining. After all, from 1800 until
1850, flax was the largest crop grown in Pennsylvania and the common-
wealth was the largest flax producer in the young country. Seeds were
used for linseed oil and the rest of the plant for linen fabric.

The flax-scutching demonstration is informative. Volunteers at stations around an enclosed pavilion demonstrate procedures used in each
stage of processing the plant for linen cloth. The plants are first dried,
then soaked in water, or retted, to loosen the outer covering of the stem.
They are dried again, then pounded in a flax brake, which breaks up the
outer coating. Next they are beaten with a paddle, or "scutched," and the
hard outer coating shatters away from the long fibers inside. These fibers
are then pulled through a hackle, or heckle, a comblike instrument that
separates them for spinning.

I was pleased to learn the origin of two words in such a short time
that morning. *Heckle* comes from the instrument that worries the flax
fibers apart. *Scutch* was a word my grandmother used jokingly when I mis-
behaved. "I'm going to give you a good scutching," she would say: a good
beating.

I had arrived in Stahlstown in time for the Sunday morning service
held by the Stahlstown Trinity United Methodist Church, the festival
organizers. Everything was on hold—the flea market, the craftspeople,
and the cooks. I broke the rules by walking around during the sermon,
scratching the ears of the horses at the wagon train encampment in the
open meadow along the road, browsing through the flea market displays,
and taking photos for my collection.

There was a low hum of anticipation as more folks arrived for the pancake breakfast. As the smells of sausage and coffee began to drift through the grove of trees, it grew to a roar. I spied a 1930s Christmas ornament at one flea market table. The price was unbelievably low for a Santa's head of that vintage. I could not put it down for fear of losing it to another buyer. But at a stand far down the row there was a green-handled soap saver I wanted for my sister's collection. I saw another customer pick it up, examine it, then stand by the table. There was a good chance she would buy it before I could get there. I could not leave the table with the Santa in my hand. It would look like theft. So I stood there, shifting my weight from one foot to the other, willing the minister to pronounce the benediction.

When the organ postlude sounded, Monticue Grove exploded into action. The worshippers became exceedingly unprayerful in their mad dash for breakfast as the flea market vendors scuttled over to their tables. I almost threw the $10 bill at the Santa Claus salesman, then left him to wrap my treasure as I raced to the other table and snagged the soap saver just as the woman returned. She had been distracted by the sausage and coffee.

Eighty people stood ahead of me in line for breakfast. The couple

---

Festival Buckwheat Cake

Dissolve two 2-ounce cakes yeast in 1 ½ gallons warm water.
Add:

    1 ½ gallons cold water   3 ½ gallons buttermilk
Stir in:

    30 pounds buckwheat flour   1 ¾ cups salt
    15 pounds white flour
Then add:

    1 ½ pints baking molasses   2 cups sugar
       (24 ounces)   3 ½ quarts cooking oil
Beat until smooth, cover, and keep in cool area. Stir down after 24 hours.

Thirty minutes before frying, add 1 cup sugar and ¾ cup soda in 4 to 6 quarts hot water.

Stir well and fry on a hot, greased griddle.

—Shirley Newell, Stahlstown

Whole-Wheat Buttermilk Biscuits

2 cups whole-wheat flour
$^1/_4$ cup wheat germ
2 teaspoons baking powder
$^1/_2$ teaspoon baking soda
$^1/_4$ teaspoon salt

5 tablespoons cold butter
   or margarine, cut into
   small pieces
1 $^1/_4$ cups buttermilk

Preheat oven to 400 degrees.

Combine flour, wheat germ, baking powder, baking soda, and salt in mixing bowl. Stir with fork to mix well. Add butter and work in with fork until mixture resembles small crumbs.

Add buttermilk, about $^1/_2$ cup at a time, stirring gently (dough will be soft). Turn dough out onto floured board and pat gently to 1-inch thickness. Cut with round biscuit cutter and arrange on ungreased baking sheet. Bake in preheated oven 10 to 15 minutes, or until tops are lightly browned.

Makes about 18 2-inch biscuits.

Applesauce-Cinnamon Corn Muffins

1 $^1/_4$ cups all-purpose flour
$^3/_4$ cup enriched cornmeal
$^1/_3$ cup sugar
4 tablespoons baking powder
1 teaspoon cinnamon

$^1/_2$ teaspoon salt
1 cup applesauce
$^1/_3$ cup milk
$^1/_4$ cups vegetable oil
1 egg

Heat oven to 425 degrees. Grease twelve medium muffin cups or line with paper baking cups. In medium bowl, combine flour, corn-meal, sugar, baking powder, cinnamon, and salt. Combine apple-sauce, milk, oil, and egg; mix well. Add to dry ingredients, mixing just until dry ingredients are moistened. Fill prepared muffin cups two-thirds full. Bake for 15 to 20 minutes or until golden brown. Serve warm. Makes 12 muffins.

Recipes reprinted with permission from Fort Allen Antique Farm Equipment Association Inc.

behind me agreed to hold my place in line while I talked to the kitchen help about the breakfast.

Frank Newell, festival chairman since 1986, told me the griddle was greased with hog fat. "We use fat off the hog we butcher for our sausage. Not much goes to waste here."

His wife, Shirley, told me about the buckwheat pancakes. "The dough is better the second day. Some of the younger folks prefer it the first day. I think it's better after it's had time to work."

"In olden times," Frank explained, "people kept a crock of batter going all winter long. They'd just dip in when they needed some."

"These are definitely old-fashioned buckwheat cakes," Shirley told me. "We use freshly ground flour. In the two days of the festival we go through fourteen thirty-gallon barrels of batter and eight hundred pounds of sausage."

After breakfast I walked over to the stage, where a husband-and-wife folk music team, Ed and Geraldine Berbaum, was working with young kids. The youngsters were playing with limber jims, dancing figures on a board, keeping time to the lively mountain music as the musicians played fiddles, guitars, dulcimers, mandolins, and spoons.

Later in the program, they taught the youngsters a Cherokee Indian step that was the basis for a hoedown. They also taught a polka that, as interpreted by mountain folks, became a clog. Finally, they danced a quadrille to a tin whistle tune.

"Any of your grandfathers who played the fiddle would have known that tune," the wife told the audience. "An old Dutchman from eastern Pennsylvania taught us that melody fifteen years ago. It's old as the hills."

I walked around the grounds that morning, stopping by demonstration areas along the way. There was a potter and a wood-fired kiln. A church bake sale offered a dozen kinds of pies, fruit puffs, sticky buns, flaxseed bread, white bread, monkey bread, pepperoni rolls, pizza, and a variety of cakes. A local Boy Scout troop was operating a cider press by the parking lot. The flax-scutching demonstration, though, was the main attraction.

❖ The festival is held the second Saturday and Sunday of September. The grounds open at 10 A.M. each day and are located on Route 711, four miles north off exit 9 (Donegal) on the Pennsylvania Turnpike, and eight miles south of Ligonier. For more information, contact the Flax Scutching Festival, Stahlstown, PA 15687, or call 412-593-2119 or 412-593-7913.

American Gold Cup
and Country Fair

Devon, Chester County

"I don't think they'll let us in," I said to Kay.

"What?" she asked as we pulled her Geo into a parking spot at the blue-and-white Devon Horse Show complex.

"Look around," I said, pointing out vehicles and show goers. "I don't think they let you in unless you have a Jack Russell terrier and arrive in a Land Rover, a Mercedes, or a Volvo station wagon."

We were attending the Germantown Hospital Equestrian Festival's American Gold Cup Jumping Competition and Country Fair. One of the legs of grand prix show jumping's Triple Crown in this country, the American Gold Cup attracts the top riders from all over the nation. The names are legendary—Norman Dello Joio, named Male Equestrian Athlete of 1992 by the United States Olympic Committee; Joe Fargis, who won an individual gold medal in the 1984 Olympic Games, guiding his mount, Touch of Class, successfully over a record-setting ninety of ninety-one obstacles; Anne Kursinski, the United States Olympic Committee's Female Athlete of 1991; Michael Matz, the all-time leading money-winning rider in the world; Debbie Stephens, who made show-jumping history in 1982 when she rode Rocky Raccoon to an outdoor high-jump record of seven feet, eight inches in Cincinnati.

The horses here are blue blood, equestrian royalty. They can trace their ancestry far back. Certain names appear repeatedly in their lineage—Touch of Class, the tiny mare that won America's heart in the 1984 Olympics; Abdullah, the legendary German stallion; and Gem Twist, known as the "Great Grey."

"It is indeed a desirable thing to be well descended," Plutarch said, "but the glory belongs to our ancestors." Accordingly, these horses are here to prove themselves. Unlike Queen Elizabeth's brood, who retain their titles regardless of their achievements, a horse is only as good as his performance, good breeding or not.

The sport of show jumping is not difficult to understand. A horse and rider must clear ten to fifteen obstacles in the show ring. Should a horse refuse a jump, fall, or knock down any portion of one of the fences, penalty points called faults are assessed. The challenge is for riders and their mounts to negotiate the course and navigate the jumps as fast as possible without incurring faults.

Riders walk the course prior to competing, determining the best line to follow, jump to jump. They have only one opportunity to do this, and no two courses are ever alike. Accomplished riders know their horses' strides and jumping styles, and as they walk the course they determine the best takeoff points for their animals at each jump. Riders also note the different kinds of jumps on the course. Some horses shy away from certain kinds of obstacles.

We had arrived in the middle of Class 16, the International Jumping Futurity for five- and six-year-old horses, in time to see Sherri Jamison take Barn Man around the course. They finished in 38.637 seconds, with eight faults. Davis Hopper's Count followed with a time of 42.491 and no faults. Kevin Maloney was next on Pog, making it around the course in 41.273 seconds with four faults. One rider followed another around the course in the September sunlight.

When that class ended, the staff cleared the ring for the next class. Tractors pulled large flatbed trailers, and staffers loaded them with pots of mums, pieces of jumps, and potted trees. Finally, the ring was readied for Class 11, the Ladies' Hunter Side Saddle–Pleasure Class.

We walked over to the warren of board-and-batten shops under the trees. Set on gravel pathways that go off at odd angles, many of the shops have cedar shake roofs, flower boxes, and colorful awnings. At Devon's shops, one thinks of Nantucket and Martha's Vineyard. They were offering oriental rugs, fine art with equestrian themes, fine jewelry, antique estate jewelry, designer sweaters, lawn furniture, saddles, custom boots, luggage, and quality toys. A caterer sold elegant fare, and there were gourmet coffee, wine, iced capuccino, and beer at other food stands. The one car dealer was displaying the latest Lexus models.

There was a dog show in one corner, where kids demonstrated their pets' talents: "This is Happy—he lies down." "Waldo is five. I'm nine. He lies down and rolls over." The prizes were big stuffed dalmatians.

We returned to the bleachers in time for Class 10, the $2,500 Amateur Owner Jumper Stake. Forty-two contestants jumped past our seats. When we left that afternoon, we were still chuckling over Devon's definition of a country fair. No doubt about it, Devon, like the horses that jump there, is top shelf.

❖ The American Gold Cup is held on the third weekend in September, from Thursday through Sunday. The show grounds are on Route 30 in Devon. For more information, write to the American Gold Cup, Germantown Hospital and Medical Center, One Penn Boulevard, Philadelphia, PA 19144, or call 215-951-8880.

Hinkelfest

Fredericksburg, Lebanon County

Hinkel is the German word for chicken. The tiny Lebanon County town of Fredericksburg owes its livelihood to the feathered, clucking creatures. Industry in the town means egg-production or chicken-processing plants, so when Fredericksburg celebrates, it pays homage to its benefactors. Hinkelfest is one big chicken extravaganza.

I arrived at Hinkelfest on a Sunday so beautiful it was almost unbelievable. The sun was as yellow as an egg yolk and cotton candy clouds sculled across the Prussian blue sky, fueled by the gentle breeze. Having no permanent home, the festival exists in a tent city at the airport on the edge of town. Food stands, dining facilities, cooking demonstrations, industrial displays, and souvenir stands are all under temporary shelters. The entertainment stage area is enclosed by a wagon train of poultry trucks parked end to end in a circle. They wear their legends proudly— Pennfield Farms and Dutch Country Egg Farms, Incorporated.

I arrived in time for the stuffed chicken breast dinner. The chicken breast was huge, and it was served with corn, slaw, a roll, a beverage, and ice cream. There was seating available, but at noon the business was heavy and the tables were full.

I was soon sorry I had eaten such a large dinner. Around the grounds was a variety of food, and all of it had clucked and crowed its way to the table: chicken corn rivel soup, chicken corn noodle soup, chicken hot dogs, grilled chicken sandwiches, chicken fried rice, chicken egg rolls, chicken burgers, chicken pizza, chicken pot pie, chicken nuggets, chicken and waffles, chicken barbecue sandwiches.

The industrial displays featured live poultry. The Dutch Country Egg Farms had about a dozen hens in a cage. Their eggs rolled to a trough below them. Another tent had an incubator: Busy beaks were chipping and chiseling the way to freedom, the newly hatched chicks were wet and exhausted, and fluffy yellow balls were toddling about. Seven other cages held chickens from one week to seven weeks old, showing their growth from egg to fryer.

One of the most interesting features of Hinkelfest was the cooking demonstration by Alletta Schadler, a Penn State Extension home economist. "I used to have to teach people how to cut up a chicken," she said. "People buy chicken parts now. So I show them how to bone chicken parts. It saves them a lot of money in the long run. One of the other benefits of boning legs and breasts is that you have the bones to make stock. Do a large stock pot at one time. Freeze it in one-cup portions or muffin tins."

After she finished boning a breast, she told the crowd, "Get nine or ten breasts and practice boning them. Otherwise you'll just gritzel it up. For those of you who aren't native, 'gritzel it up' means to make hash of something."

As she demonstrated boning a leg and thigh, she explained the process carefully and slowly, then began cooking—against all odds, I

Chicken Spinach Bake

1 10-ounce package frozen chopped spinach, thawed
1 egg
1/4 teaspoon onion salt
Crumb Mixture:
1/2 cup Italian bread crumbs
Mix and divide:
3 tablespoons melted butter

1/4 teaspoon nutmeg
1/8 cup Parmesan cheese
4 boneless, skinless chicken breast halves

1/4 cup Parmesan cheese

salt and pepper to taste

Drain and squeeze out excess moisture from spinach. Beat egg with onion salt and nutmeg. Add spinach and Parmesan cheese. Mix well.

Combine bread crumbs and Parmesan cheese and divide.

Sprinkle chicken with salt and pepper. Coat with half the bread crumb mix. Place in greased baking dish. Divide the spinach mixture. Spread on top of breasts. Sprinkle with remaining bread crumbs. Drizzle with melted butter. Bake at 350 degrees for 35 to 40 minutes.

Cheese Sauce:
3 tablespoons butter
1/8 cup flour
1/4 teaspoon salt
1 cup milk

1 cup shredded cheddar cheese
1/2 cup fresh mushrooms

Melt 2 tablespoons butter. Blend with flour and salt. Stir to form a smooth paste. Add milk. Cook and stir until thickened. Add cheese. Stir until melted. Sauté mushrooms in 1 tablespoon butter. Add to cheese mixture. Serve with chicken.

—*Nancy Peiffer, Jonestown*

Butterscotch Apple Coffee Cake

3 cups chopped peeled apples
1 cup (6 ounces) butterscotch
    morsels, divided
2 tablespoons lemon juice
2 $^3/_4$ cups flour
2 teaspoons baking powder
$^1/_2$ teaspoon salt
$^3/_4$ teaspoon cinnamon

$^1/_2$ cup (1 stick) butter,
    softened
1 cup sugar
4 eggs
2 teaspoons vanilla
$^1/_2$ cup and 1 tablespoon
    milk
2 tablespoons brown sugar

Preheat oven to 350 degrees. Grease and flour 10-inch tube pan with removable bottom. In a small bowl, combine apples, $^1/_2$ cup butterscotch morsels, and lemon juice. Set aside. In another small bowl, combine flour, baking powder, salt, and cinnamon. Set aside.

In a large mixer bowl, beat butter and sugar until creamy. Add eggs one at a time, beating well after each addition. Blend in vanilla. Add flour mixture alternately with $^1/_2$ cup milk. Spread half of batter in pan; top with half of apple mixture. Repeat layers; sprinkle with brown sugar.

Bake 60 minutes or until cake tester inserted in center comes out clean. Cool 30 minutes. Loosen cake from side of pan. Invert pan to remove cake. Cool completely, apple side up.

Glaze:

In microwave oven, melt $^1/_2$ cup butterscotch morsels with 1 tablespoon milk, stirring often until smooth. Drizzle glaze over cake.

—*Sue Werner, Jonestown*

thought. She cooked with a microwave and an electric skillet, neither of which could possibly have been working at peak performance, connected as they were to extension cords running to heaven knew where. She made a lime chicken salad, Caribbean jerked chicken, and chicken cordon bleu, sharing her products with her audience. The food was delicious.

There was a chicken and egg cook-off with sixty contest entries in several categories. The chicken cook-off was divided into legs and thighs, breasts, and one-dish or casserole categories. Egg dishes were entered in desserts, main dishes, and salads.

Hinkelfest had a small midway with six rides, three for adults and three for kids. There were also a haunted house, a fun house, a dozen games of chance, bingo, a moonwalk, a superslide, and pony rides. A souvenir booth sold Hinkelfest pottery, chicken pencils, chicken erasers, chicken carvings, and festival T-shirts.

❖ Hinkelfest runs the third full weekend of September, Friday evening, all day Saturday, and Sunday until 5. The festival is held at Farmer's Pride Airport, seven miles north of Lebanon, just off Route 22 at Fredericksburg. There is entertainment each night on the main stage. Except for entertainment and rides, the festival is free. For more information and exact dates, call 717-865-2123.

October

Falmouth Goat Races

Falmouth (Bainbridge), Lancaster County

I read the advance publicity for the Falmouth Goat Races, then read it again. It sounded like a pagan ritual, a custom that had survived long after its origins and purposes were forgotten, like Shirley Jackson's short story "The Lottery." I could imagine octogenarians saying, "My grand-pappy ran goats here, and his grandpappy before him. We've always had a goat race in Falmouth. We'll always have one."

It was not that far-fetched an idea. Even the name of the town was enigmatic. The village is called Falmouth, but the address is Bainbridge.

The origins of the Falmouth Goat Races are more interesting than I had imagined, but less mysterious. They began as a practical joke in 1980. In the Village Store on the corner, the regulars were lamenting their bad luck at the racetrack. Said Glen in despair, "We might as well bet on goats!"

The practical joker in the outfit took out an ad in the local paper for a goat race in Falmouth, listing Glen's number for additional information. People started calling to enter their goats in Glen's race. When Glen returned from work that day, his wife handed him the messages. The only way to save face was to stage a goat race. It was a cute joke that blossomed into an event attracting thousands to the thirty-house village.

It did not take long for me to recognize the spirit of fun that surrounds the event. The racetrack was a fifteen-foot-wide horseshoe. The judges' stand was a hay wagon with hay bales, pumpkins, and corn shocks piled artfully around the front. Two mountain goat trophies hung on the front; were they incentive to the runners?

The announcer called out numbers for each heat. When the gun went off, the goats' owners ran around the track with their charges on leashes. One ten-year-old fell when his pygmy goat balked. The announcer said, "You can pick him up and carry him," and the little handler did. Another goat dumped his handler and finished on his own. As number 41, a big black goat with impressive horns and a long beard, was dragged to the finish line by a twelve-year-old girl, the announcer said, "Look at the intensity. We're gonna have to put in a sandbank to stop them."

One heat followed another. Goats of all sizes and descriptions were pulled, dragged, carried, and chased by handlers of all sizes and descriptions. "I don't know how good number nine is gonna be," the announcer said. "She's being carried to the starting gate."

There was a goat auction between heats. Four kids were led to the auction block.

"This is a Swiss Alpine Mountain Climber," the announcer said of the first goat to be auctioned off. "We caught him in the Scottish Highlands."

Bidding started at $5 and rose to $25 before the proud owner carried the kid away.

"The next goat is a Moroccan Short Hair. He was actually stolen from the Sand King Omar Ishkabor. Do I hear five dollars?"

He introduced the third goat as a Polynesian Pepper Pounder trained to stomp peppercorns. The fourth, which brought $65, came to the block as a Mexican Menagine.

I talked with Michelle Fry from Hummelstown, who had just purchased two goats as pets for her children.

"I have no idea what kind they are," she told me. "I don't know anything about goats. Nothing at all."

Her mother, Ann Pinard, added, "We had a goat as a pet many years ago when my children were young. We came here to buy a goat. I guess we got good prices. One lady told us that pygmies go for as high as a hundred dollars."

There was a chicken-flying contest after the races. Two chickens were placed on a perch. Each had a string tied to its leg. On "Go" the handlers let go of the chickens and coerced them to fly—in theory.

Some chickens flew, others dropped to the ground, and still others just sat there on the perch.

"How do you get a chicken to fly?" the announcer asked. "You goose him!"

The fun started when two chickens really did fly. Two elementary children brought their pets to the perch and let them go on cue. Joleen Cramer was flying Buddy, and her brother John was flying Alfie, a white rooster. Alfie took off and did not stop. Adults scrambled after him in flying leaps. The last anyone saw of Alfie, he was headed down Route 441 like he had just seen Colonel Sanders.

There were many other attractions and activities at the Falmouth Goat Races. Country music played continually from the stage. There was a pleasant little crafts show with Indian jewelry, wooden toys, tinware, wreaths, Christmas decorations, potpourri, rustic paintings, and dolls. A children's area offered nickel-and-dime games and a petting zoo. There were hayrides, goat cart rides, and a puppet show. There was plenty of food on hand for a variety of tastes. The biggest attraction, of course, was the fun.

The Falmouth Goat Races, though not that old a country celebration, certainly have their roots in our nation's tradition. Americans have always gathered in the fall to celebrate the harvest. Laughter was at the heart of these celebrations, with silly highjinks, rowdy games, and a wealth of fellowship. The Falmouth Goat Races continue this tradition.

❖ Held on the first Saturday in October, the races begin with a kickoff parade through town at 10:30. Falmouth is four miles south of Middletown on Route 441. You will see "No Parking" signs before you turn into Falmouth. A shuttle bus runs from designated parking areas every two to three minutes. For more information, write to the Falmouth Civic Association, 211 Falmouth Road, Bainbridge, PA 17502, or call 717-367-6044 or 717-367-6801.

Apple-Cheese Festival

Canton, Bradford County

In the 1980s, Canton, a community of fewer than two thousand residents close to the New York border, realized that like many other small towns across the state, it was in trouble. Businesses had phased out and moved away, and the Rialto Theatre stood empty, a haunting skeleton reminding folks of a once thriving town. Luckily there were folks around with both memories and vision. Their "Just Say Canton! Rekindle the Spirit" program has put the community back to rights and made it a self-sufficient town beholden to no one save its own citizenry. One of the projects born of the new awareness was the Apple-Cheese Festival, capitalizing on local orchards and dairy farms.

When I arrived at Hickok Field, the rain on Saturday had turned the festival site soupy and sticky. Beth Stiner, festival chairperson, and her team had shoveled sawdust for hours, only to be met with more rain and standing water on the field.

The mud did not deter the crowd, however. As soon as the clouds pulled back, people poured in. Everyone I met was in a festive mood. Together, we jumped rivulets, laughed at muddy pant cuffs, and formed strange lines around puddles.

Business was brisk at the food stands. The "Rekindle the Spirit" program was offering roast beef and honey-dipped fried chicken dinners, including mashed potatoes and gravy, corn, applesauce, and apple pie with cheese for dessert. But by the time I got to the window, the frazzled volunteer told me that they had run out of food. The same thing happened at the chicken shish kebob stand. Before the day ended, the Canton Band Boosters had sold out of french fries, the East Canton Church had sold every one of its two thousand apple dumplings, the Canton Tops had sold all its chili and soup. The public-address system announced sell-outs all afternoon.

Given another situation, I would undoubtedly have been annoyed. Instead, I was happy for the festival organizers and civic organizations— no leftovers, and a profit!

The crafts show was good. At least 130 craftspeople were displaying and selling quality products. Dr. Marcella M. Hyde had a booth in one corner of the display building for selling and autographing her book, *Bradford County: The Story of Its People.* A retired teacher, she sells her book with a teachers' manual. I also enjoyed talking with Rebecca Bagley, a photographer from nearby Shunk. I visited with the women working on the quilt that would be raffled off.

Cheese and Apple Pockets

2 tablespoons plain yogurt	1 cup diced sweet red apple
2 tablespoons orange juice	(unpeeled)
$1/_8$ teaspoon ground cinnamon	$1/_4$ cup seedless raisins
1 cup (4 ounces) shredded Colby	16 (2-inch-diameter) mini
or cheddar cheese	pitas

In a small bowl, combine yogurt, orange juice, and cinnamon. Gently stir in cheese, apple, and raisins; set aside. Cut a $1/_2$-inch slice off the edge of each pita; fill pocket with cheese-apple mixture. Wrap individually in plastic wrap.

Apple, Sausage, and Sweet Potato Casserole

2 pounds link pork sausage,	1 28-ounce jar fried apples
cut in $1/_2$-inch rounds	$1/_2$ cup dark brown sugar
5 to 6 medium sweet potatoes,	$1/_4$ cup margarine
boiled and sliced	

Cook sausage in large skillet until brown; drain. Arrange potatoes in 3-quart casserole dish. Top with sausage. Cover with fried apples. Sprinkle with sugar. Dot with margarine. Bake in 375-degree preheated oven for 20 minutes or until it's heated through. Yields 8 servings.

One of the highlights was the tasting tent. Suppliers from Tute Cheese, Leprino Foods, McCadam Cheese, Leidy Meats, Hatfield Meats, Landman Meats, New Hope Mills, and Eastern Best Cheese were giving out free samples of bacon, sausage grillers, sausage links, apple-cinnamon pancakes, and all kinds of cheese with cups of cider. Given the situation at some of the food stands, these handouts were welcome.

Most of the entertainment scheduled throughout both days of the Apple-Cheese Festival was local, and that seemed appropriate. There were also orchard tours and a tethered hot air balloon ride. I walked away, a little muddy, saying, "What a nice little country festival!"

❖ The Apple-Cheese Festival is held Saturday and Sunday, the first weekend in October. The gate opens at 10 A.M. on Saturday and noon on Sunday, closing at 6 P.M. each day. Hickok Field is just south of Canton on Route 14. For more information, write to the Canton Area Chamber of Commerce, P.O. Box 243, Canton, PA 17724, or call 717-673-5500.

Fall Foliage Festival

Bedford, Bedford County

Heritage, traditions, values, and economic history all surface in the way folks throw a celebration. I was not surprised when my friend Linn Black told me that Bedford was once called "the town of a thousand rooms," for on the day I visited the Fall Foliage Festival there, hospitality warmed the crackling October air like a steaming mug of hot mulled cider.

Located on old U.S. Route 220, Route 30, and the Raystown Branch of the Juniata River, Bedford has been a stopping place for travelers for more than two hundred years. From the opening of Jean Bonnet's stone inn in 1780, through the gilded Victorian heyday of the Bedford Springs Hotel, to today's motels catering to Blue Knob skiers, people have found an open door in Bedford.

For years I'd heard Linn's stories about his hometown, and I finally accepted his invitation the first weekend of October for the opening day of the two-weekend-long Fall Foliage Festival. From the moment I opened my car door and began to walk the two blocks to the festival, the town worked its charm on me. Behind rows of towering trees stood houses of virtually every style and period since Washington. Most were dressed in autumn finery for Foliage Festival visitors. Along the wide pavements, light posts, telephone poles, and street signs were costumed in corn shocks. The town was so perfect that it could have been a movie set, but the tantalizing smells were very real.

In the square, at the heart of the day's festivities, I traced the origins of the aromas. The Kiwanis Club's chicken barbecue, the Bedford Rotary Club's beef barbecue, and the pig roast sent fragrant smoke signals. The smell of simmering green peppers and onions from the steak sandwich vendor wandered down the street and joined with the smell of crushed apples from the cider press on the square. Warm caramel and taffy from the apple-dipping stand sweetened the acrid exhaust fumes from idling engines. All over town, simmering potpourri attempted to overwhelm all other smells.

We spent the morning exploring the crafts show that radiated down Juliana and Penn Streets from the shady town square. Along the way, antiques shops lured us, and Linn talked about the Bedford of his childhood years. The Greystone Galleria, for instance, was once a down-in-the-heels bar and hotel; now it houses fifty antiques dealers. In the days of flattops and Butch Wax, National Antiques was the town barbershop. Founder's Crossing, which houses an upscale crafts co-op on the corner of Pitt and Juliana, was once a Murphy's Five-and-Dime store. "I can almost smell the roasted peanuts," Linn said as we walked through the warren of shops in the old building.

We left the festival for lunch and a tour of the surrounding area. At the Jean Bonnet Tavern, four miles out of town on Routes 30 and 31, clam chowder, steaming coffee, and apple pie warmed me as effectively as the merrily blazing fire on the hearth. From the Jean Bonnet, we drove up to the Bedford Springs Hotel. Once famed for its gracious hospitality, in its abandonment it now looks down its nose on the town like an aging dowager. In our rambles, we missed the Covered Wagon Parade through town, but it seemed a small price to pay for the view of the Bedford Springs Hotel against the autumn-cloaked mountainside.

Later that afternoon, we returned to the festival in time to see the quilt display at the Pioneer Historical Society and buy raffle tickets for the Bedford Needlers' quilt at the St. Thomas School. I picked a plump pumpkin from hundreds on the square before saying a reluctant good-bye to Bedford's Fall Foliage Festival.

I thought seriously about returning for the second weekend of the festival. The antique car parade promised more than two hundred vehicles, and the entertainment scheduled for Saturday was top-shelf. Most alluring, perhaps, was the Harvest Ball to be held Saturday night. Having seen how well Bedford throws a celebration, I knew that the dance would be

Mom Black's Peach Pecan Pie

$^1/_4$ cup butter   3 eggs
$^1/_4$ cup sugar $^1/_4$ teaspoon vanilla
2 tablespoons flour   1 unbaked pie shell
$^1/_2$ cup light corn syrup   1 $^1/_2$ cups diced fresh
$^1/_4$ teaspoon salt   peaches
Topping:
$^1/_4$ cup flour $^1/_4$ cup brown sugar, firmly
2 tablespoons butter, softened   packed
  $^1/_2$ cup pecans, coarsely chopped

Cream together butter and sugar. Add 2 tablespoons flour. Stir in
corn syrup and salt. Beat in eggs one at a time. Add vanilla and mix
until blended. Add peaches and pour into pie crust. Combine flour,
brown sugar, soft butter, and pecans. Mix until crumbly. Sprinkle
topping over pie. Bake at 375 degrees for 30 minutes.

wonderful. Although other commitments kept me away, my thoughts
strayed back there throughout the weekend.

❖ Bedford's Fall Foliage Festival is held in the center of town Saturday and Sunday the first and second weekends in October. The crafts
show runs from 10 A.M. to 5 P.M. all four days. Entertainment in the parking lot behind the courthouse is free, and there are picnic tables and bales
of straw for seating. Because of Bedford's many attractions, you may want
to stay for the weekend. If so, make reservations early, for Bedford's thousand rooms fill up quickly. For more information, write to Fall Foliage Festival, P.O. Box 234, Bedford, PA 15522.

National Apple Harvest Festival

Arendtsville, Adams County

It was autumn in Adams County. Along the stretch of road that winds and twists between Route 30 and Arendtsville, the busy little creek played hopscotch and leapfrog with the rocks scattered over its passageway. It caught a shower of confetti-bright leaves, trapped a few in a tiny inlet, sent a few more on an amusement-park ride rocketing downstream, and tossed the rest up on rocks.

Nature seemed to be at her most playful that afternoon, finger painting the landscape in impossible colors—scarlets, russets, bronzes, crimsons. Poison ivy set weathered barn walls afire. The sky was too blue that afternoon, straight out of the paint tube.

Here in Pennsylvania no one is fooled by Nature's whimsy—she is a cat toying with a mouse. There is always an urgency to autumn, a feeling of much to accomplish in a short season, of much to see before the days of winter's confinement. We have an appointment with winter.

As I looked around me that balmy afternoon, I knew that in a few short weeks the chilling winds would strip the leaves from the trees overhanging the creek in the narrows. The killing frost would come, but today folks were out and about.

I parked in a lot far from the main gate of the National Apple Harvest Festival that afternoon, not by choice, but by necessity. The crowd was huge. There was constant pedestrian traffic on the metal footbridge over the creek headed toward the festival. I could have waited for the "people mover," a hay wagon pulled behind a tractor, but the day was brisk, the air intoxicating, and I walked . . . and walked . . . and walked to the gate, occasionally shifting my daypack from shoulder to shoulder.

The Apple Harvest Festival is a huge celebration. It attracts folks from all over the country. Beth Burdette, cochairperson for publicity, expected one hundred thousand people over the four days of the festival. The Sunday before, twenty-seven thousand people had entered the gate. Diving into the mob of crafts-crazed shoppers, I felt a little panicky, for there were so many people in certain areas that movement was difficult.

Two buildings right beside each other were selling meals, and each had the advantage of seating. The 4-H club building featured a reasonably priced barbecued chicken dinner with chips, a pickle, applesauce, ice cream, and a beverage. The Adams County Fruit Growers Association next door had sandwiches—grilled ham, egg and cheese, grilled ham and cheese, hot dogs, barbecues, cheeseburgers, and hamburgers, plus fries, shakes, and fruit cups.

Among the many other foods at the Apple Harvest Festival, the ox roast sandwiches are legendary, and so are the french-fried sweet potatoes, dusted with powdered sugar. Many items, of course, were made from

Dutch Apple Brandy Cheesecake

1 recipe Cinnamon Crust (below)
4 8-ounce packages cream
　cheese, softened
1 cup sugar
3 tablespoons apple brandy
1 teaspoon ground cinnamon
$1/_2$ teaspoon vanilla

$1/_8$ teaspoon ground nutmeg
4 eggs
1 cup chunk-style
　applesauce
$1/_4$ cup whipping cream
1 recipe Crumb Topping
　(below)

Prepare and bake crust. Beat cream cheese until smooth. Gradually add sugar, beating well. Add brandy, cinnamon, vanilla, and nutmeg; blend well. Add eggs, one at a time, beating just until combined. Stir in applesauce and cream. Pour into cooled crust. Bake at 350 degrees for 50 minutes or until center appears nearly set. Meanwhile, prepare topping; sprinkle over cake. Bake 10 minutes more or until cake is just set. Cool 5 minutes on a wire rack. Loosen sides of cake. Cool 30 minutes. Remove sides of pan. Cover; chill thoroughly. Makes 16 servings.

　Cinnamon Crust:

1 $1/_4$ cups graham cracker
　crumbs
$1/_3$ cup ground walnuts or
　pecans

$1/_3$ cup margarine or butter,
　melted
$1/_2$ teaspoon ground
　cinnamon

Combine ingredients. Press on bottom and 1 $1/_2$ inches up sides of 10-inch springform pan. Bake at 350 degrees about 10 minutes or until golden; cool.

　Crumb Topping:

$3/_4$ cup packed brown sugar
$3/_4$ cup all-purpose flour
$1/_3$ cup margarine or butter,
　melted

$1/_2$ teaspoon ground
　cinnamon
$1/_4$ teaspoon ground nutmeg

Combine ingredients and mix until crumbly.

　　　　　　　—Joan Bucher, National Apple Harvest Board Director

Apple Fritters

1 cup flour	$3/4$ cup milk
$1/2$ teaspoon baking powder	1 egg
$1/4$ teaspoon salt	5 medium apples, diced
$1/4$ cup granulated sugar	

Combine all ingredients except apples. Stir apples into batter. Fry in oil 5 minutes for each side.

—*York Springs Jaycees*

apples: apple bread, apple butter, apple cookies, apple fritters, apple jellies, apple peanut brittle, apple pizza, apple sausage, applesauce, candied apples, fresh apples, fried apples, hot apple cider, apple daiquiris, apple crepes, and caramel apple slices. There were also soups, crab cakes, fresh roasted peanuts, soft pretzels, and lemonade.

The crafts show is one of the largest in the area. More than 350 vendors fill exhibition halls and livestock barns and line the pathways of the South Mountain Fairgrounds. There are crafts demonstrations, too. I watched a moccasin maker, a tinsmith, a potter, a weaver, and a blacksmith. I also watched apple-butter making.

Other activities appeal to all ages. Visitors could enjoy a minitractor pull, pony and steam engine rides, free orchard tours, operating antique gas engines, antique farm equipment, and a steam-operated shingle mill. Five stages offered nonstop entertainment. I stopped at the Apple Stage in Memorial Auditorium when I heard the Chambersburg Steel Band's reggae music rolling out the front door. I could only chuckle at the incongruity: displays from the apple industry of Adams County, country green walls with white curtains tied back with green ribbons, and kids in the reggae band wearing flowered Caribbean shirts.

As I started the long trek back to my car, I passed a large corral full of straw, where parents and kids were stuffing old clothing to make scarecrows. There must have been thirty under construction in the early afternoon. I wondered how the parents would carry those life-size creations to their vehicles and seat them for the ride home.

❖ The National Apple Harvest Festival is held the first two weekends in October. The festival is just eight miles from Gettysburg on Route 234, so you may want to drive into Gettysburg before leaving Adams County. For more information, write to the Upper Adams Jaycees, Sponsors, P.O. Box 38, Biglerville, PA 17307, or call 717-677-7820.

Flaming Foliage Festival

Renovo, Clinton County

I have two photos from my day at the Flaming Foliage Festival. One shows a huge complex of brick buildings—the railroad yard—starkly outlined against the brilliant autumn mountainside behind it. A fleet of retired cabooses rests beside the complex. Like the buildings, they are abandoned.

The other photo is of a brick building in town, its side facing Huron Avenue. It wears a Mail Pouch Tobacco sign, worn by years of rain and sun. A ghostly sign above it whispers, "Butter and Eggs, Dry Goods, Notions, General Merchandise."

The buildings were built when Renovo was a busy railroad center. Now they endure as monuments to the town's past. Renovo, like so many small Pennsylvania towns, is in the autumn of its life, its heyday only a memory.

I arrived in town with my friend Judi in time for the Flaming Foliage Festival's Saturday afternoon parade. At least we assumed there would be a parade, judging from all the evidence.

"Either that or the running of the bulls," Judi said.

Lawn chairs lined Huron Avenue and front porches hosted festive parties. Locals moved down the street slowly, stopping at porches as they went, sharing conversation, laughter, beer, and party foods. The entire community was out and about, enjoying the autumn afternoon.

Houses wore banners encouraging and endorsing queen contestants. "Good luck Denise!" and "Good luck Miss Bucktail!" were printed in bold letters.

We found a vantage point on Huron Avenue next to St. Joseph's Church and set up shop, unloading cameras and notepads and watching the crowd. The smell of the Emerald Hose Company's chicken barbecue on the vacant lot on the opposite corner was its own best advertisement. It hooked pedestrians and pulled them in.

The street was busy with pre-parade excitement. Vendors carried trays of mammoth soft pretzels up and down the street. We succumbed and bought two. Other vendors worked the crowd with a myriad of inflatable toys—crayons, skeletons, superheroes, cartoon characters, and walking lizards. I wanted a lizard, but Judi said she would not be seen with me walking a reptile on a stick. There is a limit to friendship, after all.

Spinach-Cheese Pie (Spanokopita)

10 ounces spinach
  (about 6 cups)
2 cups feta cheese
1 small onion, minced
$1/_2$ teaspoon salt
4 tablespoons chopped parsley
2 teaspoons dried dillweed (optional)

3 eggs, well beaten
1 tablespoon butter,
  softened
$1/_2$ cup butter, melted
$1/_2$ 16-ounce package frozen
  phyllo leaves, thawed

Wash spinach; drain and chop. Cover and cook until tender, about 3 minutes; drain. Crumble the feta cheese. Mix spinach, feta cheese, onion, salt, parsley, and dillweed; combine with eggs.

Brush bottom and sides of 12 x 7 $1/_2$ x 2-inch oblong baking dish with softened butter. Unfold phyllo leaves. Remove ten leaves; cut crosswise into halves. (Cover completely with damp towel to prevent drying.) Gently separate 1 leaf; place in baking dish, folding edges over to fit bottom of dish. Brush lightly with melted butter. Repeat nine times.

Heat oven to 350 degrees. Spread spinach-egg mixture evenly over phyllo leaves. Layer ten more phyllo leaves over filling, spreading each leaf with melted butter and tucking in sides around edges to cover filling. Cut pastry through top layer of phyllo leaves with sharp knife into six squares. Cook uncovered in oven until golden, about 35 minutes. Let stand 10 minutes. Cut through scored lines to serve. Serves 6.

Sandwich boards along the street advertised local businesses. "Streett's Tatooing and Crafts," one read. "Permanent, safe, sterilized needles. Must be eighteen or older." It was decorated with autumn leaves. Another advertised a tanning salon.

At 2, St. Joseph's chimes activated the parade. It was an extravaganza with thirty-three contestants from all over the Endless Mountains vying for the title of Flaming Foliage Queen, each seated with her escort on the back of a convertible. What a pleasure it was to see these teenagers—well dressed, clean-cut, with sparkling smiles. There were floats between the candidates—high school bands, Zembo Shriners in midget cars, and even the Mummers. The parade lasted two and a half hours, and every new spectacle brought *oohs* and *ahs* from the crowd. Even politicians on foot won applause.

After the parade we walked down to the crafts show at the Flaming Foliage Festival Park by the bridge. It was small as crafts shows go, but it had some good vendors. There were sweatshirts, T-shirts, dried flowers, spices, herb vinegars, baskets, and two displays of western wear.

The food concessions were selling interesting choices, from maple sugar cotton candy to white pizza. A Greek catering service offered spinach pie and baklava, and we succumbed again.

Route 120 was bumper to bumper for an hour following the parade, so we sat at a picnic table enjoying the flaming foliage that envelops Renovo before we started for the car.

We stopped at a convenience store and bought the local paper, the *Record,* for the schedule of events. There had been a talent show the first Saturday in October at the high school with tap dancers, vocalists, and accordion players. The queen contestants were introduced at the football game, and the Queen Coronation was scheduled for Sunday afternoon. The festival really belonged to the young people in the pageant. For them there was a prom, a banquet, and other activities.

❖ The Flaming Foliage Festival is held the second weekend in October in Renovo. The parade is your best bet for a Saturday afternoon of fun. Arrive early and take lawn chairs.

Farmers' Fair

Dillsburg, York County

One cannot drive through Dillsburg, a cul-de-sac community midway between Harrisburg and Gettysburg, during the weekend after Columbus Day. The town is closed down. There is no school that Friday. It is Farmers' Fair weekend and the streets of the town host only pedestrian traffic. I know, for I teach there.

On Wednesday afternoon, the school auditorium is closed to students. Women's Club members hurriedly decorate the stage for the annual queen's contest. Tensions run high. In Dillsburg, it still means something to be Farmers' Fair Queen.

When I leave school on the Thursday before Farmers' Fair, I always drive down Baltimore Street, through the center of town. Bleachers line both sides of the thoroughfare. The food stands are tacked together for another year's service. The town seems empty except for a few workmen hurrying around. The sounds of hammers and the whine of power saws echo through the town.

That night the middle school is as hectic as the opening night of a Broadway show. Traffic police urge motorists into parking spots. The auditorium fills up early, and choice seats are occupied an hour ahead of the curtain. Conversation roars from the auditorium into the lobby and out the doors to the pavement.

The houselights flash a warning and latecomers hurry for seats. And then the show begins. Young women from each grade level at the high school vie for the title of Farmers' Fair Queen. There are prepared speeches, impromptu speeches, costumed segments, and evening gown segments. The high school jazz band performs. The evening is glamorous and glittering.

On Friday evening, I examine the displays in the community hall. Along with the apple pie contest and the Hershey's cocoa baking contest, there are always many additional entries in myriad baking categories. I look for familiar names by blue ribbons. One does that when he knows everyone in town.

The produce contests are always fun and fascinating. There is a vegetable animal division, where contestants form animals from their produce. There are potato spiders, zucchini snakes, butternut squash turtles, tomato lobsters, and turnip pigs. Another category for children is a pumpkin animal contest. There are few rules in the contest, and an all-time favorite entry was a pumpkin porcupine, full of toothpicks. I also remember from a Farmers' Fair years ago a Tony the Tiger. Flower arranging is another division that receives my attention, and the arrangements rival those from the finest floral shops.

I leave the community hall only when I hear drums racketing down Baltimore Street, the front-runners of the Children's Parade. I hurry for a spot on the bleachers close to the reviewing stand. It is a long parade, full of costumed children, and it lasts over an hour. Etiquette decrees that the audience applaud each group in the parade. The emcee, always a local comedian, makes comments like, "Is that Igor or Al Gore?" and "Who does your hair, honey—the blind?"

Saturday is the really big day of the fair, with events and attractions all over the tiny town. There are a farmers market in the bank parking lot and a farm equipment display by the middle school. There is a 4-H steer

Blue-Ribbon Pumpkin Bread

4 eggs
1 cup oil
3 cups sugar
1 $^1/_2$ teaspoons salt
1 teaspoon cinnamon
1 teaspoon nutmeg
2 teaspoons baking soda
2 cups pumpkin (I don't use canned stuff. I cook my own and
    freeze it. Don't use canned—spices are already added. I
    don't recommend it at all.)

$^2/_3$ cup water
3 $^1/_2$ cups flour (I use
    Gold Medal.)
1 cup walnuts or pecans

Add ingredients in order listed and mix with a whisk. Bake 1 hour
at 350 degrees and test with a knife.
    Makes 3 loaves.

—Cynthia Weir

and heifer show at the athletic field close to the pony rides and petting
zoo. Around a hundred craftsworkers sell their wares by the elementary
school while the Future Farmers of America grill rib-eye steak sandwiches. Baltimore Street hosts an antique car show.

That night, the Fantastic Parade controls Baltimore Street. There are
sixteen categories for groups, individuals, floats, bands, horses and riders,
and horses and carriages.

For me, the best part of Farmers' Fair is seeing former students. Everyone comes home to Dillsburg for Farmers' Fair, even the folks who will
not make it back for the holidays. It is a large reunion, a homecoming, a
time to share the triumphs, disappointments, joys, and sorrows of the year
with the folks of your past.

Former students introduce me to their children, older now than their
parents were when they sat before me in room 100. Others discuss college
or careers.

"I wanted to tell you," a few start out, "I finished my doctorate last
year," or "Mr. Kennedy, this is my husband," "Mr. Kennedy, did you hear
about . . .?" and they keep me informed and in touch with their lives.

It is fitting and proper that Farmers' Fair falls in the heart of harvest
season. These young people, in a small way, are part of the harvest of a
teaching career.

We count on events like Farmers' Fair not to change, and when they do not, we give thanks. In an ever-changing world, these small-town celebrations offer continuity and stability. Thomas Wolfe once wrote, "You can't go home again," but he was not from Dillsburg, and he never attended Farmers' Fair weekend.

❖ Mark the third weekend of October on your calendar for Farmers' Fair. It is held in the center of Dillsburg. For more information, contact the Dillsburg Community Fair Association, P.O. Box 502, Dillsburg, PA 17019.

November

Heidlersburg Beef and Oyster Dinner

Heidlersburg, Adams County

There are firehouse dinners all over the state, but few have received as much attention—or patronage, for that matter—as Heidlersburg Fire Company's dinners. On the third Saturday of each month containing an R, the volunteer staff feeds eleven hundred to fifteen hundred people in their dining room—people from as far away as Philadelphia, Baltimore, Pittsburgh, and New York.

They do not advertise. Aside from a billboard in front of the firehouse and notices in a few local papers, their patrons advertise for them. I first heard about their dinners from Judi and Rusty Shunk. Their friends from New York City plan their visits to Carlisle around Heidlersburg's schedule, and it is a given that Saturday night dinner on the weekend of their visit will be at the firehouse.

Judi told me before I left, "It's not fancy, and it's not elegant. It's country cooking—but it's wonderful!"

Kay and I met my editors, Sally and Mark, on a November afternoon as gray as the inside of winter's own overcoat. The sky was heavy and leaden, and it promised a snow flurry before evening slipped into night. It was one of those afternoons that ride just on the edge of winter.

Each of us had plans for later that evening, and we thought that by arriving early, at 3, we could avoid the rush. But we were wrong. The parking lot at the firehouse was already overflowing.

"I had forgotten," Sally said from the backseat. "Real country people eat dinner early."

"Supper," Kay corrected pedagogically. "Country people eat *supper.*"

A crowd was milling around inside. Apparently we looked like the outsiders we were. One kindly woman advised us, "Go to the end of this hallway and stay to your left. You have to get a number before you can be seated."

We found the cashier, close to the restrooms, and paid for our meals. Party of four, tickets 242–45.

After that we waited. A hundred people sat in chairs along the wall. Two hundred more stood in the firehouse bays, all sorts of people: country people, city people, old people, young people, big people, little people—and all of us were waiting for the famous Heidlersburg dinners.

"I've never eaten oysters," Mark confessed doubtfully. "I guess I'll try them."

"Get with it," I told him. "I've tried all kinds of things I didn't like." And then I told several stories about fair foods, and how I had manned my way through under the benevolent smiles of proud fair organizers. "For the sake of the book," I reminded him. "For the sake of the book."

The afternoon dragged on. I looked out the window in time to see the first flakes of snow filter down from the heavy sky, crushing my evening's plans underfoot like a burnt out cigarette.

We invented games to amuse ourselves. We played Funny Couples. Each of us walked up beside an unlikely person and waited until he or she looked at us, and then I would snap a photo of the incongruous couple. There are photographs in my album of Sally with a mountain man, Mark with the Far Side lady, Kay with a toupeed beer drinker, and me with Miss Read, the British schoolmarm.

A man with a microphone, seated on a platform, finally called our number, and we were escorted to another hallway opening into a paneled, acoustically tiled room. Thirty tables of eight were lined up. In a matter of minutes, a policewoman allowed us to enter and a host seated us.

Immediately, our food was served, family style. We never met our tablemates formally. I had expected leisurely conversation, a few handshakes, something to inspire a note or two on my tablet. Instead we all set about the serious business of eating dinner. The beef was fall-apart tender, the oysters were a masterpiece, smothered in a sweet batter, and the filling was rich and savory. There were mashed potatoes and green beans, too. The minute a platter or bowl was emptied, another appeared. I wondered aloud how long a table could sit there eating before the fire company kicked them out.

While my companions were enjoying dessert, I went to the kitchen to talk with Rita Dick, the head cook. Eighteen volunteers were working at a breakneck pace in the kitchen that afternoon. It was a surprisingly well-choreographed crew, and I thought about my own lame efforts at dinner for four.

The crew goes through eighty-five gallons of oysters, seven hundred pounds of beef, and one hundred or more pounds of potatoes for each dinner. The beef is roasted on Monday preceding the dinner and sliced that night. Filling is made on Wednesday, and oysters are padded on Friday. It takes a week to prepare the dinner, and a staff of seventy-five, "all volunteers," Rita said.

"One time during one of our dinners, the lights went out. We called

Filling

1 ½ gallons celery
1 gallon onions
30 dozen eggs
2 to 3 gallons beef broth

14 tablespoons salt
14 tablespoons pepper
2 gallons of parsley
42 5-pound bags of bread
    cubes

Makes 14 batches.

—Rita Dick, president of Ladies Auxiliary

in generators from all the local fire companies and went on with the show. We served dinner by candlelight. When the lights went on, we in the kitchen rejoiced, but the crowd was heartbroken!"

We left that afternoon, filled to the top with Heidlersburg's beef and oysters. I did not even go back for some of their cashews or peanuts.

❖ The firehouse suppers are held on the third Saturday of each month with an R in it. Dinners are served from 3 till 7, but in Rita Dick's words, "We never turn anyone away." From Route 15 take the Heidlersburg exit toward Biglerville on Route 234 West. The firehouse is on the right about a mile from the exit. For more information, write to the Heidlersburg Fire Company, 720 Heidlersburg Road, Gettysburg, PA 17325, or call 717-528-8867. And tell Rita I send my best.

December

Dickens of a Christmas

Wellsboro, Tioga County

Charles Dickens ends his Christmas tale of Ebenezer Scrooge with these sage words: ". . . and it was always said of him, that he knew how to keep Christmas well, if any man alive possessed that knowledge. May that be truly said of us, and all of us!"

Dickens would be proud of Wellsboro, for it is a town that knows how to keep Christmas.

A year earlier my friend Linda Olsen had told me about Wellsboro's Christmas merrymaking. Her description of the event stuck in my mind. When I attended the Laurel Festival in Wellsboro late in June, one look at the town persuaded me to return in December. It would be the perfect setting for a Victorian Christmas celebration, with its gaslights, Victorian houses, and spacious park.

On the first weekend in December, Linda, her husband, Rich, and I left home early in their Jeep. Getting a room in the vicinity was out of the question—it had been out of the question since June.

Once we arrived in town and found parking, we walked around the corner onto Main into another world, nineteenth-century England. The four-block section of the street in the heart of town was blocked off. The flickering gaslights on the medial strip wore fresh pine wreaths with bright red bows. Between the lights, Christmas trees glowed and sparkled. There were horse-drawn wagons carrying passengers around the Main Street circle. Bells and harness jingled brightly with each movement. Costumed vendors lined the streets hawking their wares. It was market day, more than a century ago.

Proper Victorian gentlemen wore greatcoats, top hats, waistcoats, gloves, and spats. Fine Victorian ladies wore velvet dresses with bustles and hats plumed with ostrich feathers. There were tradesmen in shirt-sleeves, vests, arm garters, and derbies, and there were street urchins in knickers, tall socks, and snap hats.

The foods sold on the pavement that day were varied and delicious. There were hot sticky buns, steaming cranberry drinks, scalloped potatoes and ham, mulled cider, Earl of Sandwich roast beef sandwiches, cabbage and noodles, soups, chili, and cornbread. Two street urchins were selling hot dogs from boxes slung around their necks, and there was one stand specializing in Greek foods. For those folks needing a seat or a warm-up, the restaurants in town were running specials.

The crafts for sale on the street were as varied as the menu. A decoy carver was at work, and a craftsman sold reproduction candle lanterns. Many of the vendors were selling holiday ornaments, arrangements, and decorations. There were live wreaths and Christmas trees on the corner of Main and Central Avenues and ground-pine wreaths a little farther back.

We walked to the Episcopal church to see the model railroad setup. I struck up a conversation with Rich Stoving, who was making trees for his own model railroad in a quiet corner.

"I've been playing with model railroads all my life," he told me. "I retired from the New York City Board of Education a few years ago. I was an English teacher, but I ended up supervising the implementation of technology in one of the schools in the city. The moment I retired, we bought twenty-two acres and moved out here. I qualified as a conductor on the Tioga Central Railroad. So, what do you do?"

When I told him that I was also a teacher who happened to be writing a book on fairs and festivals, he said, "I'm conductor on the dinner train tonight. Why don't you bring your friends and come out with us? It's scheduled to depart at seven. Take Route 287 north of Wellsboro three miles. Look for a dirt road on the right. Ask for me."

We stayed in town just long enough to see the community tree-lighting ceremony in the park. The cold had settled in with the darkness and we bundled up in our coats. The citizens of Wellsboro carried candles, the local band played Christmas carols, and we sang the old tunes in the frosty night, the rose window of the Episcopal church glowing behind us. A local doctor delivered a short homily, the Laurel Queen pushed the switch, and the towering Christmas tree blazed with light. It was a magical evening, full of Christmas spirit.

We raced to the Wellsboro Junction. The train was already running, and doors hung ajar. Rich Stoving was waiting for us and escorted us to the Cornell Club Car. There was a tiny Christmas tree in the car, and an HO model train circled it.

Soon the train began to tremble, and we were under way. Rich came through our car calling out to everyone, "Santa Claus is at the next crossing. We're stopping to pick him up!"

Santa came through, giving gifts to the youngsters aboard. Carolers followed. I watched the lights soar by the windows.

Twenty minutes into the ride, Rich asked, "Would you like to ride in the cab?"

Before long, we were outside, stepping from the club car to the engine. The walk along the outside of the moving engine was a thrill I will not soon forget. I was every cowboy hero in every Old West movie I had watched as a kid, and I wondered whether they were as nervous as I was, or as cold.

I spent the rest of the train ride in the engine with engineer Ralph LeBlanc and brakeman Gregg Carpenter. They pointed out whistle signs that indicate where one must blow the whistle for a crossing, flag signs where folks may flag down the train for a ride, mileage signs that indicate distance to the next station, and different kinds of railroad tracks.

They told me about a little boy named Benji who lives on the train route. The engineers of the Tioga Central Railroad always blow the horn for him and he comes out and waves. One time, he jumped out of the bathtub and ran outdoors naked. When we passed his house, we blasted the whistle and Benji came out, clothed.

Bread Pudding

12 slices of bread	1 cup raisins
6 tablespoons butter or margarine	9 eggs, lightly beaten
	1 cup sugar
1 cup brown sugar	$1/_2$ teaspoon salt
$1/_2$ teaspoon cinnamon	7 $1/_2$ cups scalded milk

Lightly grease a 9 x 12-inch pan and preheat oven to 350 degrees.

Toast bread lightly and spread with butter, sprinkle with mix of brown sugar and cinnamon, and cut into quarters. Arrange in pan in layers, buttered side up, and sprinkle with raisins. Blend other ingredients and slowly stir in scalded milk. Pour over bread.

Place pan in larger pan, filled with water 1 inch deep, and bake approximately 70 minutes. Test with knife—knife should come out clean. Serve with Maple Raisin Sauce. Serves 24.

Maple Raisin Sauce:

$3/_4$ cup maple syrup	1 cup whipping cream
$1/_2$ cup raisins	

Stir together maple syrup and cream in saucepan, and bring to boil. Boil 15 to 20 minutes or until thickened, stirring occasionally. Add raisins and stir.

Yields 1 $1/_4$ cups.

—*Shirley Butler, Soldiers and Sailors Memorial Hospital Auxiliary Booth*

Bread Pudding

3 cups bread cut into 1-inch cubes

4 eggs, beaten

2 cups milk

$^1/_3$ cup sugar

$^1/_2$ teaspoon cinnamon

$^1/_2$ teaspoon vanilla

Mix eggs, milk, sugar, cinnamon, and vanilla. Put the bread into greased baking dish; pour mixture over bread. Bake at 325 degrees for 35 to 40 minutes or until knife blade comes out clean.

—*Regina Becht*

It was late when we pulled into the Wellsboro Junction and the drive home was a long one, but all of us agreed that we had had a Dickens of a day at Wellsboro's Dickens of a Christmas.

❖ Wellsboro holds its Christmas celebration the first weekend in December. Events are scheduled for both Saturday and Sunday, and the train runs throughout the weekend. Although there are activities all over town, Main Street is the heart of the celebration. The train leaves from Wellsboro Junction, about three miles north of town on Route 287. For more information, contact the Wellsboro Chamber of Commerce, 114 Main Street, Wellsboro, PA 16901, or call 717-724-1926. For reservations on the Tioga Central Railroad Christmas excursions, call 717-724-7709 or 717-724-3141.

Dill Pickle Drop

Dillsburg, York County

It was cold, the kind of cold that attacks the nose first, takes the ears, and descends quickly to the feet. And it was dark. Even the stars had not ventured out that night, so deep in the heart of winter. And it was late, the end of a trying year of being on the road almost continually, seeking out the state's country celebrations, the end of the road for me. It was New Year's Eve.

"One more," I said to my friend Deb earlier that night. "I must do one more—for the book."

It seemed an appropriate grand finale to my project. And for Deb it was a new beginning. Recently divorced, she had just moved home again, a little older, a lot wiser.

We had shared the earlier hours of New Year's Eve with my family, well fueled on my sister's seafood dinner. I wanted a New Year's Eve celebration for the book. I had several options, but loyalties prevailed. I wanted to go to the Dill Pickle Drop in Dillsburg, the town where I had spent the bulk of my teaching career. Forget New Bloomfield with its Huckleberry Drop, forget First Night in York—it was Dillsburg or nothing.

We left at eleven, dressed in every warm piece of clothing we owned. I already knew that the dill pickle would be dropped to a barrel from a fire company's crane. I had talked with the two students who had created it, Abby Mahone and Colleen Carswell.

"It was brought up at a Girl Scout meeting of leaders that someone was needed to make the pickle for the Pickle Drop," Abby had told me. "My mom is a leader and she volunteered our troop, Troop 1576 from Dillsburg."

"We started it in mid-December," Colleen said, "and we were finishing it the day before."

"M and W Hardware gave us the wire frame and we tried papier-mâché and that didn't work," Abby said. "So we taped dry newspaper around it and put the papier-mâché over that. For a while it looked so bad that we had our doubts.

"We painted it green," Colleen continued, "and it started looking better."

"A little better," Abby interjected.

"After we painted it green, we painted brown lines on it to give it more detail."

"Texture."

"Then we put on green and silver glitter. And after that was dry—"

"We put on sequins. We tried to arrange them in circles and lines so that they looked bumpy."

"Then it started to look like something," Colleen concluded.

There was a folk singer that night, and the Civic Organization sold party hats and noisemakers. We connected with the Ohrum family, friends I had known since I started teaching at Northern York County School District.

When the dill pickle dropped at midnight, the several hundred people gathered in the heart of town celebrated the New Year with cheers, applause, hugs, and kisses. It was small town life at its finest.

The Dill Pickle Drop has grown up just a bit and now has the backing of the Heinz Food Corporation. Personally, I was happy to have been a part of the first year of the celebration.

We went home that night, on to new adventures, other books.

❖ The Pickle Drop is ongoing. Be in the heart of Dillsburg by 11 on New Year's Eve. Baltimore Street closes down for the event. Have a coffee on me.

About the Author

Craig Kennedy, a former columnist for *Country Home* magazine, traveled some twenty-three thousand miles over a year and a half to research this book. During that time he says he "learned more about Pennsylvania than I ever thought possible." When he's not exploring or collecting country furniture and Victorian oil paintings, he teaches high school in York County. A Pennsylvania native, he lives in Newville.